The Imperative of American Leadership

A Challenge to Neo-Isolationism

Joshua Muravchik

The AEI Press

Publisher for the American Enterprise Institute
WASHINGTON, D. C.
1996

Available in the United States from the AEI Press, c/o Publisher Resources Inc., 1224 Heil Quaker Blvd., P.O. Box 7001, La Vergne, TN 37086-7001. Distributed outside the United States by arrangement with Eurospan, 3 Henrietta Street, London WC2E 8LU England.

Library of Congress Cataloging-in-Publication Data

Muravchik, Joshua.
    The imperative of American leadership : a challenge to neo-isolationism / by Joshua Muravchik.
    p. cm.
    Includes bibliographical references and index.
    ISBN 0-8447-3958-8 (alk. paper)
    1. United States—Foreign relations—1989–   I. Title.
E840.M873 1996
327.73—dc20   96–445
                                                        CIP

THE AEI PRESS
Publisher for the American Enterprise Institute
1150 17th Street, N.W., Washington, D.C. 20036

Printed in the United States of America

CONTENTS

ACKNOWLEDGMENTS   xi

1   INTRODUCTION   1
    America's Role   1
    Leadership for Peace and Security   2
    Limits to American Power?   3
    A Special Time   5

PART ONE
AMERICA AND THE WORLD AFTER THE COLD WAR

2   THE RETURN OF ISOLATIONISM   9
    Collapse of Confidence   9
    The 1992 Elections   10
    The Spirit of Isolationism   11
    Elite Leadership   13
    Economic Issues   15
    Distrust of American Power   16

3   THE NEW GREAT DEBATE—WASHINGTON VERSUS WILSON   20
    Washingtonians and Wilsonians   20
    Interest and Morality   22
    Future Threats   26
    Preventing War, Defending Peace   28
    American Power   30
    The Success of Idealism   33

4 CAN WE AFFORD TO LEAD? 36
America's Wealth 36
The Budget Deficit 38
Spending on Defense and Foreign Policy 38
Entitlements 39
Discretionary Spending 40
The Solution 42
The Cost of a Sound Foreign Policy 43
Military Spending and Economic Growth 45
Solving Domestic Problems 47

PART TWO
ALTERNATIVES TO LEADERSHIP

5 CAN OTHER "POWERS" SHARE THE BURDENS? 53
How Many Superpowers? 53
Japan or China as Leader 55
Europe as Leader 56
The Cold War 62
Global Issues after the Cold War 68

6 CAN WE TURN THE WORLD OVER TO THE UNITED NATIONS? 71
After the Cold War 71
Clinton and the United Nations 73
The Limitations of UN Peacekeeping 75
Problems of Multilateral Military Action 77
Conditions for Peacekeeping 79
Deficiencies of World Organizations 81

PART THREE
BOSNIA—A CASE STUDY IN ABDICATION

7 "THE HOUR OF EUROPE," 1987–1992 85
Dispute over Kosovo 85
Unrest in Slovenia and Croatia 87
America's Response 89
The EC's Diplomacy in Yugoslavia 90
Recognition of Sovereignty and Its Consequences 95
Ethnic Cleansing Begins 98

8 AGGRESSION AND INDIFFERENCE, 1992–1995   99
   The Bush Administration's Response   99
   The Clinton Administration's Response   101
   The Siege of Sarajevo   105
   NATO and the United Nations   106

9 THE LESSONS OF BOSNIA   112
   Sanctions   114
   No-Fly Zones and Safe Areas   114
   Serbian Threats   115
   Pressure on Bosnia   116
   Who's to Blame?   119
   General Rose in Bosnia   125
   Lack of Leadership   127
   What Lies Ahead?   129
   Fallout from the Conflict   130

PART FOUR
LEADERSHIP THROUGH MILITARY STRENGTH

10 REMAINING THE SOLE SUPERPOWER   135
   The Defense Planning Guidance   136
   A Defensible Strategy   137
   Clinton's Defense Policy   139
   Effects of Reduced Spending   143
   The Flaw in Clinton's Defense Plan   145
   Threat-based Planning   146
   Considerations for Planning   147
   How Much Defense?   150

11 WHEN TO USE FORCE?   152
   Criteria for the Use of Force   152
   The Gulf War   154
   Bosnia   156
   Somalia   158
   Rwanda   159
   Haiti   160
   Justification for Force   160
   Resistance to Aggression   167
   Collective Security and American Power   168
   Appendix 11A: Interstate Wars since World War II   170

PART FIVE
POLITICAL AND ECONOMIC LEADERSHIP

12 FOSTERING DEMOCRACY   173
    The Nature of Democracies   173
    The United States as Agent of Democracy   180
    Today's Role   181
    Areas of Strategic Interest   185

13 FREE TRADE   191
    New Trade Barriers   192
    Fear of Japanese Economic Strength   192
    Protectionism   194
    Japan Bashing   195
    Mimicry   195
    The Cost of Protectionism   196
    Consequences of Protectionism   198
    Argument against Strategic Trade   198
    Japan's Economic Problems   200
    Security Interests   202
    NAFTA, GATT, and the WTO   203
    American Leadership in Free Trade   204

14 CONCLUSION   206
    The Tragedy of Bosnia   207
    Our Unique Opportunity   207
    American Influence   208

LIST OF FIGURES
7-1 The Six Republics and Two Autonomous Provinces of Yu-
     goslavia before 1991   86
7-2 Croatia, with the Breakaway "Republic of Serbian
     Krajina"   93
8-1 The Six "Safe Areas" of Bosnia and Herzegovina Declared
     by the UN Security Council, 1992   104
9-1 The Partition of Bosnia and Herzegovina into the Serbian
     Republic and the Muslim-Croat Federation according to
     the Dayton Peace Accords, Signed in December
     1995   113

APPENDIX: Chronological Highlights of the Wars
    of Yugoslavia's Dissolution   211

NOTES   217

INDEX   249

ABOUT THE AUTHOR   261

ACKNOWLEDGMENTS

So many people have helped me in the course of writing this book that I fear that I shall omit to mention someone. If I do, I beg forgiveness. My first thanks go to the officers of the American Enterprise Institute—Chairman Wilson Taylor, President Chris DeMuth, Executive Vice President David Gerson, and former Chairman Paul Oreffice—who labor tirelessly to provide an unexcelled setting for research and writing. I have benefited greatly from the knowledge and insights of my colleagues at AEI, including Herbert Stein, Murray Foss, Claude Barfield, Cynthia Beltz, Richard Perle, Jeane Kirkpatrick, Marvin Kosters, Jeffrey Gedmin, Chong-Pin Lin, Karlyn Bowman, Patrick Glynn, Andrew Goldman, Lieutenant Commander Tim McGregor, Jonathan Siskin, and Randolph Stempski. During the course of working on this book I have had three wonderful assistants, Susan Alderfer, Stacey Thomas, and Amanda Watson Schnetzer, and at one critical juncture Michelle van Gilder pinch-hit. I am indebted, too, to AEI's fine librarians, Evelyn Caldwell and Murray White, and to the director of publications, Dana Lane, and of publications marketing, Virginia Bryant, with both of whom it is a pleasure to work. I must say a special word about the unfailing generosity of Mark Lagon, formerly research associate to Jeane Kirkpatrick and now with the House Republican Policy Committee, who provided me with countless resource materials.

I have benefited as well from the efforts of some very able interns. Three in particular did yeoman service for me even after their internships were formally over: Lawrence Kaplan, Dan Fata, and Peter Erickson. Others were spendid, as well: Allison Boyd, Marta Ferrer,

John Fishman, Nicolas Gentin, Sonya Hand, Christopher Hayes, Scott Kocher, Rachel Lebenson, Warren Mazer, Bethany Molinari, Daniel Nexon, and Matthew Salvetti. Jeane Kirkpatrick, Peter Rodman, Norman Podhoretz, Marshall Freeman Harris, and Jeffrey Gedmin read the entire manuscript or parts of it, and I profited from their criticisms. Others have provided me with information or favored me with conversations that were valuable to me, notably, Frank Lavin, Stephen Walker, Al Micheli, Bill Driscoll, Thomas Helde, Scooter Libby, Carl Smith, Eliot Cohen, Joseph E. Ryan, Charles Krauthammer, Dick Wilson, and Ariel Cohen.

Last, but far from least, is my wife, Sally, who comforts and encourages, advises and succors, edits and proofreads, whom I love, and with whom I have shared the inestimable joy and wonder of raising Stephanie, Madeline, and Valerie. To those three apples of my eye I dedicate this book.

The Imperative
of American Leadership

·1·

INTRODUCTION

This book is an argument. It is an argument for a certain kind of U.S. foreign policy now that the cold war is behind us. It is an argument for a foreign policy that is engaged, proactive, interventionist, and expensive.

America's Role

This argument flies in the face of the shibboleth that America cannot be the world's policeman. In truth, it must be more than that. A policeman gets his assignments from higher authority, but in the community of nations there is no authority higher than America (notwithstanding Boutros Boutros-Ghali, who for a time seemed to fancy that he commanded such a mandate). America is the wealthiest, mightiest, and most respected nation. At times, it must be the policeman or head of the posse—at others, the mediator, teacher, or benefactor. In short, America must accept the role of world leader.

This message will not fall on welcoming ears in America. Other peoples at other times have warmed to the lures of empire. But Americans have no taste for it. Never in history has so much power whetted so little imperial appetite. And while Americans always rally to their president's summons in times of danger, they also have little taste for the burdens of leadership. It took the menace of Stalin (on top of the lesson of Hitler) to draw America out of the peacetime aloofness that had been its tradition since the founding of the republic. Once the Soviet threat disappeared, that tradition of peacetime aloofness reasserted its pull on the American psyche.

Ironically, while citizens of other countries often envy or resent America's preeminence, they generally recognize that American leadership is essential. "It is really tragic to give a signal to the world that you [Americans] are not prepared to pursue your leadership,"[1] recently warned the foreign minister of Sweden, a country scarcely known for its subservience to America or its devotion to power politics. Aside perhaps from the French, the only people averse to American leadership are the Americans.

In this sense, America is akin to the philosopher in Plato's parable of the cave. Only the man who has achieved philosophic knowledge is truly fit to rule, said Plato, but having achieved it, he will resist being drawn back down to the mundane tasks of ruling. I do not mean to suggest that America is philosophic: it may be one of the least philosophic nations. But it has discovered at least some of the secrets of the good life, and Americans would rather enjoy that life than rule— or lead—others. Plato said that the philosopher would have to be compelled to rule. America cannot be compelled to lead: it can only be persuaded. That is the goal of this book.

Leadership for Peace and Security

Why does the world need leadership? To speak of leadership implies that the nations are headed in some common direction, and it is not obvious that they are or should be. Despite their diversity, however, the nations share the goal of prosperity and are to some degree interdependent in its quest. Most also share the goal of human rights, or at least pay lip service to it. Leadership is important in pursuit of both these goals. But there is a still more urgent requirement for leadership—leadership for peace and security. The world needs leadership to respond to crises, to discourage or thwart aggression, to settle quarrels, and to uphold international law. In short, leadership alone can prevent the world from dissolving into a Hobbesian chaos in which the strong prey at will on the weak.

Must we be the ones to lead? The answer is that if the mightiest nation fails to lead, world politics will lack equilibrium. America first came to primacy during World War I, although it was not yet any kind of superpower. Still, its abdication after the war created a vacuum that undermined the peace. Most of the European continent looked to France to undergird its security. France looked to Britain. Britain looked to America. But America was not there. The result was calamity. Now that America has no rival in power, abdication would be even more destabilizing. World politics could easily degenerate into a series of Bosnias, or Bosnias writ large. Could some other states summon the power to prevent or stop this dissolution? Perhaps, but if the leading nation will not act, the others will not either.

That explanation may clarify the world's need for American leadership, but does America need the world? What is the stake that justifies bearing the onus of leadership? With the demise of the Soviet Union, no force on earth can threaten America. We could minimize our political and military involvement abroad and still continue commercial relations. Adverse developments might impinge on our trade, but that would cost us only money, not lives or freedom. This is the argument of the true isolationist, and it is perfectly coherent. But it fails on several grounds. Foreign trade is not a small part of our economy but a large and growing part. If we ignore international politics, we leave our economy hostage to fate. In addition, were America to turn its back, the havoc that would ensue outside our borders would break our hearts. This spectacle might impel us to reengage, but we would find that the costs of restoring order would be much higher than the costs of preserving it. If we remain aloof, however, a rival might eventually emerge that would command sufficient economic and scientific resources to end our physical invulnerability. Thus our own security is ultimately connected to preserving the peace and forestalling the rise of a hostile imperium.

Limits to American Power?

Have we the wherewithal to do it? Early in Bill Clinton's presidency, Peter Tarnoff, the under secretary of state for policy, proclaimed that "we simply don't have the leverage, we don't have the influence, we don't have the inclination to use military forces, we certainly don't have the money"[2] to tackle various international crises. Therefore, he said, the administration's deliberate inaction on Bosnia exemplified a new foreign policy based on "setting limits on the amount of American engagement."

These assertions reflect a state of mind widespread within the Clinton administration and also within the country. But they do not reflect the state of things. Having emerged from the cold war as victor and sole superpower, America finds its influence and military supremacy greater than ever. And the country is wealthier than ever.

It is not influence or money or might that we lack, but purpose, as Tarnoff himself exemplifies. Faced with Pearl Harbor or the Czech coup of 1948, we were prepared to "pay any price, bear any burden." But in the absence of a direct attack or an imminent threat, we are reluctant to embroil ourselves in distant quarrels, to sacrifice butter for guns. Our lethargy comes not merely from selfishness but also from uncertainty. It is not obvious how best to preserve the security we now enjoy. We are unsure which foreign problems we can safely ignore and which ones will come back to haunt us. In that sense, the circumstance we face after the cold war is more like what we faced after World War I than World War II. After World War II, the danger was clear, while after World War I, it was not, but it turned out to be equally dire.

Even the Soviet threat looks a lot clearer in hindsight than it did at the time. In the 1940s, former vice president Henry Wallace and his followers argued that the conflict with the Soviets was of our making. This view went into decline after 1948, but variations of it reappeared, stronger than ever, during the Vietnam War when the likes of Senator J. William Fulbright, mentor to Bill Clinton, argued that America's problems arose from its own "arrogance of power." And even those who agreed that the Soviet Union was the problem were divided about how to respond.

Ironically, some of the most vociferous opponents of an activist foreign policy today were equally vociferous opponents of such a policy during the cold war, especially of the assertiveness of the Reagan administration. Had we heeded their counsel, we might not have won the cold war. Yet few seem to have paused to digest the lesson.

Still, without doubt today's issues are murkier. We are not weighing how to blunt the threat from a central rival but how to respond to a variety of bullies and local quarrels. There are those who say these are mere irritants, about which we need not be too concerned. If one metastasizes into a major threat, then we will respond appropriately. That is what happened in 1941 when we recognized the threat of Germany and Japan and succeeded in repulsing it. But what a price we and the world paid! Had we acted earlier, we might have saved ourselves and others untold suffering. And next time, as weapons grow ever more lethal, the consequences of belatedness might be even worse.

Accordingly, the premise of this book is the very antithesis of Francis Fukuyama's deservedly popular work on the "end of history." Although I believe that Fukuyama makes a strong case that democracy and market economics answer something innate in man, I do not believe (and neither does Fukuyama) that we are near to seeing an end to tyranny, greed, hatred, and war. I believe instead that we must struggle unceasingly to protect ourselves against those scourges.

A Special Time

We are, however, at a special time. Having lived for decades with the tensions of cold war and the specter of nuclear conflagration, today we find ourselves without a main enemy and enjoying the status of sole superpower. No force on earth could hope to defeat us in a war. That claim would have been the envy of most nations throughout history. We did not plan this. When the Soviet Union imploded, we found ourselves with a windfall of security. What to do with it? We can spend the windfall by turning our energies and funds away from foreign affairs, as Congressman Barney Frank so aptly put it, to "be nicer to ourselves"[3]—for as long as the security lasts. Or we can invest it by working to counteract hostile forces that could grow to threaten us, to dampen down turmoils that could grow into major conflicts, and to encourage the growth of democracy and trade. These burdens come with leadership. The goal of assuming them would be to strengthen the peace and prolong the high level of security we now enjoy. To advocate the assumption of burdens may seem out of tune with the prevailing wish for a smaller government. But whether or not the federal government should support the arts or generate electric power or allocate medical care, its irreducible function is to conduct defense and foreign policy.

This book makes the case for accepting those burdens and responsibilities. Part one examines the debate about U.S. foreign policy that has unfolded since the cold war ended, stating the case for American leadership and rebutting the arguments against it. Part two explores whether any conceivable substitute exists for American leadership. Part three is a case study of Bosnia, America's one great post–cold war experiment in leaving leadership to others. Parts four and five lay out the elements of a policy of leadership. These consist, first, of maintaining our military supremacy and setting sound criteria for the use of force and, second, of pursuing peaceful, long-term policies to influence global politics and economics.

PART ONE

America and the World after the Cold War

·2·

THE RETURN
OF ISOLATIONISM

Historians will long marvel at the denouement of the cold war. The Soviet Union, the mightiest military juggernaut in the history of man,[1] just upped and threw in the towel. This capitulation was not the result of any defeat on the battlefield but of a collapse of confidence on the part of its ruling elite. There is no known precedent for such a turn of events. Yet, historians may find even more amazing what happened next. The United States, the beneficiary of the Soviet forfeit, responded to its victory not with triumphalism but with a similar collapse of confidence on the part of its elite.

Collapse of Confidence

Finding itself with the unanticipated status of sole superpower, America has not asked itself what use to make of this dominant position. Nor has it even addressed the more basic question of how to preserve for future generations the unparalleled security it now enjoys, invulnerable to defeat by any other power or conceivable coalition. Instead, the American policy elite has raised its trumpet and issued a clarion call to retreat, as if embarrassed by its new power or frightened of the implied responsibilities.

This flight is unreasonable but not hard to understand. From the founding of the republic until the bombing of Pearl Harbor, the dominant motif of American foreign policy was isolationism; its most cher-

9

ished principle, neutrality. Only the threat posed by Soviet expansionism propelled America to peacetime global engagement. Once the Soviet threat abated, it was inevitable that the isolationist temptation would make itself felt anew. And just when the Soviet state imploded, the American economy sank into recession, generating a preoccupation with domestic woes.

The recrudescence of isolationism is not limited to the elites. It is if anything stronger among rank-and-file voters and among politicians who keep their ears close to the ground. It first appeared in Harris Wofford's 1991 campaign to fill Pennsylvania's vacant seat in the U.S. Senate. Running against the heavily favored former U.S. attorney general Richard Thornburg, Wofford achieved an upset, campaigning on the slogan "It's time to take care of our own." The slogan was intended as a reference not only to the end of the cold war but also to the complaint that President George Bush, in whose cabinet Thornburg had served, was absorbed in international problems at the expense of domestic ones. Once elected, Wofford eschewed the label *isolationist,* penning an article for the journal *Foreign Policy.* Yet the article only confirmed the isolationist image it was intended to dispel. "What the world needs most from the United States is that we succeed in solving our own . . . problems," it said.[2]

Wofford's protestations reflected the fact that isolationism still has a bad name, as a result of the widely accepted view that America's isolationism after World War I helped to precipitate World War II. When an isolationist position is offered in a pure or extreme form, Americans are almost sure to reject it. Thus, in the presidential primaries of 1992, only Patrick Buchanan offered an extreme isolationist position, under the slogan "Put America first," a calculated reprise of the name of the most notorious isolationist organization of the interwar years, the America First Committee. Buchanan was soundly trounced, as was Senator Bob Kerrey on the Democratic side. Kerrey did not articulate as full an isolationist program as Buchanan, but he sought to tap into the same vein by running television commercials showing himself as a hockey goalkeeper, valiantly deflecting Sonys and Hondas that the Japanese were trying to shoot into the American net.

The 1992 Elections

While Americans rejected isolationism in pure or extreme form, the impulse in the direction of isolationism was clearly reflected among the mainstream 1992 candidates. President Bush responded to attacks on his deep involvement in foreign affairs not by defending this as a necessary obligation of his office but by postponing a long-planned trip to Asia and then changing its agenda to focus on trade and "jobs" rather than on political and security issues. He floated the idea that James Baker, his closest and in many eyes his ablest deputy, would relinquish the office of secretary of state in a second Bush administration to take charge of domestic economic policy, thereby signaling a dramatic shift in priorities. And while Bush was undoubtedly concerned about the political evolution of post-Soviet Russia, he refrained from seeking any new appropriation of aid for Russia until publicly prodded by former president Richard Nixon.

Bush's electoral opponent, Bill Clinton, criticized him for some of these maladroit moves, but the isolationist pull on Clinton was manifest in his campaign's watchword, "the economy, stupid," and in his decision to deliver but a single speech on foreign policy from the time of his nomination until the election.[3] This aversion to foreign affairs carried over into Clinton's presidency, leading the *Washington Post* to report in his first year in office that the administration was planning some speeches designed to "scotch suspicions that the president is leading a retreat from the world stage."[4]

The third man in the 1992 race, Ross Perot, ran as a "populist," that is, one who attempts to rally the visceral sentiments of the man in the street against the prevailing opinions of the elites. Not surprisingly, he leaned even more toward isolationism than Bush or Clinton, eventually staking his political fortunes on a campaign against the North American Free Trade Agreement.

The Spirit of Isolationism

If the spirit of isolationism affected presidential candidates and presidents, it affected Congress even more. While President Bush proposed deep cuts in spending for national defense and other international activities, President Clinton proposed deeper ones. But both men found their proposals reduced still further by Congress. The turn away from world affairs by Congress was expressed not only in how it exercised its power of the purse but also in a spirit of indifference. As *Congressional Quarterly* reported in 1993: "As much as Republican presidents used to complain of Congress' 'micromanagement' in foreign policy, today there is the opposite concern—that Congress is not paying close enough attention."[5]

Not only was the rise of isolationist sentiment evident in the reflexes of politicians, but it was directly recorded in various public opinion polls. Surveys that ask Americans whether our country should "take an active part in world affairs" or "stay out of world affairs" continue to elicit solid majorities for participation, again showing Americans' rejection of pure isolationism.[6] But when the question is asked not about mere participation but about leadership, the answers are very different. An ABC News/*Washington Post* poll in January 1994 asked respondents to choose between these two positions: that the United States "has the responsibility to take the leading role in world affairs" or that "it needs to reduce its involvement in world affairs." Only 27 percent chose the first formulation, while 67 percent chose the second.[7]

A *Times Mirror* survey, in September 1993, asked respondents whether America should be the "single world leader" or play a "shared leadership role" or "no leadership role." Small minorities favored either extreme—10 percent for "single world leader" and 7 percent for "no leadership role." Fully 78 percent preferred the middle course of a "shared leadership role." This middle group was then asked a follow-up question: should the United States be "the most active of the leading nations," or should it be "no more or less active than other leading nations?" Fifty-one percent of the 78 percent chose the second option, while only 27 percent chose the first.[8]

In February 1995, the Chicago Council on Foreign Relations released the results of its quadrennial opinion survey, which showed, it said, that "Americans are committed to an active role for the United States in the world."[9] Most news accounts of the survey echoed this inference. But a closer look at the results suggested a different conclusion. When respondents were asked to name "the two or three biggest foreign policy problems facing the United States today," without being given a list to choose from, the three most common answers were getting involved in the affairs of other countries, spending too much on foreign aid, and illegal immigration.[10] All three concerns pointed to a wish for diminished American interaction with the outside.

The general public is naturally less knowledgeable about foreign affairs, which are by definition esoteric, than it is about domestic affairs, which more often touch people in their daily lives. This ignorance conduces to escapism. (Not that escapism is unknown on other issues, such as budget deficits, the product of an unwillingness to tolerate either an increase in taxes or a decrease in benefits.) In foreign affairs, escapism often takes the form of imagining others to have power over us and blaming them for our problems. A 1989 Gallup poll found that when Americans were asked to name the world's top economic power, 58 percent said Japan, while only half that many, 29 percent, said the United States. (In fact, Japan's gross national product was and is less than half the size of America's.) The same poll revealed that the one federal program Americans were most eager to cut to reduce government spending was foreign aid. This response was not surprising, but what was illuminating was that 50 percent of all respondents said that they believed that foreign aid was one of the two biggest programs in the federal budget.[11] In fact, it is one of the smallest, totaling less than 1 percent.

What should we make of this far-fetched response? Various surveys have illustrated a popular deficiency of knowledge about public affairs, for example, the failure of a substantial proportion of citizens to name their congressman when asked. But surely, if they stopped to think about it for a moment, most Americans must know that many more dollars are spent on things like social security, Medicare, education, and national defense than on foreign aid. The 50 percent of Gallup's respondents who judged foreign aid to be such a major expenditure suffered not so much from ignorance perhaps as from wishful thinking. It is childishly self-satisfying to pretend that our straitened circumstances arise from spending too much on foreigners rather than from spending too much on ourselves, that is, from refusing to foot the bill for the services and benefits that we demand from government.

Elite Leadership

For just this reason, in foreign policy the role of elite opinion (and presidential leadership) is so important—not that elite opinion is always wiser. For example, it tends to favor leniency toward criminals—foolishly, I believe—perhaps because members of the elite are more insulated from crime. But, by the same token, if there is one area in which the better educated, those who have studied and seen more of the world abroad, have a special contribution to make in informing their fellow citizens, it is in foreign affairs. Thus, the Council on Foreign Relations was created in 1921 as a vehicle with which members of the elite could influence public opinion in the direction of internationalism. As William Hyland, until recently editor of the council's publication, *Foreign Affairs*, explained, "A number of influential Americans regretted the U.S. refusal to join the League [of Nations]. They believed that one reason for the turn against Wilsonian internationalism was public ignorance not only about the League, but about international affairs in general."[12]

How ironic then that in the aftermath of the cold war, a moment in some respects reminiscent of the aftermath of World War I—with an empire crumbled, nationalism on the wing, and the familiar balance of power overthrown—*Foreign Affairs* began to reverberate with calls for American disengagement. And leading the chorus was none other than William Hyland, writing: "The greatest challenges are within our shores, not beyond them. . . . the current vulnerabilities of the American position [are] much greater at home than abroad. If the United States wants a new world order that reflects traditional American values and principles, then the first place to achieve this goal is in this country."[13] Hyland was so bold as to embrace, albeit gingerly, the old isolationist tradition: "'Put America first' is a dangerous old slogan," he wrote, "but in light of this decade's realities it is not altogether wrong."[14]

Hyland is scarcely alone. Indeed, never have the three major journals of foreign affairs been so at one as in their appeals since the end of the cold war for reducing America's role abroad. *Foreign Affairs,* the organ of the traditional establishment, is flanked on the Left by *Foreign Policy,* founded in the 1970s as a liberal alternative, and on the Right by *The National Interest,* founded in the 1980s as a forum for more conservative views. While Hyland expounded in his journal the wisdom of putting "America first," Charles William Maynes, editor of *Foreign Policy,* expressed a similar thought in his: "Both the American and Soviet people are having to come to terms with their own limitations. . . . Each is recognizing that the priority of the 1990s is to concentrate on domestic affairs. Each understands that as great as its power may be, in different ways each is falling behind others in critical areas."[15] At the same time, *The National Interest's* editor, Owen Harries, was singing much the same tune:

> The United States should increasingly (but not abruptly) leave Europe to the Europeans . . . . being the world's only remaining superpower is not altogether a comfortable situation to be in . . . . Unilateral initiative on this scale [of Operation Desert Storm] was a luxury the United States could once afford; no more. . . . It needs a period . . . in

which excessive demands will not be made on its resources and energy—to buy time, so that it may attend to serious domestic problems and put its house in order.[16]

Former high officials, Republican and Democrat, have taken pen in hand to prescribe similar medicine. Theodore Sorenson, the speechwriter credited with authorship of President John F. Kennedy's famous inaugural pledge to "pay any price, bear any burden, fight any foe" to ensure the survival of liberty, revisited that phrase and recommended that America reject such "global hegemonic power." Instead, it should, he said, "evolve into a pivotal, residual power" that would "transfer to independent regional security groups the primary and initial responsibility for containing those threats to security that arise in their regions."[17]

Zbigniew Brzezinski, the national security adviser to President Jimmy Carter, wrote that

> U.S. policy will have to strike a more deliberate balance among global needs for continued American commitment, the desirability of some devolution of U.S. regional security responsibilities and the imperatives of America's domestic renewal. This will require a more subtle American contribution to sustaining global security than was the case during the cold war.[18]

And James Schlesinger, who served as secretary of defense under President Gerald Ford and secretary of energy under President Carter, wrote that America "must learn . . . to husband its strength" and to be "sufficiently disciplined to select those tasks, few in number, that truly involve the longer-term interests of this society."[19]

Economic Issues

The prime themes of this campaign are economic. "America's resources are no longer commensurate with the maintenance of the exalted position it held in the postwar period," says Hyland.[20] In this view, he echoes President Bush's famous line that America "has more will than wallet."[21] Some advocates believe that foreign policy absorbs dollars that they would rather see spent on domestic issues, which the *New York Times* calls "the nation's real security needs."[22] *Foreign Policy* reports a "growing popular sentiment for investing at home much of the money that is now spent abroad to maintain America's alliances."[23] And the Carnegie Endowment for International Peace, one of the nation's venerable bastions of internationalism, sponsored a commission of eminent citizens to study America's role in the new world order, which concluded that "America's first foreign policy priority is to strengthen our domestic economic performance."[24]

Distrust of American Power

For others, economic issues are secondary. Their preference for American withdrawal begins with a distrust of American power. Owen Harries resents the "unhealthy American habit, acquired during the Cold War years, of absolute dominance, of assuming control without consulting anyone, and then complaining bitterly that others were not backing it up and sharing the burden."[25]

From a distrust of American power, it follows that a diminution of America's role is a good in itself. Thus Harries and Michael Lind write that to "realists" like themselves, "the genuine long-term interest of all great powers is best served by a world order in which no power, and no combination of powers, strives for hegemony or empire. This puts classical realists at odds with proponents of a Pax Americana."[26]

Because the advocates of retrenchment are not pure isolationists, they do not say that America should simply ignore international problems; rather, they often suggest that we should let somebody else solve them. For those of liberal bent, that somebody else is usually the United Nations or other multilateral bodies.

Thus the *New York Times* opined after Clinton's election that "the new administration also needs to ease America out of the costly role of world policeman by helping to transform the United Nations and regional groups into credible instruments for enforcing collective security."[27]

The Carnegie Endowment's prestigious National Commission on America and the New World declared that "any plausible vision for America's role in the world must include a renewed financial commitment to the United Nations," and it said that the "emphasis on collective leadership can no longer be merely a facade or an afterthought . . . we will sometimes have to yield a measure of the autonomy we have guarded so zealously during most of our history."[28] The Brookings Institution is promoting the concept of "cooperative security," which William J. Perry helped to formulate before he became secretary of defense. Its premise is the "subordination of power projection to the constraints of international consensus."[29]

Can it be "isolationist" to support the United Nations? Yes, if the aim is to substitute UN leadership, to which the United States contributes modestly, for American leadership. Charles Krauthammer has said that "multilateralism is the isolationism of the internationalist."[30] We might better say that it is the internationalism of the isolationist.

Conservatives are less likely to place hope in the United Nations; instead, some of them advocate devolving responsibilities from America's shoulders to other groups of nations. About the resistance to Iraq's occupation of Kuwait, Owen Harries wrote:

> The first mistake made by President Bush . . . was the immediate, unqualified, and unilateral commitment of American power to achieving the complete, unconditional withdrawal of Iraq from Kuwait. . . . he should have made it clear at the outset that the days of leaving it to the United States to bear the burden of responsibility and leadership— to "do the hard work of freedom"—were over. . . . [He] should have turned to the Europeans and the Japanese and said: ". . . you call the shots."[31]

And William Hyland says: "Going it alone will become an increasingly less justifiable course, and working out a redistribution of burdens will become a crucial challenge to American foreign policy."[32]

In some ways, the liberal and conservative currents in the new isolationism feed off each other. Liberals who are reluctant to condone the direct exertion of American power for American interests are often more comfortable when the United States contributes forces to missions carried out by the United Nations or undertakes military missions that are wholly humanitarian. Thus, Morton Halperin, the antiwar activist appointed to Clinton's National Security Council staff, published a book in 1992 in which he advocated the use of American troops under international auspices to resolve nationality conflicts around the globe.[33]

Michael Lind has labeled this "the politics of national disinterest," elaborating: "The less a policy benefits the nation undertaking it, the nobler the policy and the nation."[34] Conservatives find such an approach as repugnant as liberals find the use of force for narrowly self-interested reasons.

Beginning while Bush was president, the thrust of neo-isolationism came more from liberals than conservatives. But this changed after the 1994 elections, which brought to Congress a militant new Republican majority, half of whose members were first elected after the cold war.[35] The philosophy of this new majority emphasizes individualism and the dignity of self-interest, and it is tinged with populism. Many of these representatives measure any foreign policy activity by a narrow gauge of American interest. Where the liberal voices of neo-isolationism sought to reduce foreign policy accounts to augment various domestic programs, the new majority seeks such savings to fund deficit or tax reduction, while domestic programs are cut, too.

When Republicans in Congress moved to cut appropriations for some foreign policy agencies and to abolish others, Clinton branded them "isolationists." He denounced such efforts as "a frontal assault on the authority of the president to conduct . . . foreign policy."[36] Yet he himself had earlier justified giving short shrift to the war in Bosnia "because what I got elected to do was to let America look at our own problems."[37] Likewise, Secretary of State Warren Christopher complained that the cuts "would damage our nation's interests and cripple our ability to lead."[38] But in presenting his own foreign policy budget proposals a year earlier, he had stressed that "our first strategic priority is strengthening America's economic security. . . . Ensuring our nation's economic security is the central objective of this administration."[39]

The attacks by Clinton and his aides on the isolationism of the new Republicans were mostly on target, but they were also a classic example of chickens coming home to roost.

Whether liberal or conservative, those who advocate American retrenchment rarely accept the label *isolationist*. As Paul Weyrich has put it: "Isolationism is itself a conjuring trick by the internationalists, a hoodoo they call up whenever they feel threatened. . . . America was never isolationist."[40] But those who battled in the 1920s and 1930s to keep America at arms length from the rest of the world also eschewed that label. Senator Henry Cabot Lodge, leader of the opposition to the Versailles Peace Treaty of 1919, made much the same complaint as Weyrich:

> Those who . . . wish the United States to become an integral part of the European political system, use the word 'isolationist' in order to discredit those who differ with them. There is no such thing as an 'isolationist,' of course, in the United States, and there never has been.[41]

Perhaps so, or perhaps true isolationists are few and far between. But what is not scarce among Americans—neither among the public nor among the elites—is a mood of weariness with international burdens, a yearning to focus on things nearer to home, and a facile illusion that neglecting foreign policy will help us solve domestic problems.

·3·

THE NEW GREAT DEBATE—
WASHINGTON
VERSUS WILSON

Although those who today are summoning America home from its international engagements may not be much different from, or much wiser than, those who did the same seventy years ago, I have no wish to engage them in semantic argument. Rather than call them isolationists, we might call them Washingtonians (in a reference to our first president's views on foreign entanglements), surely not a prejudicial label. And we might say that the main debate over U.S. foreign policy is between the Washingtonian and the Wilsonian outlooks.

Washingtonians and Wilsonians

Throughout the cold war, or at least since Vietnam, the main divide on foreign policy pitted "doves" against "hawks." Both sides understood that the question was how to protect ourselves against the power of Soviet communism or the danger of war with the Soviet Union. Hawks believed that the answer lay in strength and toughness, while doves believed it lay in understanding and accommodation. Although labels necessarily simplify and group people together and override nuances, most national politicians and commentators fell in one camp or the other, and on this basis it was fairly easy to foretell accurately what position each would take as the theater shifted from East Asia to Central America to southern Africa to the Middle East and so on.

The great debate between hawks and doves ended with the cold war. In its place has emerged the debate between Washingtonians and Wilsonians. These embody the two contrasting answers to what—in the absence of a more specific threat like the Soviet—the generic basic question for foreign policy is, How do we keep ourselves secure?

By "Washingtonian," I mean to invoke the famous Farewell Address. To President Washington, the world outside—the operative part of which was Europe—was replete with conflict. The key to our safety was to avoid getting drawn into other people's quarrels. "Why . . . entangle our peace and prosperity in the toils of European ambition, Rivalship, Interest, Humour or Caprice?" he asked. To gird ourselves against such entanglement we needed to guard against sentimentality, that is, against "excessive partiality for one foreign nation and excessive dislike of another." In sum, look out for ourselves and avoid trouble.

The Wilsonian approach shares the premise that the world is full of conflicts. But President Wilson learned from the bitter experience of World War I how difficult it is to keep America aloof from foreign broils. His solution was that America try to shape and guard the peace, keeping itself safe by making the world a safer place. This approach sets a much lower threshold for American involvement abroad, on the theory that early intervention on a small scale may forestall a much heavier commitment later on. The Washingtonian's characteristic question about any foreign quarrel is, Does it threaten us? The Wilsonian's is, Might it come to threaten us?

Wilson is probably the most controversial major figure in the history of American diplomacy, and by using his name I risk inviting a host of tangential arguments. But the specific provisions of the Versailles Treaty are no more intrinsic to the Wilsonian outlook than any particular interpretation of the 1778 treaty with France is to the Washingtonian. Political scientist Arnold Wolfers divided the goals of states between "possession goals" and "milieu goals." The former designates tangible goods or benefits; the latter, "the shape of the environment in which the nation operates."[1] The essence of the difference between Washingtonians and Wilsonians is how much attention to give to milieu goals.

To put it another way, the question is how far from home America should begin trying to defend itself. I refer not primarily to geographic distance but to distance along the chain of contingency. Extreme Washingtonians—true isolationists—believe that American defense begins when an enemy army approaches our shores. Less extreme Washingtonians—otherwise known as "realists"—would defend key allies or pieces of geography that in hostile hands might soon translate into the approach of an enemy army. But they insist on a rather close connection. Wilsonians are willing to travel much further along the chain of contingency to confront problems whose effect on us might be indirect or several steps removed. They are more concerned about the internal evolution of states, believing that it often affects external behavior. They put more stock in the psychological effects that events in one situation may have on another, therefore caring more about the force of example and the strength of international laws and norms. They also tend to attach more importance to the power of "hearts and minds" relative to that of guns and dollars.

Interest and Morality

The difference between the two camps has less to do with the conflict between interest and morality than is often supposed. On some issues Wilsonians might give priority to a moral principle or humanitarian concern, while Washingtonians would put first an American material interest. On the question of trade with China, for example, Washingtonians might emphasize America's commercial stakes, while Wilsonians emphasize human rights. But where American security is at issue, no thoughtful Wilsonian would put other values first. On the contrary, Wilsonians argue that self-defense is completely harmonious with sound morality. They tend toward Jefferson's view that "with nations as with individuals our interests soundly calculated will ever be inseparable from our moral duties."[2]

Will Wilsonians, however, more often hazard military action where no U.S. interests are at stake? Sometimes yes. They will be more open than Washingtonians to humanitarian interventions, but the occasions for such are rare and extreme. Indeed, the cases most often discussed as ripe for humanitarian intervention are hypothetical—against Pol Pot's mass slaughter or Hitler's genocide. One contemporary tragedy where a strong case could have been made for humanitarian intervention was Rwanda, but oddly no one made the case since America had only recently been burned in Somalia, where a low-risk humanitarian mission, launched by a very non-Wilsonian president, had been spoiled by "mission creep."

On the other side, Washingtonians, in the main, would deny that their approach ignores moral reasoning. David C. Hendrickson, for example, summoning Americans to the foreign policy of the Founding Fathers, calls it a "tradition of thought and web of principle."[3]

In this century, America has tried both the Wilsonian and the Washingtonian approaches with instructive effect. After World War I, Wilson unveiled his visionary scheme, but in the end he failed to bring his countrymen behind him. The nation turned instead down the Washingtonian path. We refused to join the League of Nations, we erected trade barriers, and we focused our attention on domestic affairs. The themes behind that decision were very like what we hear today. "It is not that which is happening in Russia . . . that is bringing doubt and worry to our own people," said the famous Progressive, Senator William Borah. "It is the conditions here in our own land . . . . Capitalism must turn its eyes inwardly . . . and solve its own internal problems."[4] The other leading opponent of ratifying the Versailles Treaty, Senator Henry Cabot Lodge, said, "The United States can best serve the world, first, by preserving its own strength and the fabric of its civilization."[5]

Then, the Washingtonian path led directly to the worst catastrophe in history: World War II. Of course, there were many causes of the war, starting with Hitler's evil genius and including much folly— on the part of German politicians, British statesmen, French strategists, and the Soviet dictator. Still, had America shouldered the burdens of international engagement and enforced the terms of the Versailles Treaty, the war might never have happened.

After World War II, the pull of Washingtonianism made itself felt again. Even as Stalin spread his empire over Eastern Europe, thereby launching the cold war, America demobilized at breakneck speed, reducing its forces from 12 million to 1 million within a year. But by 1947 Americans had wakened to the Soviet threat, and we came roaring back. We embarked on the most Wilsonian of policies. Never has a country undertaken such an internationalist policy, with the possible exception of the great empire builders, and even they may not compare. We established scores of military bases around the world. We forged a dense web of entangling alliances. We remade Germany and Japan if not quite in our image then according to our lights. We carried out the Marshall Plan, on which we spent, together with other foreign aid, some 2 percent of our gross national product for six years. We fostered the United Nations and the Bretton Woods international economic regime. Above all, we adopted the strategy of containment, audaciously taking the whole globe as our chessboard, determined, as George Kennan put it in his famous "X" article, to resist Soviet expansion through "the adroit and vigilant application of counter-force at a series of constantly shifting geographical and political points, corresponding to the shifts and maneuvers of Soviet policy."[6]

The results of this radically internationalist policy were sublime. We faced the most fearsome foe the world has ever known, and we triumphed without having to fight a general war. Some "realists" may object that the post–World War II policies that issued in victory in the cold war ought not to be credited to Wilsonianism. The Carnegie Endowment explicitly contrasts Wilson's "too idealistically conceived" policies with those "after World War II [when] wise leaders tempered idealism with realism."[7] Wilson's notions about things like collective security and disarmament *were* woolly-headed, and America's postwar policies were more tough-minded, but they were not "realist" policies in the formal sense of that term.[8] They were, in the largest sense, distinctly Wilsonian. At a time when America enjoyed a nuclear monopoly, it might have sought security in military technology and separated its security from that of every other country. Instead, it took the view that its security was invested in almost everyone else's. The goal was to defend America. The strategy was to defend as far along the chain of contingency as we could get.

Moreover, not only was our postwar strategy Wilsonian, but it reached its successful climax under our most Wilsonian president since Wilson—Ronald Reagan. To speak of Reagan in this way may confuse some who, quite rightly, think of Wilson as a premier liberal and Reagan as an arch conservative or who recall Wilson's faith in international organizations and Reagan's apparent low regard for the United Nations. But "liberal" and "conservative" have little to do with it. And Wilson's attachment to international organization was but one part of his legacy—I would say the hollowest. In other respects, Reagan's policies were quintessentially Wilsonian.

One hallmark of Wilson's view was the belief in a nexus of America's security and that of many others. Reagan acted from the premise that American security was bound up with events in places far from home and in countries of little intrinsic weight: Nicaragua,

El Salvador, Angola, Afghanistan, and even Grenada. Wilson also put great store by the power of ideas and moral values in international politics, and so did Reagan, even to the point of including ideological thrusts in his speeches that were regarded as great diplomatic blunders, such as calling the Soviet Union an "evil empire." Wilson championed the spread of democracy, seeing it as a key to solving many of the world's problems. Likewise, Reagan launched the National Endowment for Democracy and succored a global trend of democratization. Above all, Reagan, like Wilson, viewed American leadership as the linchpin of world order.

Because historical events and circumstances do not repeat themselves, the success or failure of a policy in the past is no sure guide to the future. Still, the very dramatic contrast between the catastrophe that resulted from the Washingtonian approach after the first world war and the spectacular success of the Wilsonian approach after the second constitute a prima facie case for staying on the Wilsonian path as we search for a post–cold war policy.

What makes that quest so difficult is that no single palpable threat appears on our horizon as Soviet imperialism did in the aftermath of World War II. In that sense, our situation more resembles what we faced after World War I. In 1919, neither fascism nor Nazism had yet been invented, and while Bolshevism had seized Russia, few believed it could endure, much less bid for world supremacy. No one foresaw that we would spend the next seventy years fighting for our lives against these totalitarian movements. That we can identify no single such menace now does not mean that none will emerge: that failure may only show the limits of our imaginations. Moreover, whether such a menace will materialize is not written in the stars or predetermined. Our own engagement or abdication will help decide it.

Hitler and Stalin did not have to happen. They were partly of our making. It is widely appreciated that our isolationism stoked the Nazi juggernaut. Less widely appreciated is that we might have nipped Bolshevism in the bud and thus forestalled the spawning of all this century's totalitarian regimes, for it was the model the others copied. In Lloyd George's war cabinet in 1918, Winston Churchill urged that the Allies impose, either by diplomacy or by force if need be, a free, supervised election on Russia, which he was confident would lead to the defeat of the Bolsheviks.[9] But he was turned down. He recorded his thoughts in a memorandum that makes interesting reading today:

Most people wish to get free from Russia and to leave her to work out her own salvation or stew in her own juice . . . . Nobody wants to intervene in Russian affairs. Russia is a very large country, a very old country, a very disagreeable country inhabited by immense numbers of ignorant people largely possessed of lethal weapons and in a state of extreme disorder. Also Russia is a long way off. We on the other hand have just finished an important and expensive war against the Germans. . . . We wish now to bring home our soldiers, reduce our taxes and enjoy our victory. . . . We may abandon Russia: but Russia will not abandon us. We shall retire and she will follow.[10]

Future Threats

Where today may lurk the embryo of future monsters to torment us or our children, as Russian Bolshevism tormented our parents and ourselves? Perhaps again in Russia, although probably not in the form of resurgent communism but of ultranationalism or fascism or, more likely still, some completely original ideological mutation. These forces emerged in the parliamentary elections of 1993 in part as the result of Western inaction. As Jeffrey Sachs, former economic adviser to President Yeltsin, put it, "For two years, reformers in Moscow struggled for power while Western governments promised them large-scale aid. The reformers could not win without our help, but help never arrived."[11]

Or it may lurk in China, which has won almost as much Western admiration for its rapid creation of capitalism as it won a few decades ago for its rapid creation of communism. Although it may now prefer the economic theories of Friedman to those of Marx, the Communist Party still rules China, and it remains ruthless and ambitious. Nicholas Kristof, former Beijing bureau chief for the *New York Times*, observed: "China . . . has nuclear weapons, border disputes with most of its neighbors, and a rapidly improving army that may—within a decade or so—be able to resolve old quarrels in its own favor . . . . While most countries have been cutting military budgets . . . China has been using its economic boom to finance a far-reaching buildup. It seeks the influence of a great power."[12] With its vast population, if China's economy continues to grow like those of the other Asian "tigers," it could come to rival America's. If this growth is not accompanied by political transformation, then China could become a big threat to world peace. Americans of the Washingtonian school regard the issue of human rights in China as mere sentimentalism that must not be allowed to disrupt our access to "the world's biggest market" or to complicate our diplomacy. But the fate of human rights there—which means the nature of the regime—may well determine our ability to live with China in the next century.

Or our future bane may lurk in Tehran, which has succeeded in spreading the virus of Islamic fanaticism to the Sudan, Algeria, Egypt, Lebanon, and Palestine and even into Turkey. Muslims make up nearly one-fifth of the world's population, and if radical Islam becomes dominant among them, it will cause unimaginable turmoil. Yet Western governments have consistently endeavored to get along with Tehran rather than combat the virus.

Serious threats may also arise in places now hard to foresee or through a synergy of troubles in disparate places. The events that led from 1919 to 1939, from peace to war, were to some extent disconnected, but they fed on each other. Democratic regimes succumbed in Italy, then in Central and Eastern Europe; the Japanese occupied Manchuria; Hitler rose to power; Italy invaded Abyssinia (now, Ethiopia), and the West responded with feckless economic sanctions; Germany rearmed in violation of the Versailles Treaty, and the West responded with appeasement; civil war broke out in Spain. A terrible momentum built. Although today's circumstances look far less ominous, it is not hard to picture dangerous events once again reinforcing each other. North Korea begins to assemble a nuclear arsenal; Islamic fanaticism takes hold of a growing portion of the Muslim world; a breakdown of law enforcement in Russia allows more weapons of mass destruction into international circulation; from one source or the other, "rogue" regimes in Iran, Iraq, and Libya get their hands on nuclear weapons, and so do some of the terrorist groups they sponsor; Serbian nationalism metastasizes in ethnic cleansing bordering on genocide against Bosnian Muslims, giving Muslims everywhere a festering grievance at their treatment in Europe and weakening the norms of international law. Do any of these events seem unlikely? Together they make an explosive mixture.

We can deal with such an explosion when it comes, or we can do our best to prevent it by dealing with its contributory elements as they arise. That is the essential choice we face. Washingtonians would have us keep our heads down until threats loom on our doorsteps or in our front yards. Does this caricature their position? Consider this editorial from the *New York Times:* "For America to remain truly strong now, Congress has to distinguish clear and present dangers from overblown and distant threats."[13] To wait until dangers become clear and present, however, is to wait until very late in the game.

The point was underscored by a comment Colin Powell made while serving as chairman of the Joint Chiefs of Staff: "I've been chairman for 18 months . . . and I've had . . . six opportunities to use the armed forces of the United States and no one had predicted [any] of them 18 months and one day ago."[14] In an unintentional illustration of that point, in 1992 Foreign Relations Committee Chairman Lee Hamilton observed about the Gulf War that "few threats to the peace will be so clear-cut . . . as a direct military threat to the world's supply of oil."[15] What Hamilton apparently forgot was that he had opposed the Gulf War. Threats are usually much more clear-cut in retrospect than in prospect.

Preventing War, Defending Peace

The Wilsonian alternative is not to wait for "clear and present dangers" but to make every effort to defend the peace. Sometimes such a defense will entail political exertions to influence developments between or within other nations. Sometimes it will entail military action to deter aggression or to stop its development. Many of the Americans who drive around with bumper stickers urging fellow motorists to "work for peace" have in mind methods, like unilateral disarmament, that would bring results opposite to those intended. But the spirit is right. Peace is hard to come by and hard to keep. And we must labor for it, although better by arming than by disarming.

Washingtonians may respond by saying that preventing wars is hopeless, so our goal must be to stay out of them. But we have a poor record of staying out of wars. We determined to stay out of World War I and trumpeted our neutrality, only to be drawn in. We attempted neutrality of a sort again in World War II, but we were not neutral enough to satisfy Tojo and Hitler, so they made war on us. In 1950, we implied that we would not go to war on behalf of South Korea, but when it was attacked, we concluded we had to defend it. Korea and World War II might both have been averted had America acted robustly early to deter the aggressor. And the same is true, mutatis mutandis, for World War I, had Britain—which was then the leading power—so acted. (Even Vietnam was a war we tried unsuccessfully to stay out of by denying French entreaties for help in 1954, although in that case it is much harder to say what we should have done.)

Americans sometimes overlook the fragility of peace because we have suffered less from war than have most other peoples. And this good fortune can lead us to react too slowly. Columnist Robert J. Samuelson has made the point that we think too contentedly about the outcome of World War II, "the good war," from which we emerged victorious. We sometimes forget the terrible cost of having entered it so late and so unprepared. Had we fought sooner, we might have prevented the Holocaust and Soviet conquest of Eastern Europe. Indeed, Samuelson speculates, following historian William O'Neill, that had Japan not attacked us, America might not have entered the war. As a result, Hitler would likely have made all Europe his own, or he and Stalin would eventually have divided it.[16]

The urgency of working to preserve peace is magnified by the proliferation, or its prospect, of nuclear weapons. Iraq, we discovered, was very close to acquiring a nuclear bomb. North Korea, it seems, already has one or two. Neither is an advanced country. We are thus clearly poised on the brink of a substantial increase in the number of nuclear-armed states. Of course, it would be suicidal for any of these new members of the nuclear club to attack the United States, but that is hardly our only concern. Nuclear weapons in the hands of a Saddam Hussein or the heirs to Kim Il Sung could pose a very real danger to the states near to them and could also be used to deter American intervention against a local aggression. How would the Persian Gulf crisis have unfolded had Saddam already completed his bomb? Would Egypt, Saudi Arabia, and Syria have given us their cooperation in the face of such a peril? Could we ourselves have been deterred by a threat to respond to the bombing of Baghdad by a nuclear strike on an American city?[17]

We can attempt to counteract proliferation through diplomacy, intelligence, controls on the transfer of technology, and economic sanctions and even through preemptive military strikes, as Israel carried out against Iraq in 1981 and we may at some point execute against North Korea. But Edward Luck, president of the United Nations Association, argues convincingly that the prospects for success against proliferation are tied to the general level of peacefulness in the world: "Ultimately . . . it will be necessary to create conditions that reduce the demand for advanced weapons of mass destruction. That effort will entail more decisive and consistent efforts by the international community to enforce a geographically inclusive concept of collective security. A laissez-faire American approach to regional conflicts would have the opposite effect."[18]

Realists will scoff at the idea of "a geographically inclusive concept of collective security," and perhaps they are right. But their mantra that the future will mostly resemble the past takes on a macabre aspect in light of nuclear proliferation. Should we simply resign ourselves to a conviction that nuclear war will become part of our environment? Even if Luck is naive in his aspiration for collective security, the point stands that local or regional conflicts will spur nuclear proliferation, a fact that gives America a stake in their resolution.

Realists are right that the world is not transformed easily or painlessly, but it does change. Adherents of the Washingtonian approach invoke the wisdom of the Founding Fathers. But with the advent of nuclear weapons, and missiles that can carry them across continents in minutes, how different the world is today from that with which Washington had to cope. At its founding, America was a nation of 2 million, one of the smallest and weakest states on earth. Its main goal was to avoid being crushed by any of the great powers. The policies appropriate to that goal hold little relevance for our current circumstance.

American Power

America is no longer small, nor is it just one power among others. Its power has largely shaped the world we know, and its decisive weight is the ballast that provides what stability the world of nations enjoys. Imagine for a moment the world of today without the United States or in which the United States withdrew into a policy of "fortress America." We can predict that Japan would rearm, and probably "go nuclear," as would Germany. Russia, where everything else is going wrong, would be irresistibly tempted to compensate by exerting its chief asset, its supreme military power. Moderate Arab regimes would fall before the onslaught of Islamic radicalism, compelling Israel to put its nuclear arsenal on a hair trigger. Competition and mutual distrust between China and Japan and between Russia and Germany would mount. Would World War III be very far from hand?

What makes this scenario unlikely is the presence of America, which gives some measure of security all around. The basis for world peace is that there is one preeminent power, and it is peaceful and nonaggrandizing. This condition is unprecedented. At other moments in history, when a single state has been supreme, it has always been imperial. America's unique role provides a basis for hope that relative peace can be preserved for a long time.

Some Washingtonians suggest that America should limit itself to holding the balance, much as Britain did with great success on the European continent throughout the long peace of the nineteenth century. But there are major differences between Britain's circumstance then and America's today. Britain then had to balance among only a handful of players sharing a common European culture. Today's world contains dozens of states with the capacity to disrupt world peace; their interests and ambitions intersect in a plethora of ways; and their diversity is such that clashes between civilizations, some argue, may characterize the coming era.[19] To be a balancer at the fringes of such a melange is all but hopeless.

Further, America's active presence—as ally, leader, protector, law enforcer—buttresses the peace today. To withdraw to the role of balancer presupposes that states like Japan and Germany would assume the full weight of their own defense, leaving America then to balance between Japan and China, Germany and Russia, and so on. Would this be a secure peace, or a comfortable role?

Finally, when America has played the balancing game, it has not always been with happy effect. Because of our own folly and that of the other democracies, we were left with no choice but to support Stalin's Soviet Union to counterbalance Hitler's Germany. But the result was the division of Europe and forty-odd years of cold war. We balanced Khomeini's Iran by supporting Saddam's Iraq, reflagging its tankers during the Iran-Iraq War. In the end, we found ourselves having to fight a war against Iraq. In extremis a balancing policy may be necessary, but these side effects only point up the wisdom of pursuing proactive policies to forestall such situations.

Some Washingtonians argue that America lacks the strength for a more ambitious role. Thus the Carnegie Endowment's National Commission on America and the New World declaimed that "among the many ironies of the cold war [is] that the victor emerged with less power, not more."[20] The first to be taken in by such nonsense may have been Saddam Hussein. In August 1990, he annexed Kuwait to Iraq, proclaiming Iraq's determination "to continue jihad without any hesitation or retreat and without any fear from the foreigner's power."[21]

President Bush replied: "This will not stand." In the next five months, America won UN support for its position, secured the active collaboration of a few dozen states, and then made good on its pledge to restore Kuwait's sovereignty, in the process destroying one of the world's larger military machines while sustaining only light casualties.

This was not the only demonstration of America's military, diplomatic, and other national strengths in the 1990s. The Arab-Israel peace process grinds forward, mediated by the United States in a region in which it once had to vie with the Soviet Union for influence. In Africa, America rescued Somalia, at least for the time being, from auto-genocide by starvation, an accomplishment not erased by the painful circumstances of America's withdrawal. And when democracy came to South Africa, Nelson Mandela looked to a special relationship with America, notwithstanding the history of distrust between America and his African National Congress.

In Latin America, whose politics were long laced with resentment of the *Yanqui,* Mexico, which once epitomized this attitude, pinned its future on the North American Free Trade Agreement. Other regional states have begun queuing up for admission. In Europe, plans for integration, which would diminish America's influence, falter, while plans for expansion of NATO, with America at its core, move forward, pushed by Eastern European countries eager for inclusion. Meanwhile, the crisis in Bosnia became a test case of the ability of Europeans to handle European problems without America in the foreground, and the results of the test were devastatingly clear. In short, the disappearance of the other superpower left America more powerful than ever before, just as common sense would suggest, and not weaker, as the contorted logic of the Washingtonians would have it.

America is even more powerful today than it was in the immediate aftermath of World War II, although that moment is cited by many heralds of American decline as the apogee of American power. They point out that America's share of global production was larger then than before or since. But however productive America's factories, it was helpless to prevent Soviet acquisition of Eastern Europe and North Korea, and it had to struggle mightily to keep much of Southern Europe—Italy, France, and Greece—from going the same way. It failed to prevent China from joining the Communist camp, and for the next years it waged a contest for influence in the third world in which it often came up short.

America's industrial preponderance as of 1945 was an anomaly, reflecting the wartime destruction of most of the other combatants' economies. As various critics of the notion of "American decline" have pointed out, America's share of world production soon returned to its twentieth-century average of 20 to 25 percent and has remained at that level since.[22] Still, in the 1970s and 1980s many observers noted the superior economic performance of Japan and much of Western Europe, especially Germany, and predicted a relentless erosion of America's position. But in the 1990s, these other industrialized economies have suffered reverses more severe than America's, while the U.S. economy has made a strong, albeit delayed, recovery from the recession of 1991. For 1992 through 1994, America's growth rate has exceeded that of any other major industrial country.

Ben J. Wattenberg calls America "the most influential nation in history," and if this is an exaggeration, it is not a big one. America's armed forces have overwhelming strength and unique global reach. America's economy, despite all the alarms, is more than twice the size of any other nation's. The idea of democracy, pioneered by America, is more widely imitated than any other political idea; it has now been adopted by a majority of the world's states.[23] Diplomatically, America is called upon to settle issues in every corner of the world. And American popular culture—for better or for worse—has spread almost everywhere. Millions upon millions wear jeans, drink Coke, smoke Marlboros, watch *Dallas* and CNN, listen to Madonna, and want to be like Mike.

One result of these assets, but also a cause of them, is the great success (on the whole) of America's foreign policies. America was victorious in World War I and World War II, after each of which it largely shaped the peace. Then it was victorious once again in the cold war. The spread of democracy, the end of colonialism, the international economic system born at Bretton Woods, and the creation of the United Nations are all large, deliberate policy achievements of America's. In seeking wise approaches to the post–cold war world, we ought to begin by asking not how we can "change our ways" (as the Carnegie Commission recommended) but how we can continue our success. What can we learn from this great record, especially from its crowning glory, our bloodless victory in the cold war?

The Success of Idealism

For one thing, this success constitutes a loud rebuke to the "realist" school of thought. For America's foreign policy tradition is laced with idealism, especially in the twentieth century as the nation has struggled to emerge from isolation. Indeed, the most telling criticism of that tradition is that its idealism has often shaded into naiveté. The United States invested great political capital in creating the League of Nations and the United Nations. It has repeatedly sought to solve international problems through legal mechanisms that often lacked means of enforcement, such as the 1928 Kellogg-Briand Pact that "outlawed" war. It has championed principles of self-determination, human rights, democracy, nonrecognition of acquisition of territory by force, one-man-one-vote, and the like that have caused no end of irritation to the diplomats of older, more sophisticated nations and to Washingtonian thinkers like George Kennan, who decried America's "legalistic-moralistic approach to international problems,"[24] and Hans Morgenthau, who believed American foreign policy had gone relentlessly downhill since the late 1700s.[25]

In contrast, France, Britain, other European states, and Japan have been guided much more by "realist" sensibilities. This may be said even for Russia, despite the heavy overlay of ideology during the decades of communism. It was Stalin who spoke that famous realist apothegm, "How many divisions has the Pope?" And yet all of these are no more than secondary powers today, having fallen from times of greater glory, while America, the naive, reigns supreme. Could it be that, as President Lincoln said, "right makes might"?

To some extent surely it does, or at least the conviction of right makes might, because it enhances a state's ability to rally its citizens and to summon the best efforts of its leaders, officials, and soldiers. In a painstaking study of sixteen international crises spanning the period 1895 to 1973 that was designed to test various theories of international relations, Glenn H. Snyder and Paul Diesing happened on an unanticipated finding. "Perceptions of legitimacy are potent in determining bargaining power and outcomes," they wrote. "That is, the party that believes it is in the right and communicates this belief to an opponent who has some doubts about the legitimacy of its own position, nearly always wins."[26] Snyder and Diesing were using the tools of social science to rediscover what Napoleon had tried to explain nearly two centuries earlier, when he said that in warfare, moral factors are three times more important than material ones.

Right may also make might by encouraging more accommodating behavior from other states who know that they have little to fear or distrust from a righteous state. One of the sources of American influence is that many other states trust America to be an honest mediator of their quarrels, and they often welcome the presence of American forces, not fearing that they will act as subjugators. Whatever the cause, the fact that America, the idealistic, has been so successful hardly suggests that it should now follow in the more "realistic" footsteps of the has-been powers.

What we should conclude from the end of the cold war is not that the time has come to lay down our burdens. Rather it is that America can be wondrously effective pursuing a "Wilsonian," or an intensely activist, engaged foreign policy—playing the role of world leader. Unfortunately, upholding the peace is not something that can be done just one time: it is a perpetual task. Fortunately, America has proved that it is very good at this task. The question is, Does it have the will and courage to keep doing it?

·4·

CAN WE AFFORD TO LEAD?

Can we afford to be the world's leader? Can we afford all the military expenditures, the foreign aid, the multifarious activities of the Central Intelligence Agency, the U.S. Information Agency, and the diplomatic corps? Haven't we entered an era of diminished resources? Aren't we, as the chairman of the House Select Intelligence Committee put it, explaining cuts in the Clinton administration's intelligence budget request, "out of money"?[1]

America's Wealth

The answer is that we can afford whatever foreign policy we need or choose. We are the richest country in the world, the richest country the world has ever known. And we are richer today than we have ever been before. We command not fewer but more resources than ever.

Although we are rich and have been, with only minor exceptions, growing richer each year, still each year we spend a smaller part of our substance on foreign policy. We spend less on defense, less on foreign aid, less on intelligence, less on overseas broadcasting and information. And because global political trends are running so favorably, we can get away with it. Indeed, in the latter 1990s, we can finance all the components of a foreign policy of global leadership for a share of our income well below what we have spent on foreign policy throughout the post–World War II era. But we cannot do it for nothing. There are limits to how far we can cut our foreign policy budgets without abdicating, indeed without inviting trouble.

The question today is not whether we can afford to lead. Rather, it is whether we will allow ourselves to be so lulled by the disappearance of the Soviet threat, whether we will so indulge ourselves in the natural temptation for high benefits and low taxes, that we will neglect the tasks of preserving the peace. If we do, we risk having to pay for our shortsightedness many times over and perhaps having to pay for it in a coin more precious than money.

If we are so rich, why do we seem to feel poor? The most prosaic reason is that people tend to take for granted what they have. When we pray, we thank God for what He has given us. But most of the rest of the time, we think more about the things we wish for than those we already possess. In a recent lecture in a Polish academy on the issues I am discussing here, when I said that America is a rich country, my audience broke into laughter. These were educated urban people, sharing in Western culture: they read the same books, watched the same movies and TV, and were exposed to most of the same products and advertisements as Americans. With one difference: they live on an average income that is one-fifth of ours. That anyone should need to point out that America is a rich country struck them as hilarious.

Of course, taking our affluence for granted is not the only reason why Americans feel poor. For many years, we have been bombarded with statistics that purported to show that Japan and much of Western Europe had surpassed America in standard of living. These statistics were derived by comparing per capita income. Each country, naturally, measures its per capita income in its own currency. Comparisons between two countries were made by multiplying the per capita income in one by the rate of exchange between its currency and that of the other. Eventually, economists pointed out the weakness of this approach. A change in the exchange rate would suddenly change the apparent comparative incomes, although no underlying change in living standard had occurred. Most international agencies have now shifted to a more sophisticated and meaningful method of comparison called "purchasing power parities." This method makes clear that America is still by far the wealthiest country. The average American is a quarter again as affluent as the average Japanese or German and almost half again as well off as the average Italian or Englishman.

Of course, not all Americans are getting richer. In recent years the poor have been getting poorer, and the incomes of those just above the level of poverty have been stagnating. Although the reasons for this are not well understood, the trend is alarming. Also alarming is a host of domestic ills like crime, illegitimacy, and urban decay. The extent to which such problems are caused by, or can be cured by, allocation of material resources is subject to dispute. To some extent, they reflect spiritual deficiencies in our society that no increase in affluence could remedy. But none of this changes the fact that the country as a whole has been getting richer.

The Budget Deficit

The main reason, however, for all the hand wringing about how broke we are is not the state of the economy but the state of the budget. To be exact, the concern is about the *federal* budget, since state and local governments cumulatively have been operating in the black for about thirty-five years.[2] The federal government, however, is nearly $5 trillion in debt and has been running a deficit of about $200 billion each year. Economists disagree about whether a growing economy can run in the red every year without severe consequence. But most agreed that the deficit path America was on in the early 1990s was unmanageable.

The public sensed this, too, and public opinion polls began to show that Americans gave balancing the budget a higher priority than cutting taxes. This, in turn, generated great pressure to cut spending on foreign policy. President Clinton made reducing the deficit the centerpiece of his first year in office. In practice, he focused entirely on defense spending. On the domestic side, his budget proposals contained as much in the way of increases as cuts. All the net reduction came out of the hide of the Pentagon.

Spending on Defense and Foreign Policy

Republicans in Congress have criticized Clinton's defense cuts, but they have been slow to restore any of the spending. Instead, they have hacked away at other foreign policy accounts, like foreign aid and international information. When the new Republican majority in the House of Representatives pushed through the 1995 National Security Revitalization Act, they held their ranks on provisions that would reduce American financial and military support of UN peacekeeping missions, but they suffered enough defections on a provision that would have increased spending for missile defenses that it was struck from the bill. Partisan loyalty, in short, sufficed to produce unity on cutting a piece of the foreign policy budget but did not suffice when it came to voting an increase in part of that budget—even for a cherished Republican initiative.

In cutting foreign policy spending, both the president and Congress are catering to public illusions. The public wants a balanced budget but also resists increases in taxes or reductions in benefits. It would like to believe it can square this circle by cutting foreign aid. A 1995 survey asked a representative sample of Americans how much of the federal budget they thought went to foreign aid. The median response was 15 percent. When respondents were asked what they thought would be an "appropriate" share for foreign aid, the median response was 5 percent.[3] If in fact foreign aid consumed 15 percent of the budget, then cutting back to 5 percent would reduce the total budget by 10 percent, not quite enough to put it in balance but getting us most of the way there. Unfortunately, foreign aid consumes less than 1 percent of the budget. If we canceled it all, we would make only a small dent in the deficit.

Entitlements

Indeed, as of 1995 if we canceled foreign policy altogether, including the entire defense budget, that saving would not by itself have enabled us to balance the budget, at least not for long, because of the explosion of "entitlements." Entitlements are expenditures not appropriated in specific amounts, but rather as "such sums as may be necessary."

Many taxpayers would like to believe that entitlements consist mostly of welfare payments. In truth, less than one-quarter of what we spend on entitlements goes into benefits that are "means-tested," that is, aimed at the poor.[4] The Congressional Budget Office compiled a list of 115 entitlement programs that each cost more than $10 million in 1993.[5] The big ones are social security, Medicare, and Medicaid—in that order.

This book goes to press with the great budget battle of 1995 unresolved. Yet the approximate outcome is easily discerned since the differences between the Republican Congress and the Democratic president have grown narrow. It will aim toward a balanced budget in

2002 or 2003, through cutting various programs and restraining the rate of growth of others, notably the once sacrosanct Medicare and Medicaid. Whether this legislation will in fact eliminate the deficit will depend on many economic, demographic, and psychological imponderables, but it has reversed the budgetary momentum.

Even if the American government operates in the black in 2002, the problem will not be resolved. When the baby-boom generation begins to reach retirement age in 2010, the number of social security claimants will be vastly expanded, especially in proportion to the number of workers feeding the kitties that pay for them. As the baby boomers retire, social security and Medicare outlays will exceed revenues. Surpluses now in those trust funds will soon be exhausted, and then where will the retirees' benefits come from? For all the *Sturm und Drang*—and all the real pain—accompanying the 1995 budget measures, we have not yet tamed the entitlement monster.

In the postwar years, federal spending has come to consume around 22 percent of national income. Federal revenues, in contrast, have remained around 18 or 19 percent. We have coped with this disparity in two ways: by borrowing and by shifting funds from discretionary programs to entitlements.

Discretionary Spending

The historical tables that accompany the president's budget reveal the dimensions of this shift. In 1962, discretionary spending made up more than two-thirds of the federal budget.[6] Today, it makes up just over one-third. Entitlements, which then made up about one-quarter of the outlays, today make up about half. And the share that goes to pay interest on the national debt has grown from about 6 percent to about 15.

Discretionary spending covers all foreign policy functions as well as most domestic activities of the federal government that go beyond merely mailing checks to individuals. This category comprises, for instance, the administration of the federal justice system; transportation, education, energy, and environmental programs; and the general operations of the government. As for foreign policy spending, about 85 percent of this goes for the military, another 10 percent for intelligence, and 5 percent for foreign aid. Diplomatic operations take up about 1 percent, and foreign broadcasting and information, a fractional amount of that.

Foreign policy spending used to dwarf domestic discretionary spending, but today it remains just barely larger. The decline in discretionary spending over the past thirty-plus years has come, in net, entirely at the expense of foreign policy. Its share of the federal budget has fallen by more than half. Domestic discretionary spending, in contrast, has ebbed and flowed over this period. Its share climbed during the Kennedy-Johnson and the Nixon-Ford years, plateaued under Carter, fell under Reagan, and crept upward under Bush. It is now somewhat higher than it was in 1962, although the Clinton budget projects decreases in the years ahead.

Since Bill Clinton took office aiming to "rebuild" America, such decreases in domestic discretionary spending are bound to come harder to him than cutting the defense budget. But in reality, unless entitlements are tamed, all discretionary spending will be relentlessly squeezed. The 1995 budget measures cut deep into discretionary spending, but they fall short of a long-term solution.

Early in 1995, the Bi-Partisan Commission on Entitlement and Tax Reform, headed by Senators Bob Kerrey and John Danforth, published spending projections developed by the Social Security Administration and the Health Care Financing Administration. According to these projections, by the year 2012 entitlements and interest payments alone will equal the amount of all federal revenue, leaving no room in the budget for any discretionary spending—foreign or domestic—except through additional borrowing. Even new borrowing would not solve the problem for long, since the entitlements would continue to grow at a faster pace than revenue, requiring deficits larger than the economy could long sustain.

The spending restraints enacted in 1995 will push back the date at which the trend lines cross, although the effect will be attenuated by the accompanying tax cuts, and a minority report filed by commission member Peter Peterson made a strong case that the official social security and health care projections were too optimistic to begin with. Those projections assumed, for example, that the rate of increase in longevity will slow, thereby slowing the growth in the numbers of elderly.[7]

Cutting discretionary spending further cannot solve this problem: it can at best postpone the day of reckoning. In practice, that reckoning will not take the form of economic collapse. Before that happens, entitlements will in effect cut themselves. At some point, as outlays mushroom, the imperative of cuts will become irresistible. Then, however, the cuts will necessarily be drastic and likely to work real hardship on future generations of retirees. If tackled today, cuts that merely retard the growth of entitlement spending could solve the problem by spreading a modest amount of sacrifice among all population groups, excluding the poor.

The Solution

The solution to the problem will likely entail three elements: slowing health care inflation, restraining the growth of social security benefits, and adding revenues. Inflation can be restrained only through government controls or through market pressures. The Clinton health care overhaul would have relied on the former. But the Clinton plan died in part because most Americans are skeptical of government price controls, which usually have harmful side effects.

Medical Costs. The explosion of medical costs has resulted in part from the success of medicine at prolonging life: older people require more care. It has also resulted in part from the adoption of Medicare and Medicaid, as well as the proliferation of employer-provided health insurance, all of which separate the consumer of health care from the payer. Senators Kerrey and Danforth, in the report of their commission on entitlements, proposed various measures to reverse this trend.[8] They would increase deductibles, copayments, and the enrollee's share of premiums for Medicare. They would encourage competition through vouchers that could be used for the purchase of a private health plan. And they would limit the amount of tax-free health insurance premiums that employees could receive from employers. While I would not venture to assess each of these proposals or their best combination, they head in the right direction. The Medicaid and Medicare cuts passed in 1995 undoubtedly make a dent in the problem. Still, they were longer on cost reductions through administrative fiat than on reforms that would restrain prices by promoting competition and efficiency.

Social Security Benefits. We must also get a handle on social security benefits. In the past thirty years, the share of our national income that goes to pay social security benefits has almost doubled. In part, this increase has occurred because people are living longer and the number of recipients has therefore grown. But also benefits have risen steeply. The big jump came in the late 1960s and early 1970s when a Democratic Congress and a Republican president vied for elderly voters. One side offered substantial immediate hikes; the other offered to make benefits keep pace with inflation. In the end, both gifts were bestowed, so that benefits increased more than 70 percent in five years and were then indexed to preserve their value.[9]

The large increase in social security payroll deductions enacted in 1983 have made payments of these benefits possible but will not suffice into the next century. Moreover, when the large baby-boom cohort retires, the ratio of workers paying into social security to retirees drawing out benefits will drop toward two to one.[10] Either much higher tax rates or lower benefits, or both, will be required. The degree of change can be minimized by acting sooner rather than later. We can substantially slow the growth of outlays by reducing the size of cost-of-living increases, by gradually pushing back the age of eligibility to reflect the reality that people are living longer and remaining vigorous longer, and by making more benefits taxable. Here, too, we can shield the most needy recipients.

In 1995, when congressional Republicans proposed needed restraints on Medicare spending, they were attacked by President Clinton. He had already foreclosed the possibility that they would trim social security by campaigning in 1994 on the slogan, "The Republicans will cut social security," which naturally they denied. Now, he raised the accusation that they were cutting Medicare to give a tax break to the rich. This may have been demagogic, by why were the Republicans advancing tax cuts with the budget so deep in the red? Each side, it seems, has its own way of buying votes. As a nation, however, our choices about social security, Medicare, and taxes could wreck our ability to conduct foreign policy. While the Republicans have rightly criticized Clinton's deep defense cuts, their budget bill would provide no defense increases, not even to keep pace with inflation. Instead, they have taken a meat ax to nondefense international affairs spending, cutting it by one-third, before inflation. Contrast this with their controversial health and welfare proposals, which do no more than lower the rate of increase.

The answer, then, to the question of whether we can afford a foreign policy of leadership depends on whether we behave responsibly on the broader budget issues. If we do, then we can afford the foreign policy we choose. If we do not, then we might not be able to afford any foreign policy—and we would still go bankrupt.

The Cost of a Sound Foreign Policy

What would a sound foreign policy cost? In other chapters, I describe what I think such a foreign policy would consist of and explain the motive for each part. Here, I will discuss just the costs. In 1994, total spending for foreign policy—including defense, foreign aid, and everything else—fell to 4.5 percent of our gross domestic product (GDP), the lowest level since before Pearl Harbor. And it is still falling. The defense budget (which includes all intelligence) is estimated to drop to 3.9 percent in 1995 and the rest of international affairs to 0.3 percent. A further scheduled decrease in 1996 will bring the combined total to 3.8 percent.[11] That number represents a cut of well over one-third in the share of our income going to foreign policy since 1989, the last year of the cold war. This amount constitutes the long-awaited "peace dividend," hundreds of billions of dollars that have come and gone without notice, sucked into the great maw of entitlements.

The real peace dividend, some wise person has said, is peace. While keeping the peace will still cost us money, the costs ought to be lower now that the cold war is over. We can perhaps afford to drop below 5 percent of GDP, as we have done, but dropping below 4 percent, as planned, is too low. Defense expenditures have been cut too far, as have funds for some other purposes, and we have not provided for contingencies, such as in Bosnia, Haiti, Somalia, Rwanda, Mexico, or elsewhere (setting aside for the moment the arguments about specific policies toward these places). Let us then take 5 percent of GDP as a safe ceiling for spending on foreign policy in the post–cold war world. Within that ceiling, we could keep our defenses strong, continue foreign aid programs that serve our strategic interests or our humanitarian feelings, maintain our diplomatic establishment and our overseas information programs (including launching such important but modest initiatives as Radio Free Asia), and still have a little budgetary room left for the unforeseen.

Can we afford 5 percent? One way to answer this question is to remind ourselves that foreign policy is the most important part of our budget. Its ultimate purpose is to ensure our survival and safety. The core of our defense forces are there to defeat any direct attack on our country. But virtually all the rest of our foreign policy activity is designed to prevent such an attack from happening, by deterring threats and keeping the world as peaceful and friendly as possible. This goal is more important than adding another increment to our already high standard of living or building a new road or even a new school.

Of course, we should not spend without limit on foreign policy. Beyond a certain point, additional dollars may do little to increase our security and might do more to protect our health or domestic security or to improve our lives in other ways. We need another way to answer the question of whether we can afford to spend 5 percent of our income on foreign policy. Let us recall that throughout the postwar era we spent much more than 5 percent on foreign policy even though we were much less well off most of that time than we are now. From 1952 through 1963, we spent more than 10 percent every year— and sometimes as much as 15 percent—on foreign policy. For the balance of the 1960s, we averaged above 9 percent.[12] In the early 1950s, we were at war in Korea, and in the late 1960s in Vietnam. To be sure, war evokes sacrifice. But for the larger part of this span— from the mid-1950s to the mid-1960s—we were embroiled only in the relentless quotidian grind of the cold war. And yet from a far smaller income than we enjoy today, we devoted about 10 percent. To spend half that rate today is something we can easily afford.

Military Spending and Economic Growth

Of course, every dollar we spend on foreign policy is a dollar we cannot spend on domestic programs or private consumption or investment. Foreign policy spending is analogous to the money we spend out of our family budgets on insurance: we want to protect ourselves and our loved ones against contingencies we hope will not arise. Although such spending takes away from the sums available for things we enjoy, we do not hesitate to do it. Some people, however, believe that funds spent on foreign policy somehow cost us more than the lost opportunity to use the same money for other things. They suggest that in some larger way foreign policy spending is dragging us down. I have already mentioned the myth that our budgetary woes stem from foreign aid—a view more popular among the men in the street than among intellectuals. Many intellectuals, however, embrace a cognate myth, namely, that military spending is destroying our economy.

The notion was suggested twenty-five years ago by the eminent political scientist, Bruce Russett. "The costs" of military spending, he said, "may be entirely in the form of current benefits forgone or, if the nation's resource base is eroded, they may be paid largely by future generations."[13] Russett endeavored to show that a substantial amount of the funds spent on defense might have gone instead to investment, augmenting future growth. This is a reasonable point, although neither definitive nor revelatory, but the notion of an eroding resource base was a mystification. Russett implied that something larger was being lost. Seventeen years later, historian Paul Kennedy enlarged on this mystification in his celebrated bestseller *The Rise and Fall of the Great Powers*.[14] Kennedy coined the term *imperial overstretch* to argue that previous great imperia had brought about their own decline by devoting so much of their resources to empire that they wrecked their economies. America, he argued, was on the same trajectory.

Kennedy's lengthy tome offered no direct evidence to sustain its point about America, only the suggestive analogies, and his thesis has been effectively refuted.[15] Yet the thought that defense or foreign policy spending is economically harmful seems to have gained wide acceptance. A quick examination of America's economic record would suggest otherwise. Herbert Stein and Murray Foss point out that the years from 1948 to 1973 were a kind of golden age of economic growth in America. During that quarter-century, America averaged a rate of real growth per capita of 2.2 percent per year, whereas during the preceding eighty years the average had been 1.7 percent, about a quarter lower. During the years since 1973, growth has been, on the whole, lower than that.[16] Yet those twenty-five high-growth years were also the period of America's highest spending on foreign policy. We devoted just a fraction less than 10 percent of our GDP to defense and other foreign policy expenditures throughout that period. Except for the years when we were fighting World War II and devoting a huge portion of our economy to the war, in no other time have we spent anything close to that percentage on foreign policy. During the slow-growth years since 1973, we have spent less than 6 percent on it. And over many decades before World War II, the figure was less than that. I do not claim that high foreign policy spending boosted the economy: other factors likely caused the high growth. But these data certainly constitute a strong prima facie case against the notion that foreign policy spending is uniquely harmful.

Various scholars have explored this subject and found no clear relation between defense spending and economic performance. Thus, James Payne and Anandi Sahu, editors of a recent collection of studies, conclude:

> Most studies cited in this volume [*Defense Spending and Economic Growth*] suggest that defense spending has rather modest effect on the economic growth of an industrialized nation. . . . In fact, defense spending does not appreciably affect other macroeconomic variables such as real GNP, inflation and interest rates. Only for less developed countries,

does the evidence presented in this volume suggest that defense spending has a significant impact on economic growth. For the LDCs [less-developed countries] . . . military expenditures seem to contribute to overall economic growth.[17]

Exploring a slightly different question, Gordon Adams and David Gold concluded that "the economic impact of military spending is only marginally different from that of other forms of federal spending. It is not uniquely inflationary, has an unclear relationship to productivity and technological development, and does not create significantly different numbers of jobs."[18] And a 1970 study of forty-four developing countries by economist Emile Benoit found unexpected results. "Econometric analysis suggested that every one percentage point of GDP added to the defense burden might reduce the civilian growth rate by as much as 1/4 of 1 percent per annum," wrote Benoit. "Surprisingly, however, we did not find the inverse correlation . . . that might be anticipated . . . . On the contrary, the simple correlation between defense burdens and growth rates was strongly positive."[19] Increased defense spending might have had this effect, he supposed, by stimulating demand, by providing education and training to a sector of the work force, or by providing a secure environment for economic activity.[20]

The costs of foreign policy, in sum, are neither more nor less than the "opportunity costs," that is, the inability to use the money for something else. Are those costs too high? Some of the advocates of a diminished American foreign policy say that before we can be strong abroad, we must put our house in order. Those who make this argument, however, usually refrain from specifying the ills they believe most need curing or the remedy. But since this refrain can be heard from both Left and Right, we can be sure that the prescriptions are contradictory.

Solving Domestic Problems

Liberal Washingtonians want to reduce spending on foreign affairs to enlarge domestic social programs, but their conservative cousins view the growth of the federal government and many welfare programs as positively harmful. Conservative Washingtonians would use foreign policy savings to cut taxes, but their liberal cousins worry that tax cuts will only widen the gap between rich and poor (which most cuts do, since the rich pay more in taxes). Liberal Washingtonians want to "renew" America through an industrial policy that conservatives think would only distort markets and thereby weaken our economy. Conservative Washingtonians want to "put our house in order" by building more prisons to enforce more mandatory sentences, which liberals think will only produce more hardened criminals.

The reason we have not "solved" domestic problems is not that we have spent too much money or energy on international ones: it is that we do not know the solutions. Proposals—mutually contradictory—abound, but few if any have been proved valid. Nor will they ever be, since social experiments rarely can be conducted under controlled conditions. Domestic policy is more a matter of making choices and expressing values than of solving problems. We may be able to reduce unemployment or inflation or crime, but we will not "solve" them.

Most of the issues that the advocates of "domestic priorities" have in mind have to do either with prosperity or race relations, but neither is a "problem" with any finite solution. If our prosperity increases for years to come, we will still not reach a moment when we all decide we have enough. And alas, much the same can be said for race relations: even if they improve steadily, we are not likely to reach a point at which all friction or inequity disappears. If we cannot exert global leadership until these "problems" are "solved," then our wait will be eternal.

If we had applied such a standard in the past, what a mess the world would be. America lifted its heaviest international burdens in the 1940s. First, we defeated Hitler and his Axis allies. Then, we stopped Stalin's advance and entered the cold war. But our economy and the state of race relations in our country were far more doleful then than today. The army that defeated Hitler and Tojo was ruled by Jim Crow. Blacks fought only in segregated units and for a nation in whose capital most public and private facilities were likewise segregated. The economy that sustained the Marshall Plan provided Americans with a standard of living that was, in real terms, only 40 percent of what it is today. Though much is made of the inadequacies of education and health care in America now, in the 1940s Americans on the average completed nine years of schooling, as compared with thirteen today, and their lives then were about 10 percent shorter than ours are today.

Of course, some domestic problems are worse today than fifty years ago, for example, crime and illegitimacy. But what relation have these to our international efforts? Liberals cannot make a persuasive case that we could solve these problems by spending more money on them, since they have grown worse precisely as we *have* spent more money on them. Conservatives, in contrast, believe that the solutions lie in renewing moral values, a goal not likely to be achieved by renouncing international responsibilities.

Moreover, there is no clear trade-off between foreign and domestic policy, except perhaps during times of full-scale mobilization. And even here the relation is not so clear. The Great Depression lingered on throughout the isolationist 1930s only to be cured by our entry into World War II. That war also created a breakthrough on the road to racial justice, occasioning the executive order that desegregated defense plants and setting the stage for another one that desegregated the military. So we can justly say that the event that caused the greatest diversion of resources from domestic to foreign policy in our history generated unparalleled progress on our two most important domestic issues. I point this out not to suggest that we ought to seek wars to achieve domestic progress but to suggest that the interaction between foreign and domestic policy is hard to predict because it involves so many variables.

If the argument that international involvements absorb resources and energies that might be used at home has any truth, it is also true that they provide domestic benefits. Robert Hormats, former assistant secretary of state for economic and business affairs, reminds us that "America's commitments abroad are not simply a drain on its economy; many are vital to it. The United States exports 13 percent of its GNP, 20 percent of its manufactured goods and 30 percent of its farm production."[21] In practical terms, our foreign commercial ties give us a stake in the freedom of the seas, international rules of trade, access to resources and markets, and the general health of the global economy. More subtly, our status as world leader adds a certain cachet to our exports. Coca-Cola and jeans and Marlboros are no doubt good products, but they are also consumed abroad because they are symbols of America. And some nations buy our airplanes or our weapons in order to be close to us.

To blame our international activities for our domestic woes is little more than making excuses. Worse, the inverse may be true, that domestic issues are used as excuses to avoid international burdens. While it is true that we have a budget crisis, this problem is of our own making and has nothing to do with our resources. We have run budget deficits for many years now, but not forever. From 1947 through 1957, the budget was more often in surplus than in deficit; the net for those years was a surplus of about $14 billion. Yet in that era we were much poorer than today. Our average standard of living then was barely half what it is today, after adjusting for inflation. Still, we ran a surplus even while spending 10 percent of our GNP on foreign policy.

I believe that we should put our budget in balance, or better yet surplus, again today. I urge this policy not as an economic judgment since I am no economist, and I am unequipped to argue with those economists who believe we can run endless (moderate) deficits. Rather, I urge it as a matter of principle. We ought to be concerned about our character as a nation, and it is wrong to bequeath unnecessary debt to our posterity.

It is even worse to sacrifice our role as world leader through our profligacy. That is what we would do if we shortchange our foreign policy instead of reconciling our taste for benefits with our aversion to taxes. The numbers tell us that in the end this evasion would prove futile. But in the meantime, we would leave our children not only debt but also something unforgivable: a world of unnecessary insecurity and peril.

PART TWO

Alternatives to Leadership

·5·

CAN OTHER "POWERS" SHARE THE BURDENS?

One of the fondest assumptions of the Washingtonian school is that if America steps back from its preeminent role in international affairs, some other benign force will step in. The search for this alternative to American leadership leads in one of two directions. The first is toward other major powers, nations that are rich or populous or militarily strong. Rarely is it suggested that some other single nation might replace America as leader; rather, the idea is that several others will come to share leadership with America. The second direction is toward the devolution of leadership from individual states to international institutions like the United Nations. In this chapter, I shall examine the prospects for shared leadership. In the next, I shall assess the role of the United Nations.

How Many Superpowers?

Various commentators have suggested that America's special station among nations was a function of the cold war. Therefore, as columnist William Pfaff put it, "The collapse of communism has produced an unexpected result in the international order: the abolishment of superpower status itself . . . . Today there is not, as some argue, a single superpower . . . there are none."[1] This notion of the relative decline of American status, and a shift in the distribution of power from bipolarity to multipolarity, is not really new. It had an earlier vogue twenty-five years ago, when it was said that the configuration of world power was transmuting into a pentagon. China, Japan, and Western Europe were reaching the same plane as the United States and the Soviet Union. World politics in the 1970s was coming to resemble European politics in the nineteenth century under the multipolar Concert of Europe.

As President Nixon put it in 1971:

> As we look ahead 5 years, 10 years, perhaps it is 15 . . . we see five great economic super powers . . . . these are the five that will determine the economic future and, because economic power will be the key to other kinds of power, the future of the world in other ways in the last third of this century. . . . we face a situation where four other potential economic powers have the capacity [to] challenge us on every front.[2]

Three of the four others—Japan, China, and Western Europe, but not the USSR—did continue to grow economically, but that growth did not translate into political power. Now the theory of American decline and the rise of other powers has resurfaced, although it is no more convincing than before.

The revival of the belief in multiple superpowers draws on the prophecy, so fashionable in the 1980s, of American decline. Led by the historian Paul Kennedy, these prophets had the extreme misfortune of predicting America's decline just a brief historical moment before America's chief rival collapsed, making America more superior than ever before.[3] To compound their error, America's triumph appears to have resulted in part from the very thing that the prophets of decline identified as the key to its doom: defense spending, which instead of bankrupting America helped to drive its Soviet rival to bankruptcy.

The theories of American decline made much of statistics showing that America's share of the world's economic production had dropped dramatically from its post–World War II high. But as I have explained in chapter 3, this decrease was an artificial statistic. America's share of production was abnormally high immediately after the war because so many other industrial countries had been destroyed. By the time those had been rebuilt in the 1950s or 1960s, America's share had settled back to its prewar level of between 20 and 25 percent. It has stayed there since, exhibiting no downward trend.[4]

Japan or China as Leader

Still, if America's global share of production remains fairly constant, that of every other country does not necessarily remain so. On the contrary, some are experiencing more rapid economic growth, which may enable their economies to rival America's in some ways. Might they then supplant its political leadership, too? Pfaff even claimed to detect a "colonial quality" in America's relations with Japan—with America as the subordinate![5] Although for years Japan was portrayed as the emerging superpower, its economy has plateaued at a level of GNP per capita about 80 percent as high as America's,[6] and its population is half the size. Its total economy, therefore, is about 40 percent the size of America's, and its prospects of appreciably closing this gap are uncertain.

China, however, whose population is five times as large as America's, needs to achieve a level of income per capita only one-fifth of America's for its economy to equal ours in size. Given its remarkable growth rate, and given also the remarkable example of Taiwan, where the income per capita is now nearly half of ours,[7] it is easy to imagine China's economy overtaking America's as the world's largest. But trends are misleading, because they change. A lot can happen to deflect China's trajectory before it achieves economic supremacy, from events as dramatic as political upheaval to trends as prosaic as a leveling off of the growth rate. And even if China's gross economy does become as large as America's, it will still be a much poorer society, with five times as many mouths to feed and bodies to clothe and house. It will therefore have less discretionary income to invest abroad, donate, spend on arms, or otherwise use for international influence.

Even if China, or Japan, developed its economy to a size equal to America's, could it assume a commensurate share of world political leadership? The answer is no. Each lacks, to borrow a phrase from pop psychology, a capacity for empathic relationship essential to leadership. It could perhaps succeed at conquest, but leadership is less likely. Each has a distinct sense of its own special role. America, too, has such a sense. But America's sense of specialness is based on being an exemplar of universal values, whereas Japan's and China's are racial. Japan is famously insular, to the point that those born in Japan of Korean stock are not accepted as Japanese, even after several generations. China by tradition views itself as the Middle Kingdom, with the rest of the world's nations arrayed around it in subordinate positions.

The two Asian giants are therefore not well suited to play the role of protector of the international commonweal. Each is feared by its neighbors, Japan more for its past and China more for its future. Neither of them, nor their neighbors, wants America to withdraw its formidable political and military presence from East Asia because each trusts America's benign intentions more than it trusts the other's.

China, moreover, is ruled by a regime that lacks legitimacy, which retained its power only through the infamous Tiananmen Square massacre. Its government has no clear structure or rules. Its dominant figure for nearly two decades, Deng Xiao Ping, officially held only secondary offices and then none at all. As with all Communist regimes, the process of succession of rulers is something of a gang war, lacking constitutional bounds. Its rulers are sometimes admired for the role they play (or are thought to play) within China, but none is viewed as a leader on the world stage. Japan is far stronger politically than China. Its government is legitimate, and its system is constitutionally sound. Still, it has undergone a time of instability in which it seems to be making the transition from a democracy with a single dominant party to a multiparty democracy. This trend is all for the good, but it suggests that as a political system, Japan is still undergoing growing pains.

In truth, beyond the platitudes about multipolarity, few argue that Japan or China is likely soon to assume a major global leadership role. The Soviet Union, which once bulked large, exists no more, and Russia is struggling to find its own way—it is scarcely ready to lead others. If there is to be multipolarity, the most plausible candidates for sharing leadership with America are the European powers, especially the powerful and wealthy democracies of Western Europe. Are they equal to this role?

Europe as Leader

American society derives largely from Europe. And despite the chic taboo against "Eurocentrism," the truth is that Europe has been the principal center of mankind's progress. In modern international relations, Europe furnished the edifying example of the Concert of Europe, which, for the most part, maintained the peace for one hundred years.

World War I. But then in 1914 European civilization came apart, and it has never been put back together. Europe in the twentieth century has lost all sense of why and how to uphold the values that are its finest legacy to mankind and on which its own survival depends, even though, with American help, much of Europe has achieved democracy and prosperity.

Consider, first, World War I, "the Great War," which stole the flower of Europe's youth, which wrote finis to four empires, which left even the victors so damaged that they were paralyzed for decades. What were they fighting about? There were no great issues of ideology or faith. No great empire was aborning. This was a war of petty arrogance and abysmal miscalculation.

To be sure, Germany wanted its place in the sun. Which sun? The sun of empire, at least in large part. And so it sparred with the other powers over colonial possessions, which, it was discovered when scholars subsequently toted up their costs and benefits, were utterly worthless.[8] Austria's rulers, feeling their empire tottering, sent their crown prince on a goodwill tour of the heart of Serbia's *irredenta* on the holiday on which Serbs commemorated their wounded national pride. This action all but invited the terrorist attack that came at Sarajevo. Russia, after encouraging Serbian provocativeness, blanched upon discovering its predictable consequence—a dire Austrian ultimatum to Serbia, backed by Germany. But France, still smarting over its defeat by Prussia in 1871 and unable to see that another go would bring similar results, stiffened Russia's spine.

And so the folly proceeded. Eager to confront Austria but not Germany, the czar ordered a mobilization on the Austrian front alone. He was informed by his advisers that although it was possible, mobilization on one front would greatly retard mobilizing on two fronts should that later prove necessary. This absurd inflexibility demonstrated why Russian military planners were held in little regard in contrast to those of Germany, who were lionized. But were they really better? Russia's reluctant mobilization on its German front compelled Germany to invade Belgium. Why Belgium? To get to France. Why France? To get at Russia. The logic of the Schlieffen Plan, the crowning glory of Prussian military genius, rested on defeating France quickly in order to shift forces for the prolonged struggle against Russia. In the event, the struggle with France turned out to be the prolonged one, while Russia was defeated fairly easily.

Germany's invasion of Belgium sealed Britain's entry into the war, although Germany's bellicosity was premised on British neutrality. Britain, therefore, might have forestalled the conflict, had it made clear its unwillingness to stand aside.[9] But apparently, British leaders themselves figured this out only after the war was underway. The events leading up to war would make a wonderful farce, had the war not come at the cost of 20 million lives.

Rise of Totalitarianism. Yet even this cost would constitute only a prelude to what Europe would do to itself in the next years. In Russia, the war unleashed Bolshevism, a political system whose lunacy was exceeded only by its cruelty. Bolshevism battened on the noble ideal of equality: the notion that the meek shall inherit the earth resonates to the foundations of Western civilization. But the idea that a disciplined party of professional revolutionaries, obediently following a single ruler, somehow embodied "the people" was on its face absurd. Yet this system was to rule Russia and an empire covering half of Europe for decades. It exacted a toll of tens of millions killed, not counting battlefield casualties but only the murder by Communist governments of their own subjects. And it inspired a series of equally odious offshoots.

The first such offshoot was fascism, invented by Mussolini, a journalist, former Socialist, and self-glorifying skirt chaser. If Bolshevism was a bizarre perversion of a comprehensible ideal, fascism was an ideology so nebulous and inchoate that to this day it has no readily agreed meaning. The *Encyclopaedia of the Social Sciences*, the august reference work issued during the heyday of fascism, all but stammered in trying to define it. "It is difficult to isolate by abstract analysis the distinctive feature of Fascism," it said. "It is only when viewed as a peculiarly Italian phenomenon that the essence of Fascism becomes clearly delineated."[10] Today, people use the term as a label of opprobrium for unpleasant regimes or movements, but it usually remains undefined. For Mussolini's Italy, fascism meant the overthrow of democracy; a radical expansion of the powers of the state; rule by violence and thuggery; and much ballyhoo about the leader and the nation. This brew had great popular appeal across Europe, where, within a decade after the Great War, democracies succumbed to dictatorship, many of fascist tint, in a host of countries.

The most important of Mussolini's many imitators was Hitler, whose variation on the fascist theme was National Socialism. Although we recall it chiefly for its unparalleled barbarism—the terrible war it started, the assembly lines of murder it built—Nazism was also notable for its absurdity. The stiff-armed salutes, the chants of *Sieg Heil,* the goose step, the elaborate choreography, the light shows, the ridiculous mustache of its Fuhrer—all would seem embarrassing to most normal adults. But Hitler's party won the support of a plurality of voters, and his rule enjoyed great popularity for many years.

Nazism's rituals were no more baroque than its ideology, the central tenet of which was its obsession with the Jews. Setting aside the unfathomable cruelty of Hitler's genocide, the logic of it was madness. The idea that the Jews were the source of Germany's problems was demonstrably false. But even granted that German Jewry held positions or property that other Germans coveted, the thrust of Nazism's genocide was directed not against German Jews but Polish, Ukrainian, Hungarian, Romanian, and Russian Jews. That they were a special enemy of Germany's or a source of its problems was a conclusion derived of thought processes entirely beyond reason.

League of Nations. While most of Europe followed Lenin, Mussolini, and Hitler down the path of dictatorship, how did Europe's surviving democracies respond? The answer, alas, is that the record of their diplomatic achievement is covered more in shame than in glory, with the magnificent exception of Churchill. Yet it was Churchill who told us that World War II, the most destructive of any in recorded history, was "the unnecessary war." By this he meant that even given the evil aggressiveness of the Hitler regime, war could have been averted by a courageous and farsighted response on the part of England and France. Instead, these powers, which had shown little indulgence toward the fragilely democratic Weimar Republic, grew weak and craven when confronted by the Third Reich or even by lesser aggressors.

The descent of Europe (and Asia) into the maelstrom of world war began with the Japanese attack on Manchuria in 1931. That was the first test of the League of Nations as a peacekeeping instrument. It failed. "The response of the League," wrote historian Rene Albrecht-Carrie, "is best summarized in two words, evasion and inaction."[11] Instead of honoring China's appeal for assistance, the league created a study commission. After nearly a year's deliberation, it duly rebuked Japanese aggression, but no action came of it, except that Japan resigned from the league to demonstrate its displeasure and also its disdain.

The league got a second chance in 1935 when Mussolini ordered his armies to conquer Abyssinia, and its emperor, Haile Selassie, appealed to the league for help. He fared no better than China. The league declared Italy guilty of aggression but buttressed this finding only with economic sanctions that, again to quote Albrecht-Carrie, "were purposely designed to insure their ineffectiveness."[12] Mussolini himself is reported to have said that had the sanctions included an embargo of petroleum, it would have stopped the war inside a week.[13]

The collapse of the league was only a symptom of the collapse of will of the European powers. Also in 1935, Hitler had announced his orders to create a German air force and to reinstate conscription, blatant violations of the disarmament provisions of the Versailles Treaty, the architecture of European peace. The British response was business as usual. Within two months, the German ambassador, Joachim von Ribbentrop, arrived in London with a draft naval treaty that he offered to Britain on a take-it-or-leave-it basis. The British government took it, although its terms made England Germany's collaborator in the violation of Versailles. Ribbentrop recalled in his memoirs that when he reported British acceptance to the Fuhrer, "Hitler called this day the happiest day of his life."[14]

In 1936, Hitler's dismantlement of the edifice of Versailles turned from the realm of armaments to that of territory. He ordered his army to reoccupy the Rhineland, from which it was banned under the treaty. War Minister Werner von Blomberg worried that France would repel the move and that his forces would be overmatched. He secured Hitler's assent that German forces would retreat without a fight if France moved to block them, but it did not.[15]

France's capitulation over the Rhineland was symptomatic of the underlying self-contradiction in French policy throughout this period. Fearing Germany's larger population and industrial base, France sought protection in a system of alliances, with England, Italy, Belgium, Poland, Czechoslovakia, Yugoslavia, and the Soviet Union. The alliances implied mutual responsibilities, the obvious corollary of which was a strategy of forward defense: that is, France would promise to aid its allies against Germany and expect them to do likewise. But France's military doctrine was one of defense in place; its centerpiece, the Maginot line. France did not venture out to confront Germany in the Rhineland because its generals preferred to rest behind the safety of their "impregnable" defenses.

As Hitler gained steam, some of France's allies hedged their bets. Already in 1934, Poland had entered a nonaggression pact with Germany. In 1937, Belgium ended its alliance with France and soon signed a treaty of "mutual sovereignty" with Germany. Belgium and Poland were scarcely unique. From 1934 until 1939, most of the nations of Europe tried to cope with Germany's mounting assertiveness by allying with Germany or propitiating it. At the extreme, Mussolini's Italy and Stalin's USSR allied outright with Hitler, the latter more incongruously since Hitler's main alliance was the "anti-Comintern pact" and the Comintern was Stalin's main alliance.

Appeasement. Among the democracies, the approach of propitiating Hitler came to be known as *appeasement,* the term proudly coined by Prime Minister Chamberlain to describe his program, although it only took policies already in place and carried them further. It reached its apogee at Munich, where France and Germany compelled a resisting Czechoslovakia, which had entrusted its security to them, to accede to its own dismemberment, although this action violated the League of Nations charter. In exchange, Germany and Britain signed an agreement never to go to war with each other, and soon thereafter Germany and France signed a declaration of friendship and mutual acceptance of borders.

Churchill said famously of the Munich agreement that England faced a choice between war and shame. Choosing shame, he said, it would get war.[16] The capitulation meant to Hitler that the floodgates on his imperial designs had been thrown open. But Britain and France did not just get war: they got war on the least favorable terms. Czechoslovakia, whose army, geography, and arms industry could have made it a valuable ally, was sacrificed. And whatever hope may have existed of drawing the Soviet Union into alliance against Hitler was squandered. Stalin was reportedly irked by his exclusion from the Munich summit, and, no doubt more important, he was edified by the demonstration of German strength and French and British weakness. Although after Munich, Paris and London wooed Moscow, Stalin merely played along with them while directing his emissaries to begin the courtship of Hitler that was consummated in August 1939.

The Stalin-Hitler Pact inaugurated the war, but the alliance lasted less than two years until Hitler invaded the USSR. This move caught Stalin completely unprepared, to the point that the shock seems to have paralyzed him for days.[17] Eventually Hitler's forces succumbed to the coalition of his western and eastern enemies, but instead of restoring Europe to peace, Hitler's defeat only set the stage for the next mighty conflict, the cold war.

The Cold War

While Eastern Europe was relegated to colonial status during the next forty-odd years and therefore had no policies of its own, Western Europe acquitted itself better than it had during the preceding decades. When the Soviet empire collapsed, Western Europe shared with America the victors' laurels. But on the whole, Western Europe's performance during the cold war gave little sign that it had regained the élan and percipience essential to its self-preservation, much less global leadership. On the contrary, Western Europe survived the cold war as much a ward of the United States as a partner.

Of course, it was easier for America to show courage and leadership because it was so powerful. One might ask how Europe could show a like strength when it was so overshadowed by Soviet power. But this observation begs the question of why Europe was overshadowed by Soviet power. Once it had recovered from World War II, Western Europe's financial, industrial, and technological resources exceeded those of the Soviet Union. If it had summoned the will and unity, it could have defended itself against the Soviet threat without relying on America.

In practice, however, while it relied on America for protection, it also often impeded America from waging the cold war effectively. Although America's commitment to defending Europe rested on the doctrine of containment, America's NATO allies often refused to help, and sometimes deliberately hindered, America's efforts to apply that doctrine outside of Europe. And even within Europe, it sometimes seemed as if America had to drag its allies into taking the measures necessary for the common defense although it was first and foremost Europe's defense.

The one European leader who objected most vociferously to the continent's dependence on America was French President Charles de Gaulle. But the policies he adopted on this account did less to remedy the dependence than they did to hinder the West's collective defense, a defense from which France, despite its aloof posture, never entirely divorced itself. In 1966, France withdrew from NATO's military structures and expelled NATO forces from its soil. According to de Gaulle, their presence "impaired" the "full exercise of [French] sovereignty."[18] Nonetheless, France insisted that its actions were "in no way incompatible with her [France's] participation in the alliance, or with her participation, should the need arise, in military operations at the side of her allies."[19] In other words, it would continue to have a mutual defense treaty with the other north Atlantic nations like the numerous feckless treaties it had signed during the 1930s.

As President Lyndon Johnson explained in his reply to de Gaulle, NATO's integrated command was far more convincing an earnest of its members' commitment to mutual defense than a mere contractual obligation could be. Underscoring this very point was the fact that in de Gaulle's letter to Johnson, he had already begun subtly to hedge France's contractual obligation in the guise of reaffirming it. France, he said, would remain "determined, just as today, to fight beside her allies if one of them should suffer unprovoked aggression." The term *unprovoked aggression,* which soon became a staple of the French official lexicon, begged the question of whether there might be such a thing as *provoked aggression* and whether France viewed its obligation to come to the aid of an attacked NATO member as contingent on discovering whether the victim had provoked the attack.

France compounded its rebuff of NATO two years later when de Gaulle embraced the policy, first articulated by French Chief of Staff Charles Ailleret, of "all azimuths." France's independent nuclear deterrent, the *force de frappe,* would accordingly be targeted in all directions: not just against the Soviet Union but also against the NATO countries that were France's official allies. De Gaulle recalled that in the seventeenth century France had "fortified all our frontiers, the Pyrenees, the Alps, our ports and even Belgium. . . . There is no reason why that strategy, which always protected us against everything, should not be perpetuated."[20]

De Gaulle's shenanigans were an extreme case, but on the whole the Europeans were less than stalwart in their support of our prosecution of the cold war. When Kim Il Sung launched the Korean War, President Harry Truman quickly decided to try to repel the aggression, although American spokesmen and planners had previously placed Korea outside of America's "defense perimeter." America's European allies were more ambivalent. As historian James Stokesbury put it, "The British dragged their feet, the French were obstreperous."[21] Nonetheless, when the United Nations decided on military action, the NATO allies contributed forces, many of whom fought with great bravery. Still, throughout the war, the Europeans' devotion to the principle of collective security was vitiated by their unease with the concentration of America's attention on Asia, when they wanted it focused on Europe.

A more poisonous issue arose in the 1960s as America sank deeper into Vietnam. Not only did anti-American demonstrations fill the streets of Europe's capitals, but intellectual luminaries like Bertrand Russell indicted America in mock war crimes trials, and the foreign minister of France (the nation whose mess in Indochina America had inherited) declared that the people of South as well as North Vietnam were "at war with the United States."[22]

Spurred by their rejection of America's policies in Vietnam, the Europeans grew freer in their opposition to America's containment efforts elsewhere. In the Middle East, where America sided with Israel, the Europeans largely sided with the Soviet-backed Arab camp because, as they acknowledged, they felt beholden to the oil producers.[23] Thus, during the 1973 Yom Kippur War, when America undertook an emergency airlift of supplies to Israel, the NATO allies would not even cooperate to the extent of allowing American planes to land on or overfly their territory. In the only exception to this policy, the military government in Portugal (overthrown the next year) allowed access to the Azores. West Germany, moreover, blocked the loading of American arms onto Israeli ships in German ports, and Great Britain even refused to introduce a cease-fire resolution in the United Nations that America sought. The State Department spokesman complained, "We were facing . . . a critical situation that involved the U.S. and the USSR . . . the European interest in the indivisibility of security . . . ought to have been an important consideration."[24] And Secretary Kissinger added: "For two weeks while the U.S. had to make significant decisions, the Europeans acted as though the Alliance did not exist."[25]

When Middle Eastern violence overspilled the bounds of the Arab-Israel conflict and Arab terrorists (supported by the Soviet bloc)[26] began attacking European and American targets, the NATO allies were loath to resist. When a Palestinian band hijacked the *Achille Lauro,* murdering an elderly American invalid, the American government traced the commander of the terrorists to Rome and asked the Italian government to extradite him. Instead, Rome spirited him out of the country to the safety of Yugoslavia, an action that Washington called "incomprehensible" and "deeply disappoint[ing]."[27]

After notorious attacks on civilians in the Rome and Vienna airports in late 1985, America's allies would not agree to impose trade sanctions against Libya, whose government was known to have sponsored the terrorists. A West German government spokesman said that economic measures were "not a suitable instrument."[28] But a few months later, after a new terrorist outrage, America bombed Libya, and this time Bonn found that military measures were also not suitable. "Force is not a promising way of dealing with things," said Chancellor Helmut Kohl.[29] Other NATO members denounced the American action, and only Britain offered tactical cooperation. The refusal of France and Spain to allow American planes to overfly, according to Defense Secretary Caspar Weinberger, lengthened their routes by 1,200 nautical miles and increased the risk to their pilots.[30]

In the 1980s, America adopted the Reagan Doctrine, which entailed supporting anti-Communist guerrillas. America's allies were generally unsupportive, and in Nicaragua, the centerpiece of the doctrine, some even supported the Communist Sandinista regime. France, Spain, and Holland gave diplomatic support and financial aid to Managua, and France even sold it weapons.[31]

The purpose of the Reagan Doctrine was to make the cold war a two-way street: instead of fighting only defensively to prevent the spread of communism, America would attempt to overthrow some existing Communist regimes. The first Communist regime to be unhorsed was in Grenada, although this was not, strictly speaking, an exercise in the Reagan Doctrine, since it involved no insurgency, only an American invasion. America justified its action on the grounds of a breakdown of legal order and a threat to American nationals and on the endorsement of the neighboring Caribbean states. But the deeper justification was that America was defending itself globally in the cold war against an aggressive, lawless foe and was therefore compelled to put strategic considerations first. Nonetheless, America's European allies again offered little support, and even Prime Minister Thatcher, friend and ally of President Reagan's, joined in the condemnation.[32]

Containment was one aspect of Western strategy that led to victory in the cold war, and the Reagan Doctrine's effect of denying communism its aura of historical inevitability was another. Still a third was encouraging opposition within the Communist bloc. The most important opposition force was Poland's Solidarity, which originally emerged in 1979 and then was violently suppressed in 1981, only to reemerge and oust the Communist regime in 1989. When Solidarity was suppressed, with the military regime of General Woijcech Jaruszelski's declaration of a "state of war," America responded with diplomatic protests and economic sanctions. Many European governments joined in the protests, but they refused to support or duplicate the American sanctions. And some, notably the Bonn government, were so reluctant to allow the Polish repression and bloodshed to impede détente that they strove to soften even the rhetorical reaction. German Chancellor Helmut Schmidt was in East Germany meeting with its dictator, Erich Honecker, when news of the military crackdown on Solidarity was received. He told reporters that "Herr Honecker was as dismayed as I, that this has now proved necessary."[33]

If America's European allies failed to appreciate the value of such cold war tactics as opposing communism on its own turf or containing its expansion in the third world or combatting the terrorist groups that it sponsored, they were also less than clear about directly protecting Europe against the threat of Soviet arms. America constantly found itself trying to coax its allies into devoting to their own defense sums commensurate with American military expenditures, but these entreaties often fell on deaf ears.

In the late 1970s, news stories revealed American plans to develop "the neutron bomb." The weapon was described as a fiendish device that would destroy people but not property: "the ultimate capitalist weapon," it was dubbed. But after the initial sensational headlines, it emerged that the purpose of the weapon was nearly the opposite of the reported implications. NATO doctrine had long called for the use of tactical or battlefield nuclear weapons to repel a Soviet ground attack in Europe because of the Soviet advantage in tanks and other conventional weapons. One flaw in this strategy, often noted by German commentators, was that this might entail destroying Germany in order to save it. A nuclear warhead that struck a phalanx of Soviet tanks, if in a built-up area, would also destroy surrounding buildings, killing their occupants. A neutron device would transform more of the energy of a nuclear explosion into radiation, rather than blast. This feature is what made the weapon seem so frightening. But in reality, the effect would be to kill the tank crews without destroying nearby structures, therefore without killing so many civilians. Paul Warnke, one of the most dovish defense specialists in American public life (he had been the defense adviser to George McGovern), summed up the issue by quipping that the Soviets opposed the weapon not because "it would kill people rather than property, but that it would kill Russians rather than Germans."[34]

Yet although the falsity of the alarm about the neutron bomb was clear even to a dove like Warnke, Europe was skittish about the deployment. Egon Bahr, a leader of the German Social Democrats, called it "a symbol for the perversion of human thinking."[35] Chancellor Schmidt took the position that Bonn would assent to the weapons only if they were also deployed on the territory of at least one other NATO member. All the others were reluctant, however, in part because these tank stoppers made most sense deployed on NATO's front line, which was Germany. While Europe procrastinated, President Jimmy Carter lost his nerve, and plans for the weapon had to be dropped,[36] although it would have made America's commitment to Europe's defense more credible.

Fortunately, neither Europe nor America lost its nerve over the deployment of new intermediate-range nuclear missiles, a decision that proved to be a turning point in the cold war. In the 1970s, the Soviet Union threatened to upset the military balance by deploying mobile SS-20 missiles targeting Western Europe. NATO decided to counter this move with Pershing and cruise missiles aimed at the USSR. In the end, NATO's decision prompted President Gorbachev to agree to the "zero option," eliminating such missiles on both sides and rendering the large Soviet investment in the SS-20s nugatory. This agreement may have been NATO's greatest triumph, foiling a Soviet gambit that could have left Europe feeling overawed and tempted toward neutralism and appeasement. Although the European members of NATO deserve credit for their resolve, we should not forget how hard America labored to win European assent to emplace the "Euromissiles" and how difficult a political battle it was.

The decision to deploy new NATO missiles arose in part out of concerns expressed in the 1970s by Chancellor Schmidt. He worried that the disappearance of America's advantage in intercontinental missiles made it less credible that America would use them to counteract a Soviet advantage in so-called theater or intermediate-range missiles stationed in Europe. But from the outset, the idea of matching the new Soviet missiles with new Western missiles was controversial in Europe. Thus in December 1979, NATO settled on a two-track approach: to proceed toward deploying new missiles while seeking to open negotiations with the Soviets aimed at obviating the deployment. As former assistant secretary of defense Richard Perle has said: "The striking thing is that it should have been so difficult an issue in the first place. Both sides had long had intermediate range weapons. When the Soviets decided to modernize theirs, they didn't ask us to negotiate about it. Why should modernization of ours have been contingent on asking them to negotiate about it?"[37]

Yet even NATO's two-track approach scarcely dampened the controversy. By 1980, Strobe Talbott reports:

> The combination of Soviet threats and overtures did not fall on deaf ears in Europe. There was powerful parliamentary opposition to the deployment in Belgium, Holland, and West Germany, and the European anti-nuclear movement was beginning to build up steam in other countries as well, including Italy and Great Britain. . . . Even Schmidt now seemed uncomfortable about the 1979 decision. When the Soviets floated yet another in their series of proposals for a permanent freeze on medium-range nuclear weapons in Europe, there were hints out of Bonn that Schmidt's government might welcome the idea. Schmidt had a slightly different freeze proposal of his own: . . . a moratorium on new deployments that would permit no new SS-20s in exchange for no [modern NATO missiles] at all.[38]

In 1981, tens to hundreds of thousands of protesters marched in virtually every NATO capital against the missiles. A demonstration in Bonn drew 250,000, the largest in West German history.[39] Schmidt remained faithful to the NATO policy but lost control of his own party, the Social Democrats. And his coalition partner, Free Democrat Hans-Dietrich Genscher, the foreign minister, faced a similar predicament, although Genscher had more success at holding off his internal opposition.[40] In the end, the Social Democratic turn against the Euromissiles impelled Genscher to bring down the government, leading his party into a new bloc with Helmut Kohl's Christian Democrats. The Kohl-Genscher government kept West Germany clearly behind NATO's two-track policy. But for West Germany, as for Belgium and Holland, it was a close call. (These three and Italy and England were the only five NATO countries designated for Euromissile deployment. The other ten had already been ruled out for a combination of technical and political reasons.)

Global Issues after the Cold War

Since the cold war's end, the European states' responses to global issues continue to present a mixed picture, as far as demonstrating the capacity for leadership in upholding world peace. When President George Bush called forth an international coalition to reverse Iraq's conquest of Kuwait, America's NATO allies rallied to the cause. Indeed, according to published accounts, Prime Minister Margaret Thatcher stiffened Bush's resolve early in the crisis. "This is no time to go wobbly, George," she is reported to have warned him in a private exchange.[41] But on some other issues, the European countries have evinced the same shortsightedness that has marred their diplomacy for so much of this century.

When Iraq was defeated, the world learned that its program for building nuclear weapons, as well as other weapons of mass destruction, was far more advanced than other governments had realized. The technological means for this accomplishment had been furnished recklessly by many countries including the United States, but mostly by West Germany and France.[42] Yet even this revelation had little sobering effect, as these two and other European nations have pursued commercial relations—including the trade of militarily relevant high technology—with Iran and other rogue regimes.[43] They have also pressed for lifting the sanctions that bar them from resuming such commerce with Iraq. French and other European companies, some apparently with government support, have gone so far as to negotiate new oil deals with Baghdad to be implemented as soon as the sanctions end.[44] Such actions are compromising the world's security out of petty greed.

Equally petty has been the reluctance of Western Europe to liberalize trade with Eastern Europe.[45] As the states of the former Warsaw Pact make the painful transition to market economies, what they need most is markets to replace the defunct Soviet Union, which was their main trading partner. Opening markets would, as always, dislocate or damage some sectors within the European economies, but in the end it would redound to their net economic benefit while it would also help ensure continental stability by helping the newly liberated states get on their feet.

Finally, confronted with the first massive postwar violation of the peace within Europe—the Serbian aggression against Croatia and Bosnia—Europe has shown itself woefully unequal to the challenge, as I shall examine in detail in part three.

My point in this brief review of the past eighty years of diplomatic history is not to denigrate Europe but to argue that it has demonstrated that it is not able to shoulder substantial burdens of international leadership. Indeed, since 1914, when the lights went out all over Europe, as Lord Grey put it, Europe has been incapable of sustaining its own security, much less anyone else's. It has been the cockpit of two world wars and the birthplace of demonic political movements. Even its better parts have been dominated by pitiful illusions and moral lassitude.

In drawing this invidious comparison of America and Europe, I do not suggest that the American record is flawless. In some of the issues on which I find Europe wanting—such as the neutron bomb fiasco or Bosnia—Washington was a full partner in the failure. Some of Europe's weakness may be laid at America's feet for its ham-handed handling of the Suez crisis in 1956. And many other aspects or episodes of America's twentieth-century diplomacy richly deserve criticism, especially the interwar isolationism when America turned its back on the very peace of which it had been the architect, paving the way for catastrophe. Still, despite these and other errors, America's record, seen in broad sweep, is one of success and effective leadership, through two world wars and the cold war.

Although it has indulged in flights of naiveté, from sponsoring the "outlawry of war" in 1928 to investing overly large hopes in the United Nations, America has shown a vision of the global well-being that others have not. Of course, America guards its own interests. Of course, too, it has no monopoly on idealism. But more than the states of Europe, America has perceived a connection between its own well-being and the common good, and this is the bedrock of leadership. It is not to be found in the Old World.

·6·

CAN WE TURN THE WORLD OVER TO THE UNITED NATIONS?

If no other country is capable of lifting some of the burdens of leadership from America's shoulders, what about the United Nations? Now that the cold war is over, can it at long last play the role of supranational authority upholding the peace? The former American ambassador to the United Nations, Jeane Kirkpatrick, posed this question as soon as the Soviet Union stopped acting like an enemy. She wrote in 1990 that for the first time since the founding of the United Nations, "Soviet officials now read the U.N. charter as it was written to be read. . . . Apparently the age of doublespeak has passed. If that is indeed the case, we will finally see how useful the United Nations can be."[1]

After the Cold War

As the cold war drew to a close, the good offices of the United Nations helped lay to rest various of that conflict's local episodes, as in Namibia, Cambodia, El Salvador, and Nicaragua. Estimates of the world body rose accordingly. "The United Nations is suddenly alive again and doing useful work," observed the commentator Morton Kondracke, no starry-eyed romantic.[2] Then an American-led coalition, operating under the aegis of the UN Security Council, reversed Iraq's aggression into Kuwait. At last the United Nations seemed to be coming into its own. In January 1993, a Bush administration report concluded that "the United Nations has been given a new lease on life, emerging as a central instrument for the prevention and resolution of conflicts and the preservation of peace."[3] Later that year, the U.S. Commission on Improving the Effectiveness of the United Nations—a body appointed by President Bush and the leaders of Congress—concluded, in the words of its spokesman, Congressman James Leach, that "the U.N. [is] finally beginning to function as its framers intended."[4]

UN activity increased dramatically. In 1992, Secretary-General Boutros Boutros-Ghali reported that the United Nations had undertaken fourteen new peacekeeping operations in the preceding four years, as compared with a total of thirteen operations in its first thirty years.[5] Current operations, he said, involved some 50,000 soldiers in the field under the UN flag, and by the end of 1994 this number had grown again by half.[6]

In his 1990 article, Kondracke had speculated that Secretary-General Javier Perez de Cuellar might have "paved the way for a successor . . . to make the U.N. the worldwide security guarantor that its founders envisioned."[7] Boutros Boutros-Ghali must have been reading those words, because upon succeeding Perez de Cuellar, that is exactly the mission he set for himself. "The machinery of the United Nations, which had often been rendered inoperative by the dynamics of the Cold War, is suddenly at the center of international efforts to deal with unresolved problems of the past decades as well as an emerging array of present and future issues," he said. And he exhorted the world "to seize this extraordinary opportunity to expand, adapt and reinvigorate the work of the United Nations so that the lofty goals as originally envisioned by the charter can begin to be realized."[8]

The new secretary-general published a fifty-page manifesto, *An Agenda for Peace,* in which he proposed that the United Nations activate the long-moribund provisions of the charter for creating a permanent UN military force consisting of ready units earmarked by the member states and a military staff committee. This force, he said, would be designed for missions more ambitious than traditional UN peacekeeping, missions of "peace-enforcement," which would include "respond[ing] to outright aggression, imminent or actual."[9] Boutros-Ghali even foresaw the possibility of "preventive deployment" within torn countries "when the government requests" in order "to alleviate suffering and to limit and control violence."[10] The goal, said

Undersecretary-General Vladimir Petrovsky, was to create a "pax U.N."[11]

Clinton and the United Nations

Boutros-Ghali's aspirations struck a responsive chord in Bill Clinton. During the 1992 presidential campaign, Clinton advocated the creation of a "new, voluntary U.N. Rapid Deployment Force."[12] After the election, his appointees as secretaery of state and ambassador to the United Nations both reiterated this concept in their confirmation hearings. For Clinton, the idea of a newly assertive United Nations held the promise of alleviating America's burdens and leaving him free as president to "focus like a laser" on the domestic economy, as he pledged to do. Ambassador Madeleine Albright explained that "multilateral action" offered a "third alternative" between the repugnant extremes of "self-absorption" and "hyper-activity,"[13] that is, between isolationism and playing world policeman. And Clinton declared that "U.N. peacekeeping holds the promise to resolve many of this era's conflicts."[14]

That Clinton truly looked to the United Nations as a major element of American security policy was shown in an interview he gave to the *Washington Post* in 1993. Warning of the need to resist isolationism, Clinton said, "We have to . . . build a consensus for what our role in the world will be and how we will define it and how we will work with the United Nations and how we will develop the peacekeeping capacity of the United Nations, how we will define our interests." The context for this exercise, said Clinton, was this: "We've simply got to focus on rebuilding America."[15] In other words, as an alternative to isolationism, the Clinton administration looked to a heavy reliance on the United Nations to provide a kind of poor man's internationalism. America would not turn its back on the world, but it would not bear too many burdens, either. The *Washington Post*'s Jim Hoagland put it: "Keeping the United Nations as a credible alternative to a Pax Americana is as important for Clinton's Office of Budget and Management as it is for the State Department."[16]

The Clinton administration, however, was soon brought up short by the turn of events in Somalia. There, on October 3, 1993, a company of U.S. Army Rangers, the cream of American soldiery, was decimated by Somali irregulars who had been regarded as mere bandits. True, the Americans in Somalia had been under American command, and their mission that fateful day was conceived by American officers. But they were in Somalia under the aegis of the United Nations, and their general mission there was largely shaped by Boutros-Ghali. From the time that President Bush had dispatched U.S. forces to Somalia in December 1992, a kind of tug of war had been waged between the UN secretary-general and the American government. While the Americans wanted to feed the starving and leave, Boutros-Ghali wanted them to stay long enough to put Somali society back on its feet. The goal, as a Security Council resolution that he engineered phrased it, was "reestablishment of national and regional institutions and civil administration in the entire country."[17]

Because it invested more hopes in the United Nations than had its predecessor, the Clinton administration allowed itself to be drawn along further by Boutros-Ghali. The State Department's coordinator for Somalia, David Shinn, said before the October debacle that UN forces "basically are recreating a country. This has never been done before in the history of the world, at least the modern world."[18] And in August 1993, when four Americans were killed in what proved to be a preview of the October events, Ambassador Albright had staunchly exhorted Americans to "stay the course and help lift [Somalia] and its people from the category of a failed state into that of an emerging democracy."[19]

But when word reached home of the deaths of the Rangers, punctuated by news photos of the body of one being dragged through the streets of Mogadishu, a cry of protest went up in Congress. Why were Americans fighting and dying in Somalia, the representatives wanted to know; and they demanded that the troops be brought home at once. It was all President Clinton could do to secure congressional agreement to six months' grace to effectuate a gradual withdrawal.

Even before the deaths of the Rangers, the situation in Somalia illustrated the flaw in the Clinton administration's early thinking. It turned to the United Nations to reduce America's burdens, but the United Nations itself was dependent on America. The world body possesses no power of its own beyond what member states lend to it. The other member states will naturally look to the most powerful member to take the lead. And that country will feel pressure to lead even if it has doubts about the mission. Thus, an empowered United Nations is as likely to add to America's burdens as to alleviate them.

Perhaps out of recognition of this bind, the Clinton administration began even before the October killings to backtrack from the large role it had ascribed to the United Nations. According to the

National Journal, the National Security Council had decided in September to revise a draft Presidential Decision Directive that had "called for U.S. troops and treasure to be committed to multilateral peace operations on a scale never before contemplated."[20] The Somalia events undoubtedly lent momentum to the revisions.

The Limitations of UN Peacekeeping

By May 1994, when a revised directive, PDD-25, was signed, and a nonclassified version released, the emphasis was on recognizing the limitations of the United Nations and ensuring that its reach not exceed its grasp. The public version said: "Peacekeeping can be a useful tool for advancing U.S. national security interests in some circumstances, but both U.S. and UN involvement in peacekeeping must be *selective* and more *effective* [emphasis in original]. . . . It is not U.S. policy to seek to expand either the number of UN peace operations or U.S. involvement in such operations."[21] Ambassador Albright explained: "The one sentence summary of our policy is that it is not intended to expand UN peacekeeping, but to help fix it."[22] And the Clinton administration revealed that it had already blocked proposals for UN peacekeeping operations in Burundi, Georgia, and Angola.[23] By the end of the year, Ambassador Albright was boasting that "[U.S.] policy is working" and that "as a result, the total number of UN peacekeepers . . . [is] the lowest in almost two years."[24] Suddenly, it seemed, the goal of U.S. policy was not to expand UN operations but to contract them.

By the beginning of 1995, even Secretary-General Boutros-Ghali was grudgingly backing away from some of the loftier goals of his *Agenda for Peace.* In a paper titled "Supplement to an Agenda for Peace," he acknowledged that in "certain areas . . . unforeseen, or only partly foreseen, difficulties have arisen."[25] Among these, he said, was "the availability of troops and equipment," which "has palpably declined as measured against the Organization's requirements. . . . For example, when in May 1994 the Security Council decided to expand the United Nations Assistance Mission for Rwanda . . . not one of the 19 governments that at that time had undertaken to have troops on stand-by agreed to contribute."[26] More broadly, he added:

> One of the achievements of the Charter of the United Nations was to empower the Organization to take enforce-

ment action against those responsible for threats to the peace, breaches of the peace or acts of aggression. However, neither the Security Council nor the Secretary-General at present has the capacity to deploy, direct, command and control operations for this purpose, except perhaps on a very limited scale. I believe that it is desirable in the long term that the United Nations develop such a capacity, but it would be folly to attempt to do so at the present time when the Organization is resource-starved and hard pressed to handle the less demanding peacemaking and peace-keeping responsibilities entrusted to it.[27]

The severity of these problems was suggested by Boutros-Ghali's further complaint that in peacekeeping, "the contributing Governments [should] ensure that their troops arrive with all the equipment needed to be fully operational. Increasingly, however, Member States offer troops without the necessary equipment and training."[28] He may have had in mind the example of Bangladeshi forces assigned to protect the "safe area" of Bihac in Bosnia who had almost no weapons, but this instance would hardly be the only illustration of the failure of governments to take UN missions seriously. In August 1993, after the attack that killed four Americans in Somalia, Ambassador Albright acknowledged, "It's no secret that U.N. command and control problems arose in Mogadishu during recent fighting, but those problems, primarily with the Italian forces, are being worked out."[29]

They were not worked out. A month later, seven Nigerian soldiers were killed and seven others wounded in an ambush. According to the *Washington Post,* Italian UN contingents had achieved their own *modus vivendi* with the faction responsible for the attacks on UN forces:

> Nigerian commanders . . . accused the Italian troops of standing by as the Nigerian soldiers—arriving at the checkpoint in open pickup trucks—were being cut down by a torrent of automatic weapons fire. [The] commander of the Nigerian contingent here said of the Italians: "They deliberately left the Nigerians alone. There was no doubt about it." [He] said Italians stationed near the ambush site refused to open fire to assist the Nigerian troops, and at one point in the firefight even asked the beleaguered Nigerians to move away from an Italian armored

vehicle so as not to draw fire to it.

There was no immediate reaction from Italian commanders to these charges, but officials in Rome suggested that provocative U.N. tactics in the campaign against Aideed had brought on the attack.[30]

It was not only the Nigerians who encountered problems of coordination among UN forces in Somalia. When the U.S. Rangers suffered their debacle in October, they were pinned down in Mogadishu. Their extrication required armored vehicles, but America had none there. American commanders therefore sought help from available Pakistani tanks and Malaysian armored personnel carriers but received a mixed response. As the *Wall Street Journal*'s Pentagon correspondent, Thomas Ricks, recounted in a book review: "The Pakistanis refused to take the lead in the convoy. . . . [Later], as the Rangers were crossing the city to safety, their Malaysian escort vehicles began speeding away, forcing the Rangers to run behind them in what they now remember as 'the Mogadishu Marathon.'"[31] Senator Sam Nunn commented, in understated dismay, "It is very unusual for the United States to be in a position where we cannot really rescue our own forces in a situation like this."[32]

In addition to these problems, Senator John Warner, a member of the Senate Intelligence and Armed Services Committees, revealed that "we've already seen two serious recent compromises of U.S. intelligence during U.N. peace operations—once in Somalia and once in Iraq."[33]

The lessons of these experiences were not lost on UN members. In June 1994, when France decided to try to alleviate the bloodletting in Rwanda by setting up havens for refugees, Washington agreed to seek a UN endorsement. "But French officials said that while U.N. backing would be welcome, France does not want its soldiers to be shackled by restrictions that have rendered U.N. soldiers ineffectual," reported the *Washington Post*.[34] The newspaper quoted a senior French official's explanation: "We realize we could get drawn into hostile fire. So we want to be sure that our troops have the means and the mandate to protect themselves and the refugees."

Problems of Multilateral Military Action

These experiences in Somalia, Bosnia, or Rwanda are not isolated episodes. They point to underlying weaknesses in the United Nations that mock its founders' hopes that it would be the bulwark of world peace. The fundamental weakness was defined by Britain's former ambassador to the United Nations, Lord Caradon: "There is nothing wrong with the Charter, only with the members."[35] The United Nations remains a collection of states, many of which are neither law-abiding nor peaceful nor legitimated by the consent of those they govern. The composition of the UN Commission on Human Rights, which, although it rotates, invariably includes representatives of the most brutal governments on earth, poignantly illustrates the problem.[36] But even if all the 180-odd member states were ruled by civilized regimes, it would still be difficult to achieve concerted, forceful action among them. Henry Kissinger has said: "U.N. multilateralism can work only if all nations share a common perception of a danger, are willing to run the same risks and agree on a common strategy. [Otherwise] multilateral machinery becomes paralyzed, and indeed is likely to favor the side capable of creating *faits accomplis*."[37]

This account may overstate the difficulties of multilateral action in theory (do all members really need to run the same risks?), but in practice, it is unfortunately accurate. Experience shows that the all-important chapter 7 of the UN Charter has been utterly ineffective. That part deals with "actions with respect to threats to the peace, breaches of the peace, and acts of aggression." The first response to such depredations prescribed in the charter is economic. Sir Anthony Parsons, another former British ambassador to the United Nations, has summarized the experience:

> Mandatory economic sanctions have been imposed unanimously (no Cold War division) on five occasions—on Southern Rhodesia between 1965 and 1979; on South Africa (an arms embargo) since 1977; on Iraq from 1990; on "Yugoslavia" (an arms embargo) since September 1991; and on Serbia (comprehensive) since June 1992. On all these occasions, albeit for different reasons in each case, they have proved ineffective. They are either circumvented or they take too long to work or they create suffering amongst the innocent while the guilty remain unregenerate.[38]

When economic sanctions fail, as they have always done, the charter envisions military action; but these provisions, set forth in articles 42 through 49, remain a dead letter. They provide for the creation of a Military Staff Committee consisting of the chiefs of staff, or their representatives, of the five permanent members of the Security Council. This committee is supposed to assist the Security Council in undertaking military action "to maintain or restore international peace and security," and for this purpose all member states "undertake to make available" to the Security Council military units "on its call."

Although the Military Staff Committee has been brought into nominal existence, none of the other provisions has ever been acted upon. Even in the case of Iraq's invasion of Kuwait, Ambassador Parsons observes, "no serious attempt . . . was made to activate the Military Staff Committee . . . , still less to put Operations Desert Shield and Desert Storm under the control of the Security Council. The United States and its allies were in effect given *carte blanche*."[39] Parsons's crucial point is that this failure to involve the Military Staff Committee or the Security Council was no mere oversight or slight of the UN machinery:

> It is in fact hard to see how a large-scale, logistically complex and minutely planned operation such as Desert Storm could in practice have been organized by a Committee . . . comprising American, Russian, Chinese, British and French Officers, while so diverse a body as the fifteen-member Security Council would have been hard put to . . . "plan the application of armed force," even to maintain the minimum of military security required with Cuba and Yemen present at the table."[40]

Conditions for Peacekeeping

The futility of the UN machinery that was designed to uphold the peace does not mean, however, that the United Nations cannot engage in "peacekeeping." In UN parlance, the term *peacekeeping* has assumed a specialized, narrow meaning. Peacekeeping operations are those undertaken between adversaries who are able to agree on a compromise but still distrust one another. The peacekeeping forces do not need to be stronger than those of the local parties because they are not there to subdue anyone, just to act as observers and as a buffer. They help to assure each side that the other is not cheating and to provide early warning if the peace is broken. If, however, either side wishes to renounce the peace, the peacekeepers are powerless to stop them. Thus, in 1967, when Egyptian President Gamal Abdel Nasser demanded withdrawal of UN forces in the Sinai, the United Nations complied with such alacrity that Nasser himself was by some accounts surprised. He may have assumed that the United Nations would not call his bluff. In 1982, when Israel invaded Lebanon in pursuit of Palestine Liberation Organization forces, Israel did not bother to request withdrawal of UN contingents; it merely brushed them aside. Croatian forces did the same in 1995 when they recaptured the breakaway Republic of Serbian Krajina.

The reason for the upsurge in peacekeeping operations in the late 1980s and early 1990s was not so much that the end of the cold war allowed the United Nations to function better, although this condition surely contributed. Mainly, the end of the cold war brought an end to a variety of local conflicts fueled by the cold war, such as those between Soviet allies and American allies in Central America and southern Africa. Once Moscow and Washington had reconciled, and each urged its clients toward peace, settlements were achieved. Then, and only then, could UN peacekeepers play their part in overseeing the separation of forces, the surrender of weapons, the holding of elections, and the like. President Clinton, therefore, had it backwards when he declared in 1993 that "U.N. peacekeeping holds the promise to resolve many of this era's conflicts."[41] In truth, UN peacekeeping can be effective only after conflicts have been resolved. The resolution may not go deep, the parties may not view it as eternal, but they must prefer it to further fighting.

Clinton's error, however, did not occur in a vacuum. The upsurge in peacekeeping operations encouraged "mission creep," which was fueled by Boutros-Ghali's expansive goals. He began to speak of "new modes of peace-keeping"[42] and also "peace-making," "peace-building," and "peace-enforcement."[43] But to undertake peacekeeping, or some variant of it, when there is no peace to keep, requires a force capable of subduing the local forces. In Bosnia, Somalia, and Rwanda, the United Nations lacked either the will or the capacity for such action.

These unhappy experiences do not negate the value of UN peacekeeping, but they remind us that it is limited to cases where all parties genuinely desire peace. Thus, however useful, "peacekeeping" does not begin to address the weightiest question of international relations, which is how to uphold peace in cases where one or more parties do not want it, or want it only on their own terms.

It is not only the United Nations that has learned this lesson.

Before it, the League of Nations learned much the same. The league mediated several disputes successfully, sometimes deploying peacekeepers. As British Foreign Minister Austen Chamberlain is supposed to have said, however, "The League could make a contribution when sparrows were quarreling but was of little avail when eagles were fighting"[44]—or, he might have added, when eagles were feasting on sparrows. Thus, Japan's attack on Manchuria, Italy's on Abyssinia, and the Soviet Union's on Finland found the league impotent—not that the league refused to act. In each case, it slapped the miscreant on the wrist, a "punishment" that elicited only a self-righteous reaction. As a British Foreign Office minute put it, the league was "a forum where the utmost provocation is given with the least possible practical effect."[45]

Because of the widely shared judgment that the league had been a failure, when the United Nations was created, "many of its features were indicative of a conscious effort to avoid the deficiencies of the previous world organization," writes Innis Claude, the leading student of international organizations. The founders "stress[ed] the newness of the leaf that had been turned, the hopeful freshness of the start that was being made."[46] Now, fifty years later, it is painful to see that the United Nations has overcome few of these deficiencies.

Deficiencies of World Organizations

Do the deficiencies, then, inhere in any particular structure of the world organizations—or in their very conception? We have now seventy-five years of experience with these bodies. When the League of Nations proved ineffectual, we blamed the absence of the United States. When the United Nations proved ineffectual, we blamed the cold war. Now that the cold war has been over for some time and the United Nations still seems largely ineffectual, we may be running out of excuses. We may have to acknowledge that such world bodies cannot live up to their expectations.

Only twice in these seventy-five years has either world body responded forcefully to repulse a major violation of the peace: in Korea in 1950 and in Kuwait in 1990. Each was a UN action in name only. Both were in practice American actions, supported by allies, with UN endorsements. The military procedures spelled out in the charter were not followed, and neither General MacArthur nor General Schwartzkopf reported to the Security Council.

There is a lesson in this. Boutros-Ghali was on exactly the wrong track when he said, "This Organization may emerge as greater than the sum of its parts."[47] The United Nations cannot be, as Richard Armitage has put it, an "organism—a sort of superstate."[48] It can be only a forum where states do business with each other and perhaps where they establish law, weak though it is. As Innis Claude acknowledged years ago, "The establishment of an international organization does not involve the creation of an autonomous will [but] of a mechanism to be placed at the disposal of states."[49]

To treat the United Nations as an autonomous entity is worse than futile: it invites evasion of responsibility. In that way, it can prove to be, contrary to Boutros-Ghali, less than the sum of its parts. The United Nations can solve no problem for which its individual members are unwilling to accept the costs and risks of solving.

This is not to say that the United Nations is useless. But its de facto functions are likely to be more valuable than its de jure ones. It can serve as a kind of public square conducive to the conduct of diplomacy. It can be a good place for the United States to round up a posse.

To the extent that its formal structures inhibit American action, however, the United Nations can be positively harmful, not only to America but also to world peace, of which American power remains the main bulwark. In the normal course of diplomacy, American power is constrained because that power is not infinite and Washington must take into account the views and interests of others. But UN structures add further, artificial constraints. Thus, in the Security Council, America holds a veto, but so do four others, none of whom is America's equal in power and most of whom are not as public-spirited, either.

Where it constrains American power (or where America uses the United Nations as a cover for its own abdication), the United Nations is unlikely to offer anything in its place. The best contributions of the United Nations to peace have come not in replacing of American power but in sanctifying its exercise, as in Korea and Kuwait.

Just as the democracies of Western Europe can be valuable allies of America but do not provide an alternative source of leadership, so the United Nations can be a useful adjunct to American leadership—by providing a suitable arena—but not a substitute for it.

PART THREE

Bosnia—A Case Study in Abdication

·7·

"THE HOUR OF EUROPE,"
1987–1992

If any other nations are to shoulder burdens of leadership, the ones most suited to do so are the wealthy and powerful democracies of Western Europe. And if there is one place where they are most equipped to take on this role, it is in Europe itself. When Yugoslavia began to blow apart, European leadership was put to the test. The United Nations, too, became involved. The United States could not remain completely apart but, soothing itself that others were in charge, chose to play a secondary role. The result has been a demonstration of what international relations will look like in the absence of American leadership. (The appendix to this book gives a chronology of events in Yugoslavia 1987–1995.)

Dispute over Kosovo

The war in Bosnia began in 1992, fighting in Slovenia and Croatia in 1991. But the fragmentation of Yugoslavia began in the late 1980s and was hastened by the crumbling of the Soviet empire (see figure 7–1). As in the Soviet Union and Czechoslovakia, the reaction against decades of Communist repression took form not only in struggles for democracy but also in a resurgence of nationalist yearnings. In Yugoslavia, the region called Kosovo became the first focus of conflicting claims. The center of ancient Serbia, Kosovo had come to be populated overwhelmingly by ethnic Albanians, a demographic circum-

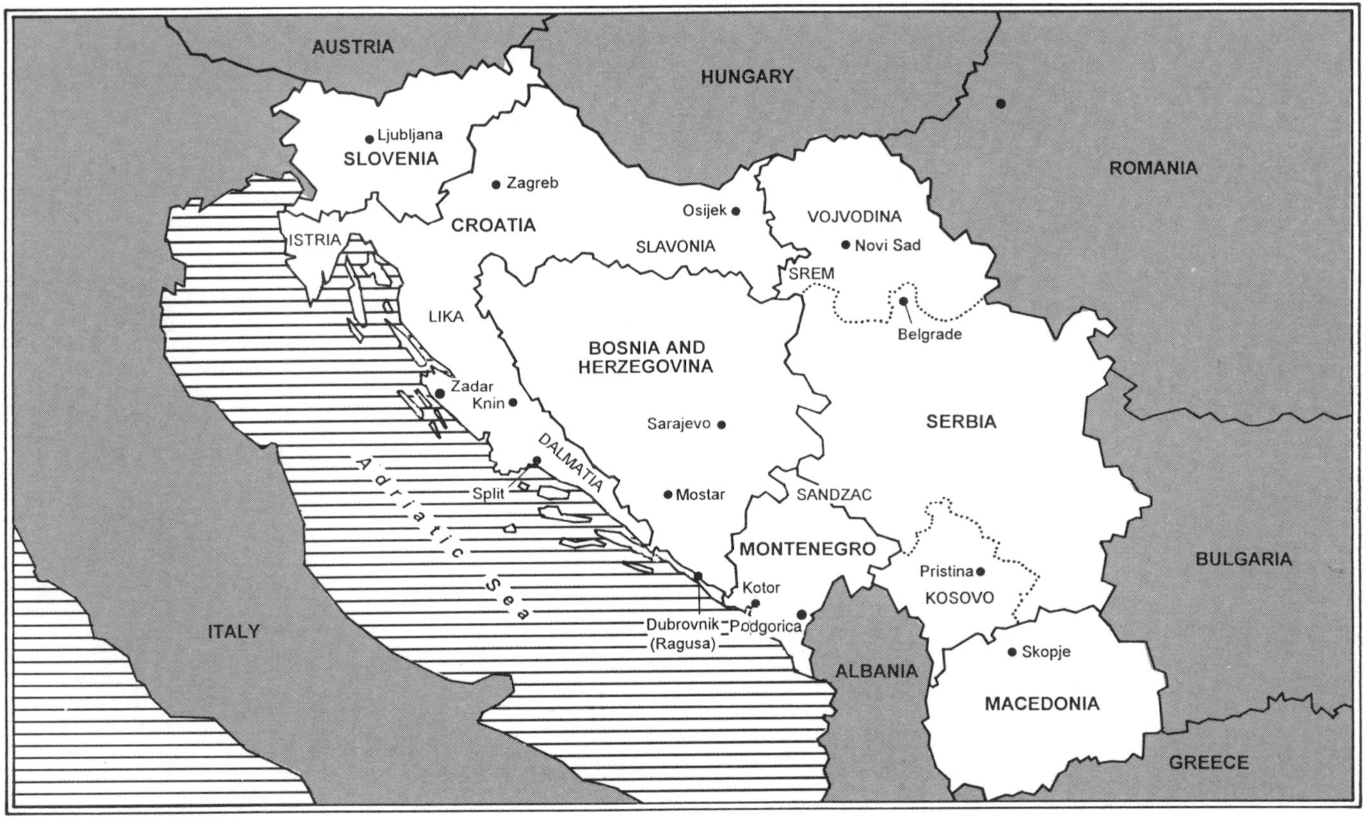

FIGURE 7-1: THE SIX REPUBLICS AND TWO AUTONOMOUS PROVINCES OF YUGOSLAVIA BEFORE 1991

stance that led to its designation as an autonomous region under Yugoslavia's 1963 constitution. In time, Albanians sought greater outlet for their sense of distinctive identity, while Serbs sought to reassert their claim to the territory.

Out of this cauldron emerged Slobodan Milosevic, headman of the Communist party (officially, the League of Communists) of Serbia. Milosevic seems to have sensed before others the declining salience of communism as a legitimating ideology. Accordingly, he transformed himself into the avatar of Serbian nationalism, stealing a march on the nationalist movements that emerged in Yugoslavia's non-Serb republics. As early as 1987, Milosevic established his nationalist credentials by ousting Ivan Stambolic, the man who had been his patron, from the presidency of Serbia on the grounds of being too conciliatory toward Kosovo's Albanians. Such moves not only hastened the rise of nationalism among Yugoslavia's other groups but envenomed it.

In early 1989, Milosevic maneuvered to abolish Kosovo's status as an autonomous region to bring it directly under Serbia's jurisdiction. (He did the same for the country's other autonomous region, Vojvodina.) This move denied Kosovo's Albanian population even such nominally independent representation as it had enjoyed under the system Tito created. The Albanians protested, but such outcries only inspired intimidating demonstrations by Serbs orchestrated by Milosevic's government. These culminated in June 1989 in a vast rally staged in Kosovo to commemorate a Serb nationalist holiday. There, Milosevic told the crowd that, as in the past, Serbs "are again engaged in battles and quarrels. They are not armed battles, but this cannot be excluded yet."[1] The harshly repressed Albanians could do little to respond to such threats. But non-Serb nationalities elsewhere in Yugoslavia had wider options.

Unrest in Slovenia and Croatia

Militancy matched militancy. In Croatia, Franjo Tudjman, an old Communist leader, perhaps emulating Milosevic, emerged now as an extreme nationalist. His party won Croatia's first contemporary free election, held in April 1990, just as proindependence forces had prevailed in elections in Slovenia a few weeks before. Late that year, Croatia's Serb community declared autonomy, voters in Bosnia and Herzegovina's first free election divided along ethnic lines, and Serb voters elected Milosevic president.

A classified CIA analysis warned of the possible violent disintegration of Yugoslavia. But according to David Gompert, then a U.S. official working on this issue, "American attempts in 1990 to get the Europeans to face the dangers were brushed aside: an American proposal to consult in NATO was declined, with the French accusing the United States of 'overdramatizing' the problem."[2] The Iraqi aggression in Kuwait absorbed America's attention, while the Yugoslav crisis deepened. Milosevic declared that if Yugoslavia became a confederation, Serbia would demand territory from the other states, and soon after he declared the Krajina region of Croatia, populated largely by Serbs, a "Serbian autonomous region." Croatian leader Tudjman's strategy was to deflect Serb ambitions southward while aggrandizing his own. In a March 1991 meeting, he and Milosevic agreed to divide the republic of Bosnia and Herzegovina between them.[3] Despite these rumblings, in April a team of three European foreign ministers visited Yugoslavia and expressed optimism that the country would succeed in solving its problems.[4]

In May, matters came to a head when Serbia blocked the scheduled rotation of the presidency, an office that, by constitutional design, changed annually. It now had come the turn of the Croatian member, Stipe Mesic. As head of state, he would have had a degree of authority over the armed forces—and it was precisely this authority that was repugnant to Milosevic and other Serb nationalists within the Yugoslav army. The Serb obstruction upset the fragile balance among the republics, prompting Slovenia and Croatia to threaten to secede from Yugoslavia by June 26.

In the face of these centrifugal forces, the Bosnian leader, Alija Izetbegovic, labored, mostly with the support of Macedonian leader Kiro Gligorov, to hold Yugoslavia together. Although both men wanted greater independence for their republics, they preferred the context of a Yugoslav federation, fearing that complete separation would leave them as prey for Serbia and Croatia. Izetbegovic, the only leader of a Yugoslav republic who had not been a Communist,[5] strove to find a formula that would accommodate the conflicting goals of Serbia, Croatia, and Slovenia. He even for a time lost the support of Gligorov, who thought Izetbegovic was making too many concessions to Serbia.[6] But his conciliatory efforts within the Yugoslav federation proved no more availing than his attempt within Bosnia and Herzegovina to find a *modus vivendi* with Bosnian Serbs.

America's Response

America, too, sought to preserve the unity of Yugoslavia. In February 1991, a State Department official testified to a Senate Subcommittee that "United States policy toward Yugoslavia is founded on support for unity, democracy, dialogue, human rights and market reform. The United States has long supported the unity, independence and territorial integrity of Yugoslavia."[7] Another high official, Assistant Secretary of State for Human Rights Richard Schifter, explained: "We would like to achieve stability [in the Balkans], and a breakup of the Yugoslav federation would be a serious setback."[8]

In May, in response to the crisis over the rotation of the Yugoslav presidency, the State Department issued a detailed statement that held "the leadership of the Serbian Republic responsible for the crisis" and called "strongly" for the "timely completion of the transfer of constitutional authority . . . to Stipe Mesic."[9] But despite pointing a finger at Serbia, the department reiterated American support for Yugoslav "unity" and warned that "the U.S. will not encourage or reward secession."[10]

With the crisis simmering, U.S. Secretary of State James Baker traveled to Yugoslavia in June where he met with the leaders of each of the republics. In addition to advocating democracy and peaceful resolution of conflicts, he stressed America's opposition to breaking up Yugoslavia. According to news reports, he told the leaders of Slovenia and Croatia that America would not recognize them as independent states "under any circumstances."[11] Two days later, the European Community backed Baker, voting unanimously not to recognize Croatia and Slovenia if they seceded.[12]

But within days, despite these pleas and warnings, the parliaments of Slovenia and Croatia passed declarations of independence, although they held open the possibility of continuing to belong to Yugoslavia if it were transformed into a loose confederation. The Bush administration reacted sharply, saying it would ignore these "unilateral steps" that "could have some very tragic consequences."[13] And Deputy Secretary of State Lawrence Eagleburger branded the declarations "a threat to the stability and well-being of the peoples of Yugoslavia."[14] A day later, the Yugoslav army initiated operations in Slovenia, and Slovenian Defense Minister Janez Jansa declared that "Slovenia is at war" with the federal government.[15]

Jansa blasted Baker's stance during his visit as "the last 'green light' needed for the aggression on Slovenia."[16] Members of the Bush administration have vigorously denied that Baker conveyed any such message,[17] but the Serbs might have interpreted his remarks to their own liking. As the *Economist* put it, Baker's strong endorsements of Yugoslav unity may have "encourage[d] some of Yugoslavia's generals in the belief that the West would not object—and might even reward them—if they moved to keep Yugoslavia in one piece."[18] Kenneth Juster, one of the former State Department officials who have refuted the "green light" allegations, concedes, however, that the Yugoslav leaders might have been emboldened in their actions by statements at the outset that "the U.S. would not be prepared to use ground troops in Yugoslavia."[19] Indeed, three weeks before Baker's visit, the Belgrade daily, *Politika*, in a story repeated by the Yugoslav news agency, Tanjug, quoted General John Galvin, the American commander in chief of NATO, as saying that "Yugoslavia is not within NATO's defense zone."[20]

For all the controversy about the effects of Baker's visit on the Yugoslav parties, the more important effects may have been those they had on him. The *Economist* expressed what others reported as well: "Wearied by the lies and evasions of all Yugoslavia's leaders, America's secretary of state, James Baker, washed his hands of the crumbling Balkan federation . . . and left the EC [European Community] to handle it."[21]

It is unlikely, however, that Baker was acting solely from pique. Several veterans of the Bush administration agree that fatigue from the Persian Gulf crisis constrained America's response to Bosnia. Gompert puts it: "Following the Gulf War, a leading role in Yugoslavia would have implied that the United States could and would act as international policeman."[22] Both George Kenney, who resigned from the State Department to protest its Bosnia policies, and former State Department counselor Kenneth Juster, who was close to the formulation of those policies, speculate that the response to Yugoslavia might have been different had Yugoslavia preceded Kuwait as the first post–cold war crisis.[23] But whatever the cause, Baker's failed mission undoubtedly marked a critical turning point: the launching of the great experiment. From then on, the Yugoslav crisis was Europe's to solve; America took a back seat.

The EC's Diplomacy in Yugoslavia

The shifting of responsibility was the result as much of a European pull as an American push. During the cold war, Europeans had chafed at American dominance, while Americans complained about disproportionate burdens. Now, both sides sought redress: the European Community was not just willing but eager for its turn at the plate. As its designated representative, Lord David Owen, has put it:

> There was a feeling that Europe could do it all on its own. . . . Europe wanted to stand on its own feet—Yugoslavia was the virility symbol of the Euro-federalists. This was going to be the time when Europe emerged with a single foreign policy and therefore it unwisely shut out an America only too happy to be shut out.[24]

Europe's excitement over its new diplomatic importance was expressed even before Baker arrived in Belgrade. The Berlin meeting of the Conference on Security and Cooperation in Europe (CSCE) that preceded Baker's visit had passed a resolution on Yugoslavia, prompting British Foreign Secretary Douglas Hurd to exult that this was "the first time the 35 countries have issued an opinion on a member state with little diplomatic flummery. This is a sign of what can happen when European states act as a sort of Congress of Europe."[25]

Slovenia. When fighting commenced in Slovenia on the morrow of Baker's mission, the EC responded quickly, dispatching a delegation of three foreign ministers. "This is the hour of Europe, not the hour of the Americans," declared one, Jacques Poos of Luxembourg.[26] After meeting with all sides, the mission worked out a compromise, which, according to Italian Foreign Minister Gianni De Michelis, "show[s] that on the political level, we already have a rapid reaction force."[27] And De Michelis made a point of reporting that the United States and the Soviet Union had not been "consulted" but merely "informed" of the mission.[28] EC Commission Chairman Jacques Delors was more blunt: "We do not interfere in American affairs. We hope they will have enough respect not to interfere in ours."[29]

American diplomacy worked to underscore the special European role in handling the Yugoslav crisis. David Gompert reports that "the United States deferred to the Europeans' wish that transatlantic coordination take place in EC-U.S. channels instead of in NATO."[30] And when some Europeans first suggested taking the issue to the United Nations, Washington's reaction was chilly. "The U.N. has no role in Yugoslavia," said U.S. Ambassador to the United Nations Thomas Pickering. And another senior official told the *Washington Post,* "The Europeans themselves have put a lot of hope in the idea that the CSCE should become the primary mechanism for resolving disputes on the continent. To go to the U.N., before the CSCE has been given a chance to show what it can do in the first crisis to come before it, would doom it from the outset."[31]

Initially, the EC foreign ministers' mission seemed successful. They secured Slovenia's and Croatia's agreement to suspend their declarations of independence for three months and Serbia's agreement to allow the Croat, Stipe Mesic, to assume his turn as president of Yugoslavia. Their efforts to achieve an end to hostilities, however, faltered. Fighting did come to a halt in Slovenia, essentially because the Serbs who dominated the federal government and army were ambivalent about holding on to Slovenia, especially after it offered surprisingly stiff resistance in the field. But hostilities flared in Croatia, a much more portentous battleground.

Croatia. Whereas few Serbs resided in Slovenia, Croatia was home to a substantial Serb minority, who, armed by their Serb brethren in the Yugoslav army, of which most of the Croatian Serb fighters were recent members, launched a war to wrest their territories from Croatia's jurisdiction. The EC debated interposing a military force but was unable to reach agreement. Instead, it sent a few score observers whose white uniforms and utter impotence led the locals to dub them the "ice cream men." Putting the best face on this failure, EC President Jacques Delors commented: "The Community is like an adolescent facing the crisis of an adult. . . . If it were 10 years older, it might be able to impose a military peace-keeping force."[32]

Meanwhile, the Serbs grew bolder. More and more, the Yugoslav army shed the pretense of neutrality and joined with Serb irregulars in attacks on Croat soldiers and civilians. This aggressiveness culminated in the bombardment and destruction of Vukovar and Dubrovnik. In August, the *Economist* reported from Belgrade:

> Mr Milosevic's plan, unveiled this week though known in outline for several years, would create a rump Yugoslavia, without breakaway Slovenia, or Croatia (except for bits that Serbia claims) if it too insisted on quitting. This would leave Serbia in control of Vojvodina and Kosovo . . . as well as of Montenegro and of most of Bosnia-Hercegovina: or so Mr Milosevic hopes.[33]

The "bits" of Croatia, however, turned out to be more than a quarter of its territory (figure 7–2 shows Croatia with the breakaway

FIGURE 7–2

Croatia, with the Breakaway "Republic of Serbian Krajina"

"Republic of Serbian Krajina"). A few weeks later, the *Economist* reported from Krajina's declared capital, Knin:

> The self-appointed rulers of Croatia's breakaway Serb enclave . . . take out the map. Soon, one of them says, all this will be ours, indicating with a sweep of the hand a Greater Serbia stretching from the border with Bulgaria to the Adriatic. . . . To the obvious objection that the republic of Bosnia and Hercegovina separates Krajina from Serbia, the men of Knin have a quick reply: Serbs in Bosnia and Hercegovina will soon declare union with Serbia.[34]

As fighting escalated, the frustrated Europeans turned to the UN Security Council. On September 25, the council voted to embargo arms deliveries to all of Yugoslavia. This resolution was introduced by France, England, the USSR, Belgium, and Austria following a presentation by the Yugoslav foreign minister, and it enjoyed the active support of the government of Yugoslavia. It is inconceivable that Belgrade did not foresee the impact of this vote.[35] The disintegration of Yugoslavia was well advanced. The Serbs had already appropriated virtually all the assets of the Yugoslav army and had distributed weapons to their cousins in Croatia and Bosnia and Herzegovina.[36] Therefore, the embargo could have only the effect of disabling the Serbs' victims. And yet the Western members of the Security Council were apparently oblivious to this predictable outcome; their suspicions were not even aroused by Belgrade's stance. It is hardly likely that they secretly intended to abet Serb aggression. More likely, theirs was a reflexive response: alarmed at the shooting, they sought to staunch the flow of guns.

Also in September 1991, the EC began a peace conference at The Hague under the chairmanship of Lord Carrington, a veteran diplomat. But it got nowhere. A month into its deliberations, the three-month suspension of Slovenia's and Croatia's independence elapsed, and both proceeded toward secession. Slovenia introduced its own currency, and Croatia's parliament voted to vacate Yugoslav laws within its territory.

Sovereignty and Minority Rights. Still, Lord Carrington made a final effort, submitting a novel proposal: Yugoslavia would remain a loose federation with international "personality"—that is, with the status of a state under international law—but each member republic could also exercise international personality should it wish. The other republics accepted this proposal,[37] but the Serbs did not, nor did they accept a subsequent version revised in light of their objections. At bottom, they would not accept a plan that provided for sovereignty of the various republics but not for sovereignty of minority groups within the republics. The Serbs found this omission quite unjust, but it is hard to see how, except in rare cases, minority groups anywhere can be granted sovereignty (as opposed to autonomy). The Serbs themselves had announced their intention to go to war rather than to grant sovereignty to minorities within Serbia, notably the Albanian majority in Kosovo whose claim to independent status seems at least as compelling as that of the Serb minority in Croatia or Bosnia.

Indeed, the vexing issue of minority rights was taken up by the EC at the peace conference. A five-member commission of eminent jurists was formed under the leadership of the French constitutional justice Robert Badinter. As hopes for a resolution of the Yugoslav crisis waned, pressure built for recognition of the republics that were breaking away. The Badinter Commission undertook to examine the claims of republics seeking recognition and to establish criteria under which the members of the EC might grant it. Among the key criteria was respect for the rights of minorities.

Recognition of Sovereignty and Its Consequences

Within the EC, pressure for recognition came primarily from Germany, which sympathized with Croatia and Slovenia. Germany believed that the threat of recognition was the only effective leverage held against Belgrade. And if this plan failed, Germany believed that recognition would give the conflict international status, as opposed to the status of a civil war. The German Foreign Ministry argued that the only alternative to an outright military response to "Serbia's policy of hegemony" was to "further internationaliz[e] the conflict . . . through formal recognition of the threatened republics in order to thwart any hopes Belgrade might have [that its] faits accomplis achieved through the use of force [would be] tolerated."[38] The German government believed, the German historian Wolfgang Krieger explains, that such recognition "would deter Serbian forces from expanding the conflict and that the international community—meaning the CSCE, the United Nations, the EC, or all of them combined—could exert effective pressure to end the hostilities."[39]

Opposition to recognition came from Britain and France, as well as from the United States, and initially from President Izetbegovic of Bosnia and Herzegovina. Izetbegovic feared that a Yugoslavia without Slovenia and Croatia would be tantamount to Greater Serbia, in which Bosnia would be swallowed up. Bosnia and Herzegovina's alternative would be to secede itself, but this, he foresaw, would be a perilous course. John Newhouse reported that "Bosnia's leaders pleaded with Western capitals to withhold recognition of Slovenia and Croatia,"[40] but their pleas fell on deaf ears. Serbian rejection of Lord Carrington's proposals cut the legs out from under those in the EC who opposed Germany's push for recognition of Slovenia and Croatia.

Germany's Role. Moreover, at this moment coincidental political factors enhanced Germany's leverage within the EC on the subject of Yugoslavia. In December, as the Yugoslav crisis deepened, European leaders convened in Maastricht for the famous summit that set Western Europe on the fast road to integration. Of all the major European powers, Britain was the most skittish about integration, and at Maastricht, it won German support on several issues of concern. In the process, it acquired a political debt that was paid at the window of Yugoslav diplomacy. Indeed, the *Economist* claimed that there was an explicit quid pro quo: "In return for German help at the Maastricht summit on European union, Britain's prime minister, John Major, gave the German chancellor, Helmut Kohl, his word that Britain would back Germany's line on Croatia. . . . [France] preferred to go along than risk the blame for breaking ranks."[41]

In mid-December, the EC, maintaining unity while acquiescing to Germany, announced that its members would recognize Slovenia and Croatia, effective one month later. Within a few days, however, Germany proceeded to announce recognition on its own, arguing that the EC's target date was only a final deadline.

This early recognition constituted another blow to the EC's tattered dignity. During these months of fighting in Croatia, the EC had secured the combatants' agreement to cease fire—more than a dozen times, each accord utterly futile. During the siege of Vukovar, an EC mission to relieve the civilian population was driven off by Serbian attacks, and discussions of forceful action in response to the bombardment of Dubrovnik led nowhere.[42] In early December, some European diplomats leaked a scathing report written by EC peace monitors (the "ice cream men"). The *Economist* reported that "the monitors come down unequivocally against the Serbs and the[Yugoslav] army."[43] They even recommended the "selective show and use of force—to intimidate and hit the [Yugoslav army] in places where it hurts."[44]

The only show of force that ensued, however, was in the opposite direction. A month after the report was leaked, a Yugoslav air force fighter plane shot down a helicopter carrying five of the EC monitors. "The white-painted helicopter was clearly marked and had given notice of its flight plan," noted the *Economist.*[45]

On top of these embarrassments, the EC's decision to recognize Croatia made a mockery of the Badinter Commission. Only one day earlier, the commission had reported that, from a legal and human rights standpoint, two Yugoslav republics were qualified for recognition: Slovenia and Macedonia, but not Croatia. Nonetheless, the EC recognized Croatia, while refusing to recognize Macedonia on the grounds that Greece did not like its name.

American Neutrality. While these tragic-comic events unfolded, America remained resolutely in the background and as neutral as possible. In October a State Department official had testified to Congress that "the bottom line . . . is that the world community cannot stop Yugoslavs from killing each other so long as they are determined to do so."[46] While the EC imposed economic sanctions on Serbia and its satellite, Montenegro, the United States imposed sanctions evenly on all six Yugoslav republics. And when the EC announced its intention to recognize Slovenia and Croatia, Washington refused to go along, but minded its place. "We continue to place a high value on the European Community's leading role in seeking a political settlement of the Yugoslav crisis, as mandated by the CSCE," declared the State Department.[47]

The EC's actions helped to draw both Macedonia and Bosnia and Herzegovina into the vortex. In its mid-December meeting, the EC announced its willingness to recognize not only Croatia and Slovenia but any Yugoslav republic requesting recognition before December 23, provided it met the Badinter Commission's criteria.[48] Both Macedonia and Bosnia and Herzegovina duly joined the queue. Not coincidentally, on the same day that Bosnia requested recognition, Bosnian leader Izetbegovic appealed to the United Nations to station peacekeepers on his soil.

The Badinter Commission told Bosnia's leaders that popular support for their republic's independence would have to be demonstrated in a referendum. The referendum, held on February 29, 1992, yielded an overwhelming vote for independence, but, ominously, the vote was boycotted by the republic's Serbian minority, whose leaders had already declared their community autonomous. How solidly the Bosnian Serbs supported this stance we will never know, because the armed and ruthless Serbian militants brooked no dissent within their own community.

Ethnic Cleansing Begins

In late March, Bosnian Serbian forces, supported by the Yugoslav army, launched their attack against Bosnia's non-Serb population and government. Some accounts later claimed that the offensive was begun in response to Western recognition of Bosnia and Herzegovina, but recognition only came on April 7, some two weeks after the fighting had begun. Both the EC countries and the United States extended recognition to Bosnia, and Washington coupled this action with recognition of Croatia and Slovenia, which it had withheld until then.

In the weeks that followed, the fighting in Bosnia reached a savagery that eclipsed the battles in Croatia. These had come to a halt in January followed by the emplacement of a UN peacekeeping force. The Serbs were sated, although they had not achieved all their territorial goals, and the Croats, although they had mounted a resistance, were, for the time being, too weak to recoup.

In Croatia, the Serbs had fought largely to wrest territories inhabited by Serbs from the jurisdiction of Zagreb. In Bosnia, the Serbs now fought to seize land largely populated by non-Serbs. The goal was not merely sovereignty but spoliation; not merely to resist rule from Sarajevo, but to transform lands that had long been Muslim into Serbian lands. Therefore, the energies of Serbian fighters were aimed less at enemy armies than at civilians. With this horrific process, a new term entered into the world's lexicon of barbarism—*ethnic cleansing*.

·8·

AGGRESSION AND
INDIFFERENCE,
1992–1995

As war—and worse—engulfed Bosnia, the international community at first remained inert. After more than a month, the United States and the EC countries withdrew their ambassadors from Belgrade to register their displeasure, although even this gesture required weeks of diplomatic debate. At the same time, the EC withdrew its monitors from Sarajevo because the city had become too dangerous.[1] The United Nations was even more cautious than the EC. France, Germany, and Poland joined in proposing the dispatch of UN peacekeepers, but Secretary-General Boutros Boutros-Ghali, basing his decision on a report from his envoy, Cyrus Vance, rejected the idea.[2] He also refused to blame the Serb side for the violence. Instead, the United Nations concentrated on removing its own personnel from harm's way in Sarajevo.

The Bush Administration's Response

As for America, the first grim reports from Bosnia impelled Washington to reconsider its back-seat role, at least to the point of attempting some back-seat driving. Secretary of State Baker worked the transatlantic phone lines to secure the diplomatic break with Belgrade. Although he got his way on this measure, the resistance he encountered, both from allies and within his own government, reportedly recon-firmed his inclination to keep the Bosnia problem at arm's length. Anonymous U.S. officials told the *New York Times* that "Secretary Baker has decided to disengage from the issue" and that "there is no policy on Yugoslavia now, other than to follow the lead of the Euro-pean Community."[3] This zigzag pattern—reflecting on the one hand the inability to ignore the problem and on the other the refusal to become deeply involved—came to characterize U.S. policy.

As shells rained on Sarajevo and other Bosnia locales, Baker ex-coriated the international community for tolerating the Serb attacks. He said to a gathering of foreign ministers in Lisbon, "Anyone who is looking for reasons not to act, or arguing somehow that action in the face of this nightmare is not warranted at this time . . . is on the wrong wavelength."[4] The kind of intervention that Baker had in mind was not military; it consisted of various economic and diplomatic sanc-tions. The United Nations promptly adopted such measures, but they were greeted with defiance by the Serbs, who renewed their shelling of Sarajevo, which had been briefly halted, and for good measure started bombarding Dubrovnik again.[5]

The *Economist* reported from the Lisbon meeting that "if [sanc-tions] fail, Mr Baker says, it could become necessary to consider mili-tary measures as well."[6] But when President Bush was pressed on this possibility some days later, he dampened expectation of any forceful action: "I'm not prepared to give up on the sanctions at all," he said.[7] He also took the occasion to suggest the limits to America's new assertiveness. "The EC, which is right there in the neighborhood, tried to have an effective role. It now appears that a U.S. . . . . catalytic role is important," he said.[8]

Even as the United States adopted a more active part in facilitat-ing humanitarian deliveries to Bosnia, President Bush belittled the cri-sis and America's interests in it. "I don't think anybody suggests that if there is a hiccup here or there or a conflict here or there that the United States is going to send troops. Yugoslavia's a good . . . ex-ample."[9] Since no one had suggested sending troops, Bush was knock-ing down a straw man to signal his aloofness from Bosnia. In August, as Bush proposed UN authorization of the use of force to protect aid convoys into Bosnia, the *New York Times* reported that he and other Western leaders made clear "that they have no intention of being drawn deeper into the war. . . . Pentagon officials have said that contingency planning makes no provision for the two kinds of assistance repeatedly requested by the Bosnian government: American air strikes . . . and an airlift of American arms."[10]

However circumscribed the steps that America was willing to take, the European powers were even more cautious. They had ceded leadership on the issue, but America had not assumed it. By the second half of 1992, America was deep into its presidential election campaign. Foreign policy is often placed on the back burner during these periods, and in 1992 the American electorate was particularly focused on domestic issues.

After the election, the lame-duck Bush administration revisited the Bosnia issue. In December 1992, Lawrence Eagleburger, acting secretary of state and former ambassador to Yugoslavia, proposed exempting Bosnia from the international arms embargo. According to David Gompert, Bush adopted this proposal at the urging of Arab states, but England and France blocked it.[11]

Critics of the administration challenged the seriousness of this eleventh-hour initiative. According to Stephen Walker, one of the State Department officers who eventually resigned to protest policy toward Bosnia, Eagleburger took none of the usual steps to make something come of his proposal."[12] Indeed, weeks later, Eagleburger was still apportioning blame evenhandedly among all sides in Bosnia. "It's Serbs, it's Croats, it's Bosnian Muslims, the whole panorama. If you're intent on killing each other, don't blame it on somebody else," he said.[13]

The Clinton Administration's Response

Bill Clinton became president in 1993, having criticized George Bush during the election campaign for too timid a policy on Bosnia. The first question the new administration faced on Bosnia was its response to the Vance-Owen plan unveiled in January. Cyrus Vance and Lord Owen, representing respectively the United Nations and the EC, proposed to divide Bosnia into ten cantons, three dominated by each of its three predominant ethnic groups and one neutral canton embracing the capital, Sarajevo. Most governmental authority would devolve to the cantons. The Bosnian Serbs rejected the plan, but the Muslim-led government rejected it more strongly, believing it to be a ratification of ethnic cleansing and a formula for dismantling the state. In early January, Izetbegovic traveled to Washington to implore Americans to oppose "appeasement," but neither President Bush nor president-elect Clinton would agree to see him.

On February 10, Secretary of State Warren Christopher announced the new administration's policy. He was eloquent in denouncing the carnage and expansive in identifying the American interests at stake, but he abjured military measures. He nominally rejected the Vance-Owen plan by observing that it "had not been accepted by the parties," but he embraced the "Vance-Owen negotiations" and announced that "the weight of American diplomacy" would now be brought to bear in support of them.

In the weeks that followed, this weight was felt mostly by the Muslim side. Through a combination of threats and inducements President Izetbegovic was persuaded to accept the plan. (America airlifted supplies to desperate Muslim communities, and it is reported to have promised military aid in the event that the Muslims accepted Vance-Owen and the Serbs did not.)[14]

Once Izetbegovic had signed on, the ball was in the court of the Serbs. On the ground, perhaps emboldened by Christopher's rejection of military measures, they ratcheted up their sieges and ethnic cleansing of Muslim communities, climaxing in the strangulation of the town of Srebrenica.

At the diplomatic table, they pirouetted around the international mediators. In January, Bosnian Serb leader Radovan Karadzic had announced his support of Vance-Owen, but on April 3, the self-proclaimed Bosnian Serb parliament rejected the plan. Two days later, however, Karadzic wrote to the UN Security Council denying that the rejection was categorical. On April 26, the parliament rejected the plan again, despite a major new concession by Owen.[15]

Lift and Strike. On May 1, in the face of Serb obduracy, the Clinton administration announced the president's decision to proceed with the use of American air power against the Serbs and to seek a lifting of the arms embargo against the government of Bosnia. The secretary of state, it was added, was leaving for Europe to secure the support of America's allies. The very next day, Karadzic signed the Vance-Owen plan and referred it once again to the Bosnian Serb parliament. But within days the press reported that Christopher was meeting opposition in Paris and London to the "lift-and-strike" proposal. And the New York Times reported in a front-page headline, "Prompt Military Reprisal Unlikely If Serbs Shun Pact, U.S. Aides Say."[16] A day later, the Bosnian Serb parliament once again rejected Vance-Owen, voting instead to put it quickly to a referendum. In the face of this "unexpected rejection of [the] international peace plan," the *Times* reported that President Clinton "said he wanted 'to see what happens over the next few days' and suggested that the Bosnian Serbs might yet change their minds."[17] On May 15, the Bosnian Serbs voted overwhelmingly against the plan, and Karadzic proclaimed it dead.

"Safe Areas." Faced with this bold Serb defiance, President Clinton chose to fold. Rather than use the Serbs' behavior as a basis for insisting that the Europeans go along with his lift-and-strike proposal, Clinton decided to fall in behind his recalcitrant allies. On May 22, a Joint Action Program was unveiled on behalf of the United States, Russia, France, England, and Spain. This program, initiated by Russian Foreign Minister Andrei Kozyrev, abandoned any thought of aggressive resistance against the Serbs and focused instead on designing six "safe areas"—Sarajevo, Tuzla, Bihac, Srebrenica, Zepa, and Gorazde—in which Muslims could find refuge (see figure 8-1). Bitterly, Izetbegovic likened these to "reservations" for the Muslims.

What exactly was safe about the safe areas remained elusive. The Security Council authorized the use of force to protect them,[18] but when additional forces were sought for this mission few countries responded. Some Muslim states offered forces, but this offer was spurned.[19] Such UN forces as were available for the safe areas were placed under rules of engagement that called for the use of force only if they themselves were attacked but not if attacks were directed solely against the Muslim civilians under their aegis.

Clinton's Retreat. Having tiptoed up to the line of military action in Bosnia and then flinched, the Clinton administration spent the next months trying to define down the importance of the crisis to America. In February, Christopher had argued that America had a range of "direct strategic concerns" at stake in Bosnia and that the conflict there was crucial "if we hope to promote the spread of freedom or if we hope to encourage the emergence of peaceful multi-ethnic democracies."[20] In June, however, he declared that Bosnia "involves our humanitarian concerns, but it does not involve our vital interests."[21] Some days later he referred to it in terms redolent of Neville Chamberlain's infamous description of Czechoslovakia, calling it "a humanitarian crisis a long way from home, in the middle of another continent."[22]

In June, in the wake of the West's retreat, Serbia and Croatia

FIGURE 8–1

THE SIX "SAFE AREAS" OF BOSNIA AND HERZEGOVINA DECLARED BY THE
UN SECURITY COUNCIL, 1992

brokered an alliance. It called for a final division of Bosnia into three ethnic parts in which a small area would be left to the Muslims. The EC hastened to endorse this approach, Lord Owen commenting, "We have to make the best of what has happened on the ground."[23] And soon the United States fell in line, albeit with more hand wringing. Although noting that he would prefer to see Bosnia preserved, President Clinton allowed disingenuously that "if the parties themselves agree" to its dismantling, "the United States would have to look very seriously" at it.[24] But the parties would not agree because the government of Bosnia, withstanding enormous pressure, refused to acquiesce in the abolition of its country.

For its stubbornness, Bosnia received an ever colder response from the West. In July, Secretary Christopher responded blandly to a question about whether the United States was prepared to see the fall of Sarajevo: "The United States is doing all that it can consistent with our national interest."[25] According to former State Department officer Stephen Walker, "The next day, predictably, more shells fell on Sarajevo than in any other point during the siege, to date."[26]

Thus encouraged, the Serbs tightened their stranglehold on the Bosnian capital until in August the United States found the situation intolerable despite Christopher's having recently washed his hands of it. This time, the United States secured NATO's assent to threaten the Serbs with airstrikes. The Serbs pulled back slightly from two strategic peaks from which they had besieged and bombarded Sarajevo, and the threat evaporated.

Throughout the remainder of 1993 the war wore on, assuming a confusingly triangular contour. With the Bosnian government largely bereft of its hopes of rescue by the West, Bosnian Croats, backed actively by the armed forces of Croatia, asserted themselves increasingly as an independent force. On various fronts, the (mostly Muslim) forces loyal to Sarajevo fought Serbs or Croats, while on others the Serbs and Croats fought each other.

The Siege of Sarajevo

Despite the slight Serb pullback of August and the designation of Sarajevo by the United Nations as a safe area, Serb forces continued to shell the city almost daily. NATO did nothing in response on the grounds that these attacks remained below an undefined threshold of intensity. Then, on February 5, 1994, a shell landed in an outdoor market in Sarajevo, slaughtering at once sixty-eight people and wounding hundreds others. President Clinton said he was "outraged," and he threatened military retaliation. But in the next breath he began to vitiate the threat: he called on the United Nations to "urgently investigate" who had fired the shell.[27] Since the Serbs had been shelling the city continuously for nearly two years, there was little mystery about who had fired the fatal round but also little prospect of conclusive proof.

Defense Secretary William Perry hastened to weaken the threat further by explaining that even if the Serbs had fired the shell, it still had to be determined whether this attack constituted "strangulation" of Sarajevo, for that is what America had pledged to prevent. "If this action is seen as strangulation and we cannot prevent that, we will definitely consider stronger action," he declared.[28]

Instead of retaliating, Clinton initially sought to use the horror to catalyze greater pressure on the Bosnian government to yield new concessions in the continuing peace talks.[29] But a few days later, NATO, acting at American behest, demanded that all heavy weapons be removed from within a 20-kilometer radius of Sarajevo within ten days. Any weapons not either removed or placed under UN control, it declared, would "be subject to NATO air strikes which will be conducted in close coordination with the U.N. Secretary General."[30]

NATO and the United Nations

NATO's determination to work hand-in-glove with the United Nations, however, soon generated ambiguities. Four days into the ten day deadline, the chief UN spokesman in Bosnia said: "This is a NATO ultimatum; it is not a UN ultimatum."[31] In addition, the word *control* became a focus of controversy. UN officials took the position that they could "control" Serb heavy weapons without necessarily taking possession of them. After a few days, journalists reported a compromise in which some Serb heavy weapons would be allowed to remain within the 20-kilometer zone but "the United States would insist on physical measures to prevent the guns from being fired, and [officials] said NATO would conduct airstrikes if the measures were breached."[32]

When the deadline passed, the *Washington Post* reported that the Serbs had fallen short of meeting its terms, but "top NATO and U.N. officials both said . . . that there was now no need for airstrikes because there had been virtual compliance."[33] A day later, however, the *New York Times* reported from the exclusion zone that UN soldiers were "controlling" Serb heavy weapons merely by watching them from a distance through binoculars.[34] And within a few months, the *Post* reported that Serbs had retrieved by force some of the weapons that had been surrendered to UN control and had moved others back into the "exclusion zone."[35]

Gorazde. While the bulk of Serb heavy weapons within 20 kilometers of Sarajevo were moved, most of these were not turned over to the United Nations. They were taken to other fronts such as Gorazde, a Muslim town in eastern Bosnia, which became the Serbs' next target. As in Sarajevo, Serb gunners rained shells upon the civilian population, wreaking death and mayhem. Initially, American officials ruled out any military measures to protect Gorazde's 65,000 inhabitants, although it was one of the six designated safe areas. When asked about the prospective fall of Gorazde, Secretary of Defense William Perry declared flatly: "We will not enter the war to stop that from happening."[36] But a few days later, American policy changed, at least rhetorically. National Security Adviser Anthony Lake announced that "neither the President nor any of his senior advisers rules out the use of air power to help stop attacks such as those against Gorazde."[37]

NATO's First Attack. Three days later, after Serbian forces pushed into the outskirts of Gorazde, two U.S. jets conducted NATO's first ever ground attack mission. But when the attack hit only a tent and one or two light vehicles, the Serbs emerged defiant, intensifying their bombardment.[38] In response, the United States persuaded NATO to issue an ultimatum to the Serbs, modeled on the Sarajevo precedent, demanding a withdrawal of their forces from Gorazde and their heavy weapons from within 20 kilometers of it. When the April 22 deadline passed unobeyed, the NATO commander asked UN authorization to attack Serbian forces, but this was refused by Yasushi Akashi, the top UN official in Bosnia.[39] The Serbs, however, did pull back shortly after the deadline, averting a NATO attack. Despite Serbian cheating and probing, NATO seemed at last to have established that it was prepared to use some degree of force to protect at least some of the proclaimed safe areas.

Proposed Division of Bosnia. This achievement, however, had its price.

To secure NATO's assent to military threats, Washington, it turned out, had agreed to a new diplomatic initiative: dividing Bosnia into two parts; a Serbian part comprising 49 percent of Bosnia's territory and a joint Muslim-Croatian part comprising 51 percent. This proposed union of Muslim and Croat territories was the fruit of an agreement, brokered by America in March, between the Bosnian government and the Bosnian Croats and Croatia. Bosnian Muslims and Croats agreed to cease fighting each other, to pool their territory, and to link their combined territory in some way with Croatia. Until then, American policy had not envisaged or condoned partitioning Bosnia. The new initiative, although purporting to keep Bosnia whole, was a long step toward partition. The *Washington Post* explained America's shift:

> Creation of the map is the result of a major change of heart within the Clinton administration, which had said it would never endorse a map, much less pressure the Bosnian factions to agree to one. However, the Americans agreed to help design such a solution in exchange for the acquiescence of Europe in general, and France in particular, to use NATO airstrikes as a threat to deter Bosnian Serb attacks on the capital, Sarajevo, and the besieged Muslim enclave of Gorazde.[40]

The plan was sponsored by five powers—the United States, Russia, Britain, France, and Germany—constituting a "contact group," which now took center stage in the diplomacy. The map they drew was presented to the Bosnian parties, who were told to take it or leave it by July 30. Any party not accepting the deal by that deadline would be subject to penalties. For the Bosnian government, the penalties mattered little: it could not afford to buck the international community since it was dependent on that community for humanitarian aid and small measures of protection. But for the Serbs, the question of penalties was important. Washington failed to persuade the contact group to agree on the one penalty that might have worried the Serbs: lifting the arms embargo against the government of Bosnia. Instead, reported Secretary Christopher, "the agreed options include tightening the sanctions, enforcing existing exclusion zones more strictly, and identifying new ones." Then he added awkwardly, "Should these steps fail to bring the Serbs to accept the plan, the parties recognize that the pressure to lift the arms embargo may be irresistible."[41]

When July 30 arrived, the Bosnian government and its Croatian allies had accepted the plan, but the Bosnian Serbs had not. Secretary Christopher flew to a meeting of the contact group in Europe, telling reporters en route that he hoped to persuade his colleagues to pressure the Serbs by setting still another deadline for their compliance.[42] But even this indulgent step was too tough for the contact group. Instead, it agreed to seek tighter economic sanctions on Serbia, while promising to reduce existing sanctions if Serbia would help win cooperation from the Bosnian Serbs. In a demonstration of their disdain for the contact group, the Bosnian Serbs resumed the strangulation of Sarajevo and renewed ethnic cleansing in outlying areas.[43]

Negotiations with Milosevic. Thus rebuffed, the contact group turned its focus to Belgrade and seemed to make some progress in this direction. Serbian President Milosevic denounced the Bosnian Serbs for their recalcitrance and announced that he would cut off the material support that had sustained their war efforts, but his prior record on this left foreign diplomats skeptical. A team of international observers thus duly set out to verify that this time Belgrade really had closed the supply routes to Bosnia.

The observers, however, were placed under severe constraints by Milosevic on the claim that a low profile was less likely to evoke a backlash from extreme Serb nationalists. Milosevic would allow only the emplacement of 135 civilians to oversee the 375-mile-long border.[44] These monitors were not empowered to inspect vehicles crossing from Serbia into Bosnia but only to look over the shoulders of Serbian officials controlling the borders; if they saw something suspicious, their only recourse was to record the license plate number. Moreover, they were not present at all on the long border between Serb-held Bosnia and the Serb-held Krajina region of Croatia.[45] There were, in short, many ways to violate Milosevic's embargo of the Bosnian Serbs. Soon, Secretary of Defense Perry reported: "We have incomplete reports that indicate that that's been partially but not fully complied with. . . . Certainly not a complete stoppage."[46] In return, the world's economic sanctions against Serbia were softened.

Despite the added leverage against the Bosnian Serbs from the presumed Serbian embargo against them, they did not budge. Indeed as the summer of 1994 turned to fall, their violations of the exclusion zones protecting Sarajevo and Gorazde intensified, as did their ethnic cleansing and direct attacks on UN peacekeeping forces. In response, the contact group offered them new concessions.

According to the revised contact group proposal, the Serbs would be allowed to confederate their 49 percent of Bosnia with Serbia. This change was justified on the grounds that the plan already allowed the Muslim-Croatian portion to confederate with Croatia. Because Muslims constituted a vast majority within that part of Bosnia, however, Croatia was unlikely to swallow it. But confederation on the Serb side undoubtedly implied the absorption of Serbian Bosnia into the so-called Greater Serbia.

Throughout the first half of 1995, the West pursued Serbian cooperation through carrots rather than sticks. The contact group plan was no longer "take-it-or-leave-it," but merely a "basis for negotiation." The embargo against Serbia could be lifted if only Belgrade would recognize the *borders* of Bosnia and Herzegovina (even if it refused to recognize the Sarajevo government). But none of these offers were taken. When, instead, the Serbs intensified their bombardment of Sarajevo, NATO airplanes bombed some Serb ammunition dumps. In defiance, the Serbs took between 300 and 400 UN peacekeepers hostage.

NATO ceased at once its attacks, and after a few weeks, in mid-June, the hostages were released. The release, however, was preceded by a series of secret negotiations between the Bosnian Serb commander, Ratko Mladic, and the chief civilian UN official in the region, Yasushi Akashi, and its chief military officer, General Bernard Janvier. At first, UN spokesmen denied the claims of Serb leaders that in return for the hostages, Akashi and Janvier had pledged that NATO would undertake no new bombing.[47] But after a week, UN officials and Western diplomats conceded to reporters that such a deal had in fact been struck.[48] It was soon to have devastating consequences.

A month later, in mid-July, Serbian forces surrounded the safe area of Srebrenica. The town's small contingent of Dutch UN peacekeepers appealed for NATO airstrikes. In Zagreb, wrote the *New York Times*:

> General Janvier . . . convened his top military advisers. . . .
> The general asked for advice. The response was nearly unanimous: airstrikes. The United Nations' credibility was at stake. Srebrenica was a safe area. It had to be defended . . . . General Janvier was unpersuaded. He announced that he would sleep on it. He left his aides "aghast," as a United Nations official put it.[49]

Janvier had kept his bargain with Mladic.

For his part, Mladic led his men into Srebrenica, driving out its

Muslim inhabitants and systematically butchering some 5,000–10,000 males taken prisoner. Then the Serb force rolled over the nearby safe area of Zepa and began to menace Gorazde.

After teetering on the brink of complete collapse, Western will stiffened, and representatives of the United States, Britain, and France delivered a formal ultimatum to Serb leaders in Belgrade, threatening actions more forceful than any previously taken if the other safe areas were attacked.

At about the same time, the beginning of August, the government of Croatia, acting with open American approval, launched a lightning offensive against the Republic of Serbian Krajina. Meeting little resistance, it quickly regained control over the entire area (except a small slice of land, eastern Slavonia, directly abutting Serbia), and the Serb residents fled to Serbia or Bosnia. Although the Croatian government had been threatening to take such action, and had repeatedly sought the removal of UN buffer forces, its thorough victory surprised Western leaders who had nurtured exaggerated images of Serb military prowess.

Perhaps emboldened by the Croatian example, NATO responded to a Serbian artillery attack against downtown Sarajevo that killed dozens in late August by launching its first substantial strikes against the Serbs. These continued for a few weeks until most Serb heavy weapons had been pulled back beyond 20 kilometers from Sarajevo.

At the same time, a combined offensive by Bosnian government, Bosnian Croat, and Croatian government forces recaptured swaths of territory from the Serbs in western and northern Bosnia. As a result, the balance of holdings between the Serbs and the Muslim-Croat alliance approximated the 51-49 percent division envisioned in the contact group plan. In late September 1995, the three sides formally agreed to a framework for settlement devised by Assistant Secretary of State Richard Holbrooke. In October, a cease-fire took effect, and in November, the presidents of Bosnia, Serbia, and Croatia, meeting in Dayton, Ohio, under the chairmanship of Holbrooke, initialed a set of agreements ending the Yugoslav wars. These agreements were formally signed in Paris in December. While preserving the legal international personality of Bosnia and Herzegovina as a single state, the Dayton accords divide the territory according to the 51-49 formula into two "entities," one Muslim and Croat, the other Serbian. A peacekeeping force of some 60,000 soldiers under the auspices of NATO and including some 20,000 Americans was dispatched to keep the two sides apart. Whether this peace will endure remains to be seen.

·9·

THE LESSONS OF BOSNIA

The Dayton negotiations succeeded because the Croats had achieved their goals in battle, Serbian boss Milosevic was ready to settle for 49 percent of Bosnia, and the Bosnians were worn down by war and by Western pressure. (Figure 9–1 illustrates the results of the agreement reached by the warring parties in Dayton, Ohio, in November 1995.) The deal, however, may turn out to be nothing but a pause: war may resume once the U.S.-led peacekeeping forces depart. Or it may last, in which case it will be a deliverance from war, but that will be its sole justification, for it will not be a just peace. It divides Bosnia according to the 51-49 percent formula. Bosnia and Herzegovina would nominally remain a single state, but it would comprise two entities, one Bosnian and Croatian, the other Serbian. The latter would continue to be called Republika Sepska and would be free to associate in some way with Serbia while the former associated with Croatia.

This peace will ratify the fruits of the Serbs' aggression, granting them de facto sovereignty over half of Bosnia. Because the various lines will be drawn on the basis of ethnicity, it will constitute a victory for the principle of intolerant nationalism over the pluralism that was once the glory of Sarajevo. The bitter taste of Christian-Muslim enmity will endure, stoking the fires of Islamic radicalism. And international humanitarian law, which seemed to have grown stronger in the decades since Nuremberg, will most likely be shredded. The UN war crimes tribunal for Bosnia has brought indictments, but the evidence is overwhelming that the ultimate authority behind

FIGURE 9–1

The Partition of Bosnia and Herzegovina into the Serbian Republic and the Muslim-Croat Federation according to the Dayton Peace Accords, Signed in December 1995

the whole criminal enterprise has been Slobodan Milosevic, now elevated by Western policy to the status of chief peace partner. If the negotiations succeed, they will necessarily entail the exoneration of Milosevic, and if he is exonerated, it is hard to see how the actions against those who did his bidding can go forth. In short, what lies ahead is either more war or a peace that is unjust and corrosive of the sinews of world order. The choice between these two melancholy alternatives will not much change the lessons to be drawn.

Sanctions

The international community's response to Serb aggression has been a litany of empty threats and feeble acts. Early in the Yugoslav crisis, when Bosnia was still at peace and Serbian aggression was still focused on Croatia, the *Economist* reported: "At the end of their patience, the Europeans threatened last week to impose economic sanctions unless the combatants stopped fighting and agreed to talk."[1] Sanctions were imposed, but the effect was nil.

Fighting continued for months until a combination of Serbian satiation and Croatian resistance brought it to a halt. The sanctions were observed largely in the breach, but even had they been effectively enforced, they are unlikely to have deflected Serbia from its nationalist mission. Months after the sanctions began, Serbia, unfazed, launched its attack on Bosnia.

After that attack, the EC and the United Nations imposed more sanctions. When successive rounds of futile tightening of sanctions accomplished nothing, the outside powers considered loosening sanctions, thinking a carrot might be more effective than a stick. Thus in late 1993 the *Economist* reported that "France and Germany recently suggested that, if the Serbs would agree to give up a little more Bosnian territory, the UN might begin to lift its sanctions."[2] And in October 1994, after Serbia embargoed the transport of military supplies to Bosnia, albeit without full enforcement, sanctions on Serbia began to be eased.[3]

No-Fly Zones and Safe Areas

After the first few months of the siege of Sarajevo, the *Economist* reported:

> Western onlookers have grown steelier in their determination to end the siege . . . . On June 26th the UN . . . told the

Bosnian Serbs that they had 48 hours to stop bombarding the city, and to place their heavy weapons where they could be monitored by peace-keepers. If they did not do so, the Security Council would determine "what other means would be required" to deliver humanitarian supplies.[4]

But all such portentous declarations signified nothing. In October 1992, the UN declared a "no-fly" zone over Bosnia, modeled on those imposed on northern and southern Iraq, but when the Serbs violated it, the UN responded by . . . counting the violations! It counted 1,484 of them[5] until, in February 1994, NATO jets spotted six Serb aircraft attacking Bosnian government facilities and shot down four. This sent a warning against conducting ground-attack missions within Bosnia. But the Serbs' use of aircraft to transport personnel and supplies continued unabated.

As for other forceful measures, the Security Council voted in June 1993 "to ensure full respect" for the "safe areas" it had proclaimed a month earlier. But in fact those six cities were bombed, invaded, fired upon by snipers, and besieged time and again with little opposition, until finally Srebrenica and Zepa were abandoned to genocide. This ultimate measure of the protection afforded by the UN Protection Force had been prefigured in January 1993 in the death of a single man. Hakija Turajlic, the deputy prime minister of Bosnia, was traveling in a UN armored vehicle escorted by French troops when Serb gunmen stopped the vehicle and shot Turajlic to death while his French UN escorts dutifully observed.[6]

Serbian Threats

The Serbs also sought to exploit the outside world's pusillanimity by making threats of their own. When in March 1993 the United States inaugurated airdrops of humanitarian supplies to Bosnian civilians, Karadzic penned an "Open Letter to the American People" objecting to this aid and implicitly threatening terrorist attacks against America. "The tragic and deplorable terrorist incident at the World Trade Center is fresh testimony to the extraordinary volatility and immediate dangers of direct involvement," he warned.[7]

The principal targets of Serbian threats were the UN peacekeepers. When the Security Council voted late in 1992 to declare a no-fly zone in Bosnia, the *Economist* reported that "Britain worries lest the Bosnian Serbs retaliate against its 2,400 soldiers protecting relief supplies. And with good reason: Radovan Karadzic . . . has said the troops would come under attack if the flight ban were enforced."[8] Then, when the humanitarian airdrops began, the magazine reported that "the British and the French, who have contributed 4,600 of the UN aid protectors or peacekeeping troops in Bosnia, were nervous that Serb reactions to the air drops might imperil their men."[9] In January 1994, as the West grew impatient with the bombardment of Sarajevo, Karadzic "warned that Serbian forces could attack U.N. troops in Bosnia in retaliation for NATO air strikes."[10] Then in November 1994, as Serb forces closed in on Bihac, a Bosnian Serb representative warned General Rose in a phone conversation, a tape of which was leaked to the press: "Don't mess about. . . . If you hit us this means all-out war. This has come from the head of state, president Karadzic. He is in a furious mood."[11]

Perhaps to justify its timidity, the West enthralled itself with grandiose recollections of the Yugoslav guerrilla resistance to Germany in World War II and projected this military prowess onto the Bosnian Serb armies.[12] This ignored the fact that many of those loyal to the Bosnian government were also the progeny of resistance fighters. More important, there was no reason to suppose that the effectiveness of Yugoslav guerrillas who fought Hitler was something that ran in their blood rather than a function of the urgency and justice of their cause. The just-cause factor would now work more to the advantage of the victims of ethnic cleansing than to that of their despoilers. The absurdity of the West's lionization of the Serbs was demonstrated by Croatia's easy rout of the Krajina Serbs in August 1995.

Pressure on Bosnia

Unwilling to oppose the Serbs, but eager to restore peace, the international community found itself bringing pressure on the Bosnian government to capitulate. In mid-1993 when the Serbs and Croats agreed on a plan dividing most of Bosnia between them and leaving a small fragment for the Muslims, a State Department cable reported that UN officials were threatening to withdraw their humanitarian mission unless the government accepted the carve up.[13] The EC negotiator, Lord Owen, even tried to undermine the Bosnian government for its recalcitrance by bringing into the negotiations the Muslim strongman of the town of Bihac, Fikret Abdic, who was openly aligned with the Serbs, as an ersatz representative of the Bosnian Muslims.[14]

Then in August 1993, in the wake of the crisis over the strangulation of Sarajevo, when NATO tiptoed up to and back from the threshold of airstrikes, Warren Christopher wrote to Izetbegovic urging him to accept the partition plan.[15] Late that year, the *Economist* reported, "The West Europeans are letting it be understood that, if the Bosnians alone obstruct a peace and continue to fight, they will consider pulling out the troops who protect the convoys that feed Bosnians."[16] Early the next year, as a new crisis mounted over the shelling of Sarajevo, the *Washington Post* reported an "acrimonious exchange" between Washington and Paris when "Christopher rejected what U.S. officials interpreted as a French plan to pressure Bosnia's Muslim-dominated government into accepting the loss of huge amounts of territory to Serb and Croat factions."[17]

Encouraging Surrender. In April 1994, following the crisis over the siege of Gorazde, "two of the highest ranking U.N. officials in Bosnia" (Yasushi Akashi and General Michael Rose, although they would not allow their names used) gave a press conference. They lambasted the United States for giving heart to the Bosnian government, making it less likely to give up. Akashi complained about the presence of Joint Chiefs of Staff Chairman John Shalikashvili and UN delegate Madeleine Albright at the opening of the American embassy in Sarajevo. "If anything emboldens the Muslim government to fight on, it's things like this," he said. "They can point to that and say, 'See, the Americans are with us.' We can only hope that the failure of NATO to come to their aid around Gorazde will convince them that the U.S. cavalry isn't around the corner."[18] (Since it had been Akashi himself who had blocked airstrikes at Gorazde, this comment shed startling light on his motivations.)

Moreover, the two officials said, according to the *Washington Post*, that "they saw no way for the three Muslim enclaves established last year as U.N. 'safe areas' in eastern Bosnia to continue to exist amid a sea of Serbs. 'Their only option is to be moved out or to submit to living under Serb rule,' the military officer said of the more than 100,000 Muslims living in Gorazde, Srebrenica and Zepa."[19] This, from the commander in charge of keeping those Muslims "safe"!

Arms Embargo. The most important way that the international community pressured the Bosnians to accept peace at any price was by maintaining the arms embargo that kept them at a permanent military disadvantage. As Yugoslavia broke up, Serbia took control of virtually all of that country's military assets, which were substantial. Part of them were distributed to Serbian forces in Croatia and Bosnia. Not only did the Bosnians enjoy no such inheritance, but in 1991 Izetbegovic, in seeking to preserve peace, complied with the demand of the Serb-dominated Yugoslav government to disarm the Bosnian home militia. From early in the conflict, the Bosnian government has been able to field forces outnumbering its Serbian adversary, but they have been no match in arms. Even as they have acquired small arms, they have remained desperately unequal in heavy weapons, which are harder to smuggle.

The embargo violated at least the spirit of Article 51 of the UN Charter, which declares that "nothing in the present Charter shall impair the inherent right of individual or collective self-defense."[20] It was imposed on Bosnia through the backdoor, so to speak. In September 1991, in response to the fighting in Croatia, the UN Security Council banned arms shipments to Yugoslavia. Yugoslavia was then still legally whole, and Bosnia was still at peace. Once Slovenia, Croatia, Macedonia, and Bosnia seceded and were recognized by other states and admitted into the United Nations, the embargo did not logically apply to them. But Secretary-General Boutros-Ghali declared in a report in January 1992 that the embargo should apply to all the Yugoslav successor states, and later that month the Security Council endorsed that construction.[21]

In December 1992 the Bush administration reversed itself and endorsed lifting the embargo. While the administration believed it had established a cooperative approach with Russia on this issue, France and Britain remained opposed.[22] They said they feared retaliation against their troops serving in Bosnia on behalf of the United Nations. But in May 1993 the Bosnian government announced that, if forced to choose, it would prefer a lifting of the embargo to the continued presence of the United Nations. Still, Britain and France were adamant, usually backed by Russia and intermittently by Germany.

Washington, however, continued to advocate lifting the embargo but often only halfheartedly. In November 1994 the United States introduced a motion in the Security Council to lift the embargo on Bosnia, which President Clinton had agreed to do to forestall legislation to lift it unilaterally. But Washington did little to lobby for it, and the motion failed. Months earlier, Deputy Secretary of State Strobe Talbott had tipped the administration's hand by testifying before the

Senate Armed Services Committee that "it is our view that, at this point in the diplomacy, a lifting of the arms embargo, unilateral or multilateral, is not called for."[23]

While the diplomats dithered, the Bosnians went on dying. According to various news reports 200,000 have died.[24] The executive director of the UN's World Food Programme put the number between 150,000 and 200,000.[25] More conservative U.S. intelligence estimates put the figure lower but still appallingly high. The director of Central Intelligence's Interagency Bosnia Task Force calculated 115,000 killed, 26,000 missing, and 167,000 wounded as of March 1, 1994. It also calculated that the majority of Bosnia's population has been displaced, more than one-quarter of it fleeing abroad and more than another quarter forced to find refuge within Bosnia.[26] Who is to blame for the international community's execrable performance? The answer is almost everybody.

Who's to Blame?

Of the five major outside powers who make up the contact group—Germany, France, Britain, Russia, and America—none has reason to be proud of its part.

Germany. Germany was a major actor early in the Yugoslav crisis, taking a special interest in Croatia. Germany's pressure for early recognition of Croatia and Slovenia led the EC to create the Badinter Commission. When the commission reported that Croatia had not met its criteria for recognition, Germany persuaded the others to grant it anyway. Chancellor Kohl called this a "great triumph for German foreign policy."[27]

The German Foreign Ministry makes a strong case that its only motive was to exert pressure to counter Serbian nationalism.[28] But even if its motives were the best, Germany's tactic failed, and when it did, Germany was unable to take practical responsibility for the consequences. John Newhouse charged that "Germany's leadership lost interest in Yugoslavia after pushing recognition past its partners."[29] Even if he exaggerates, Germany's constitution—and its ghosts—prevented it from taking any forceful part in repelling aggression in Yugoslavia. During the course of the war in Bosnia, Germany has seemed to engage with the issue intermittently. In June 1993, at American insistence, it urged the EC to support lifting the arms embargo on

Bosnia, but it was rebuffed, and soon it joined the ranks of those who opposed lifting it.[30] Later that year, it helped to turn aside proposals to impose sanctions on Croatia like those imposed on Serbia for its intervention in Bosnia.[31] But through most of the Bosnian conflagration, Germany has remained passive, although its early diplomatic assertiveness had helped to ignite it.

France. France, in contrast, is never passive. But the engine of its exertions over Bosnia, as in so much else, seems to have been fueled by little other than *amour propre*. As the *New York Times* put it, French foreign policy "has had the same objective since . . . the 1960's . . . to convince Washington, Moscow and its European partners that France is a great power."[32] With the cold war having suddenly ended, French policy accordingly focused on two goals: removing the overarching presence of the United States from Europe and preventing Germany from emerging as the continent's dominant power. As the Yugoslav crisis unfolded in 1991, France proposed "interposing" a force to keep the peace: not just any force, but one under the banner of the West European Union (WEU), a body comprising nine of the twelve members of the EC. The WEU had never played a significant military role before and therefore was a less natural candidate for any such mission than NATO. But the proposal seemed less designed to rescue Yugoslavia than to build up the WEU as an alternative to NATO, free of the United States.

When the Bosnian war began, the West was slow to respond until Secretary Baker castigated those "looking for reasons not to act." The *New York Times* reported that "his remarks appeared to be directed at some European countries, especially France and Greece, that seem to be holding up any European consensus decision on sanctions against Serbia in the civil war engulfing Yugoslavia."[33] Sanctions were soon adopted, and a month later, to demonstrate French concern, President Mitterrand made a surprise high-profile helicopter flight into besieged Sarajevo to bring a "message of hope." But, again, the true message may have been more about France's ambitions than Bosnia's hopes. In international bodies, France was now maneuvering against any military intervention for the same reason that months earlier it had proposed military "interposition." The *Economist* explained: "Mitterrand fears that an American share in any military action would demonstrate the necessity of NATO, which he would not like."[34] And when the UN Security Council agreed to apply sanctions, reported

John Newhouse, "France, which didn't favor applying tough sanctions against Serbia, insisted on excluding the no-successor-state measure [denying Yugoslavia's UN seat to the rump Yugoslavia consisting of Serbia and Montenegro] as its price for going along with the rest of the package."[35] A few hours after Mitterrand dropped dramatically into Sarajevo, he flew back out, and France resumed its adamant opposition to any strong measures against Sarajevo's tormentors.

France's policy during most of the war was that the Bosnian government should recognize that it had been defeated and accept whatever terms it could get from the victors. French and American diplomats repeatedly crossed swords over Washington's reluctance to bring pressure on Sarajevo to concede and Paris's reluctance to act against the Serbs.[36] When, in October 1994, the Bosnian government launched its first successful military offensive, French Foreign Minister Juppe denounced it as "unacceptable."[37]

Britain. Britain's approach to the Bosnian tragedy has been similar to France's, but, naturally, without the flamboyance (and without the ulterior goal of driving America from Europe). At moments when Paris has seemed in danger of deviating from its policy of denying help to Bosnia, London has hastened to call it back in line. Soon after Mitterrand's visit to Sarajevo, British Foreign Secretary Douglas Hurd hurried to that city to deflate any false hopes. He assured the Sarajevans that the West would take no forceful action on their behalf.[38] In 1993, as Washington pressed President Clinton's lift-and-strike proposal, the *New York Times* reported: "When the British heard that the French had told Mr. Christopher that they did not reject arming the Bosnian Muslims 'in principle,' urgent telephone calls from Foreign Secretary Douglas Hurd and Defense Secretary Malcolm Rifkind to their French counterparts followed. The British won assurances that the French had not softened their position."[39]

According to former National Security Council official David Gompert, "The British . . . insist[ed] that they would participate in the U.N. Protective Force (UNPROFOR) only if the United States did not introduce air power, lest it anger the Serbs."[40] At every critical juncture subsequently, Britain has argued that Western action might endanger its UNPROFOR soldiers. Not only has it opposed, on these grounds, NATO airstrikes and lifting the arms embargo but also enforcing the UN's declared no-fly zone and even airdropping food and medicine to starving civilians.

Of all the Western diplomatic eminences involved, Hurd and

Rifkind have been the most outspoken against any assistance to Bosnia. In addition, two leading Britons who have performed prominent roles on behalf of international agencies—Lord Owen for the EC and General Rose for the United Nations—have been widely regarded as tilting toward the Serbs.[41] In contrast, Britain did supply the single most eloquent Western advocate of aid to Bosnia in the person of former prime minister Margaret Thatcher. Her appeals were greeted with a display of male condescension all the more remarkable for the fact that her detractors' stature was so much less than her own. "Emotional nonsense," said Rifkind.[42] (This put-down apparently seemed so perspicacious to Warren Christopher that he borrowed it, calling Thatcher's approach "a rather emotional response.")[43]

Russia. Russia has chosen the Bosnian crisis as an occasion for reclaiming its seat at the table of great power diplomacy. When, in February 1994, NATO verged on launching airstrikes against Serb forces shelling Sarajevo, Russia won a last-minute compromise: emplacing Russian troops as peacekeepers, who were greeted by the Bosnian Serbs as allies.[44] When in April 1994 NATO replied to Serb attacks on Gorazde with symbolic airstrikes, Russian President Yeltsin protested. "I insisted to Clinton time and again that such decisions cannot be taken without prior consultation between the United States and Russia," he said.[45] Yeltsin undoubtedly felt pressure from the extremist politician Vladimir Zhirinovsky, who called for Russia to bomb NATO bases in Italy in retaliation.[46]

Secretary of State Christopher minimized the disagreement. "I'm sure that we and the Russians share the same goal," he said.[47] But the Russian role was different from the American. Moscow veered between being a mediator and being an advocate for the Serbs. David Owen likened the two powers in this way: "We have a balance . . . with, on the one side, the Russians, who are traditionally arms suppliers to and allies of the Serbs, and the United States, now casting itself as the friend of the Bosnian Muslims."[48]

The analogy was false. America held no special brief for the Muslims. U.S. defense of the Bosnian government's position was only incidental to upholding basic principles of international law—against aggression and for human rights. And insofar as Yugoslavia had been a Serb-dominated state, it was not Russia that had been its traditional ally but America, ever since the Tito-Stalin split of 1948. Indeed, America had helped protect Yugoslavia against Russia, or rather the Soviet Union. As the famous Yugoslav writer Mihajlo Mihajlov (himself of Russian extraction), has pointed out, the notion "that there is a long, historic friendship ... between Russia and Serbia" is a "myth."[49] Mihajlov concedes that the Russian and the Serbian Orthodox churches were historically close, but today's leaders of Serbian nationalism and their Russian supporters are scarcely known for their religiosity.

What really seems to motivate Russian support for the Serbs is pan-Slavism, that baneful instrument of pre-Soviet Russian imperialism that did so much to ignite World War I.

America. In light of the performance of the European powers, it would be satisfying to be able to report that America had behaved better; but, alas, if it has, it has only marginally. The Bosnia crisis unfolded in a presidential election year when George Bush was smarting from charges that he had neglected the nation's domestic well-being in favor of foreign policy. In response, he kept Bosnia's tragedy at arm's length, welcoming Europe's claim to leadership. During the presidential campaign, Bill Clinton challenged Bush's inert posture on Bosnia, suggesting he would take a more muscular approach. But once in office, Clinton declared his aversion to the Bosnian issue. "I don't want to have to spend any more time on that than is absolutely necessary," he said.[50] Many months later, a dismayed State Department official—a former head of the Yugoslav desk—told the press that he had been party to a conversation between two of the department's highest officials that had occurred around the same time as Clinton's comment. The two had explained the administration's inaction on the basis that "failure in Bosnia would destroy the Clinton presidency" and that any strong action imperiled "the fragile liberal coalition" that Clinton represented. This account was confirmed by another witness.[51]

The EC. If individual governments responded ineptly to the Bosnia crisis, international bodies performed no better. I have already related the unhappy story of the Vance-Owen plan, the main fruit of the combined diplomatic efforts of the EC and the United Nations. A closer look at the records of these two bodies offers only further discouragement. From the onset of the Yugoslav crisis, the EC, though aspiring to diplomatic leadership, found itself divided. Germany and Italy sympathized with Croatia and Slovenia; England and France more with Serbia.[52]

This was only the beginning of the tangled knot of divergent views and objectives within the EC. Although England and France were at one in their sympathies in Bosnia, they were divided over France's efforts to activate the West European Union and push America away from Europe.[53] Greece was the strongest partisan within the EC of the Serbian cause, sharing with Serbia the Eastern Orthodox faith and a history of conflict with Muslim states. But Greece's paramount concern was to oppose diplomatic recognition by anyone of the independence of Macedonia, whose name, in Greek eyes, constituted a kind of copyright infringement. Spain, meanwhile, led the fight against recognition of any secessionist republics, fearing this would legitimate its own Basque separatists.[54] The susceptibility of the EC's policy to the influence of extrinsic considerations was illustrated by the *Economist*:

> There may be more to the EC's caution over Bosnia than an honest appraisal of the difficulties involved. . . . To the British and Germans, the need to conclude a new GATT agreement is obvious and urgent. . . . In which case, why should the British and Germans fall out over Bosnia? Far better to be friends against the French over trade. Especially because . . . Bosnia surely proves that the Community is nowhere near "a common foreign and security policy" anyway.[55]

The United Nations. In contrast to the EC, the United Nations asserted itself forcefully—but to what end? Secretary-General Boutros Boutros-Ghali's initial response to Bosnia was that it was a "rich man's war."[56] As a war among Europeans, it was presumably less deserving of UN attention than conflagrations in the third world. As casualties mounted, this stance was not long tenable, and soon Boutros-Ghali denied he had ever made the comment.[57] Whatever his words, he and his subordinates labored tirelessly to thwart assistance to Bosnia. It was Boutros-Ghali who first interpreted the arms embargo on Yugoslavia to apply to all its successor states, a stance subsequently ratified by the Security Council.

In early 1994, as the strangulation of Sarajevo and other safe areas drove the West to the brink of airstrikes against the Serbs, Boutros-Ghali announced his opposition to any such action.[58] Then he modified his position by saying he was prepared to order strikes to protect UN forces.[59] It was clear if not explicit that he was not willing to extend this protection to Bosnians. Even this position was more robust than the frequent policy of the United Nations of turning the other cheek to Serb attacks. In July 1993, the Serbs destroyed ten vehicles of the French UN contingent. In November of that year, they abducted two clergymen from UN vehicles in which they were being safeguarded. To such attacks and provocations, the UN response had been conciliatory.

Even after Boutros-Ghali's putative change of heart, the procedures and conditions he imposed thwarted any strong action. In April 1994, U.S. National Security Adviser Anthony Lake complained publicly about incidents in which requests by UN commanders for air support had been mooted by "a protracted decision-making process," which General Shalikashvili had called "tortuous, at best."[60] When UN forces did manage to use their weapons, their actions were severely constrained. A Danish contingent returned fire against Serb tanks attacking them but "spared three Serb T-55 tanks because, while . . . infrared detectors found the Serbs' aiming systems turned on, they also determined that the enemy tanks' barrels were cold. Under the restrictive U.N. rules of engagement, only guns actually caught in [the] act of firing may be hit," reported the *Washington Post*.[61]

General Rose in Bosnia

Such restrictions on their freedom to protect their own forces led to the resignation of a series of UN officers: General Cot, the commander for the Balkans, and Generals Morillon and Briquemont, successive commanders for Bosnia. Briquemont was succeeded by General Rose, who, within his first month on the job, had an experience similar to those that had frustrated his predecessors. According to the *Washington Post*, he "requested NATO airstrikes to defend U.N. troops facing a mortar attack in northeastern Bosnia but was turned down by the top U.N. officials in the Balkans."[62] Unlike his predecessors who had seethed over the constraints, Rose quickly fell into step with Yasushi Akashi, Boutros-Ghali's delegate in Bosnia and the man who had nixed the airstrike Rose requested. Over the course of 1994, Rose and Akashi became the living apotheoses of UN policy.

Favoritism toward Serbs. On the heels of the Gorazde crisis, Rose and Akashi held the infamous press conference at which they denounced the Bosnian government for prolonging the war and the American government for giving them the courage to do so. As for the Serb part in all the unpleasantness, "both officials," reported the *Washington Post*, "insisted that Serb forces . . . were ready for peace."[63]

On another occasion, Akashi had singled out Bosnian Serb leader Radovan Karadzic as "a man of peace" with whom he had a "friendship."[64] Rose, meanwhile, was reported to harbor a certain admiration for the Bosnian Serb military commander, Ratko Mladic. Both Karadzic and Mladic have been indicted by the International Criminal Tribunal for the former Yugoslavia for genocide, crimes against humanity, and war crimes.[65] According to the *New York Times,* "Officials close to [Rose] say he has been pushed toward greater sympathy for the Serbian position by . . . the realization that in General Mladic, the skillful but ruthless commander of the Bosnian Serbs, he had an interlocutor who was a real officer."[66] This was the same Mladic who was to supervise personally the slaughter of thousands of prisoners at Srebrenica.

Late in August, American Lieutenant General Wesley Clark, head of the Pentagon's Office of Strategy, Plans and Policy, was embarrassed by the release of a photograph showing him socializing with Mladic. The two officers were playfully wearing each other's caps. A U.S. official lamented to the *Washington Post*: "It's like cavorting with Hermann Goering."[67] Clark was in Bosnia to meet with its government, but while there, said the *Post,* "he was invited to meet Mladic by Lt. Gen. Michael Rose." London's *Daily Telegraph* surmised that Rose hoped that Mladic would help sway Clark against lifting the arms embargo on the Bosnians.[68]

The longer Rose stayed on in Bosnia, the more sympathetic he seemed to grow toward the Serb aggressors and the harsher toward their Bosnian victims. When Bosnian government forces trying to loosen the siege of Sarajevo attacked Serbian forces from within a demilitarized zone, Rose publicly threatened to call in NATO airstrikes against the Bosnians.[69] In a meeting with Bosnian President Alija Izetbegovic, Rose went further, according to a report in *U.S. News and World Report,* warning that he would order NATO to "carpet bomb" Bosnian positions.[70] In contrast, a month earlier, Rose's spokesman had explained his decision to limit airstrikes against the Serbs to symbolic attacks against individual, unmanned, obsolete targets: "You have to use force in a proportionate, precise and relevant way."[71]

When Rose's threat of airstrikes against the Bosnians rang hollow (who, exactly, would bomb Bosnian government forces at Rose's behest?), Rose sent UN ground forces to drive the Bosnians out and blow up their bunkers and trenches.[72] Although the Bosnians were violating the zone, no such action had ever been taken against the Serbs. In the face of the Serbs' more frequent violations, the United

Nations always seemed to come up with an excuse for inaction. According to the *Washington Post,* for example, "When the United Nations reported Bosnian Serb forces were firing heavy weapons into the Gorazde zone, UN officials said airstrikes were not requested because the guns were only targeting Bosnian Muslim military positions."[73] But, in contrast, when Serbs shelled and strafed civilians in Sarajevo on November 8, killing three children and a woman, Rose's spokesman explained that no airstrikes were called for because "the attacks are not militarily significant."[74]

Disinformation. When UN forces discovered a Serbian position outside Sarajevo that had been overrun by government forces who killed twenty Serbs, the United Nations announced that the dead had been executed, their corpses mutilated.[75] Akashi even protested formally to Bosnian president Izetbegovic, while the Serbs threatened bloodcurdling retaliation. But in the face of strong Bosnian denials, the United Nations confessed error, acknowledging that the twenty had been battle casualties and none were mutilated.[76] This may not have been the only time that Rose's command made false allegations against the Bosnians to distribute war guilt more equally and thus dampen calls for action against the Serbs. *Los Angeles Times* correspondent Carol Williams reported being told by UN sources after a vicious Serb sniper attack on Sarajevo civilians, "Rose's office ordered UN public affairs workers to doctor the next day's 'situation report' to suggest Bosnian government forces were behaving just as badly."[77]

Rose's sympathies and antipathies were also displayed by a photo he kept on his office wall of a medical vehicle apparently destroyed in a NATO airstrike on Serb positions. It was glossed with the sarcastic caption, "Nice one, NATO." *New York Times* correspondent Roger Cohen, who obviously thought it revealing of Rose's mindset, reported it.[78]

The story is worse than Cohen realized. Albert Wohlstetter discovered, through inquiries with the U.S. and UN military commands, that the photo was a fraud, a crude bit of Serbian disinformation. No medical vehicle was hit by NATO. Rose knew it to be such but kept it hanging anyway.[79]

Lack of Leadership

Rose's evident hostility toward NATO was only a dramatic example of a pervasive problem. In the absence of a government or agency willing and able to lead the international community in responding to Bosnia, many things fell between the cracks and much effort was squandered working at cross-purposes.

When the Bosnian Serbs rejected the Vance-Owen plan, for example, America sought, but failed to secure, agreement on retaliatory action. The *New York Times* observed: "The suspicion grows, and no one bothers to deny it with much fervor, that each side is just as happy, all things considered, to put its proposals on the table and let the other reject them."[80] Six months later, the diplomatic initiative shifted to Europe, but the *Economist* perceived much the same temperament: "'If it goes wrong, it won't be our failure.' That was the limited ambition behind the latest European peace initiative for Bosnia, as summed up in Geneva this week by a senior German diplomat."[81] A year later, after yet another fruitless transatlantic meeting, the *Washington Post* reported:

> "There were three ways the meeting could end," a U.S. aide said. "We could issue threats that no one took seriously. We could break up in disarray. Or we could have this wishy-washy communique. We decided on the last."[82]

While America and Europe played pass-the-buck, NATO and the United Nations did Alphonse and Gaston. In early 1994, as the crisis over the siege of Sarajevo intensified, NATO leaders reiterated their threat of airstrikes if called for by the United Nations. A few weeks later Boutros-Ghali announced that he had authorized his deputy to request airstrikes.[83] A few days later, the infamous marketplace massacre took sixty-eight lives and galvanized calls for action. In response, Boutros-Ghali wrote a letter to NATO, asking it to authorize airstrikes. "According to U.S. officials," said the *Washington Post,* "Boutros-Ghali is asking NATO to decide first whether to make warplanes available for punitive bombing and then whether they would choose to bomb in response to last week's attacks or simply to be ready for the next one."[84]

In the event, there were no airstrikes. But then the Serbs turned their strangulatory energies on Gorazde, provoking NATO's first pinprick attacks. In their aftermath, "administration officials said, in effect, that they have given the senior U.N. commander in Bosnia . . . virtual carte blanche to call in airstrikes whenever he deems them necessary," wrote the *Washington Post.*[85] But a week after that, Boutros-Ghali went back to square one, asking NATO to authorize airstrikes.[86] Christoph Bertram summarized the military arrangement:

> Since NATO's members were not sure that they really
> wanted to expose their military to the conflict, [they] built
> in a safety catch: . . . specific authorization by the secretary
> general, who in turn delegated the decision to his represen-
> tative . . . . In short, NATO has made an organization un-
> willing to use force the guardian of its ability to use force.[87]

Thus, not only did each government and international body behave poorly, their collective contribution was worse than the sum of
its parts. These are the bitter fruits of America's bold experiment in
leaving leadership to others. Not since Neville Chamberlain tried out his
theory of "appeasement" has a foreign policy idea been put to the test
with clearer results.

What Lies Ahead?

While the full consequences of our failure to prevent Bosnia's devas-
tation cannot yet be tallied, this episode has without a doubt been a
fiasco. The Bosnians have paid a fearful price already. As many as
200,000 may have died; untold thousands more have been wounded,
raped, beaten, starved. More than a million have lost their homes.

In time, the rest of us are likely to pay as well. Even if the fighting in Bosnia is over—a big if—that will not end the quest for Greater
Serbia. Serbia will work to absorb the Bosnian Republika Serpska
and may go after chunks of Macedonia or try to ethnically cleanse
Vojvodina, which lies within Serbia but is largely populated by Hun-
garians.

In particular, it is hard to imagine that the Serbs will rest content
with the current situation in Kosovo, Serbia's historic heartland, which is
today 90 percent Albanian. The Milosevic government has, by means of
firings and harassment, encouraged Albanians to emigrate, and it has
forced Serbs who have fled Croatia to settle there. Only a violent campaign of ethnic cleansing, however, as fierce or fiercer than the one in
Bosnia, could restore Kosovo's Serbian character. This attempt would
almost surely bring in Albania, which has already recognized Kosovo's
independence, declared by its Albanian majority, and has explicitly threatened intervention. War between Serbia and Albania could quite easily
involve their respective allies, and mutual enemies, Greece and Turkey.

The war in Bosnia, moreover, has set a dire example. The territories of the former Soviet empire are rife with conflicting national

yearnings. Democratic, or even minimally civilized, norms are weak, and these lands harbor many ambitious and unscrupulous men watching to see how the likes of Milosevic and Karadzic fare.

The bonds that might restrain them have been weakened. NATO, the cornerstone of America's security architecture, has allowed itself to be humiliated. America, by acting impotent, has squandered the capital it earned in defeating Iraqi aggression. The already threadbare fabric of international law has been frayed further, just when the passing of the cold war gave hope it might be rewoven. The example of Serbia's aggression, if successful, will embolden other predators. Czech President Vaclav Havel put it:

> The demons we thought had been driven forever from the minds of people and nations are dangerously rousing themselves again, and are surreptitiously but systematically undoing the principles upon which we had begun to build the peaceful future of Europe. . . . Europeans continue to suffer and die in the former Yugoslavia, and with them is dying the hope that Europe will be able to bring these horrors to an end.[88]

Russia's vicious attack on Chechnya was likely encouraged by the flaccid Western response to Bosnia. The Chechnyan attack, unlike the Bosnian, is not a violation of international borders, but in addition to being another humanitarian calamity, the Chechnyan affair has weakened prospects that Russia will continue on a democratic path.

Fallout from the Conflict

The West's apparent indifference to the suffering in Bosnia, where Muslims have been murdered and humiliated for being Muslims and mosques have been destroyed and desecrated, is bound to inflame opinion in the volatile Muslim world. Muslims make up one-fifth of mankind, and extreme Islamic fundamentalism constitutes the one anti-Western ideology that is still on the rise. It is in power in Iran and the Sudan, it constitutes an imminent threat to regimes in Algeria, Afghanistan, and Egypt, and it is a substantial force in Jordan, Lebanon, Palestine, and even Turkey.

The militants contrast America's tolerance for Serbia's aggression with our devastating reaction to Iraq's, offering it as proof that the "Great Satan" is the enemy of Islam. We may say that the two situations are different, but the strength of the analogy in the eyes of Muslims is proved by the fact that Turkey and Egypt, our two closest Islamic allies, have both made a display of reducing their cooperation with us on Iraq because of their embarrassment over Bosnia. The Islamic government of Iran, meanwhile, has exploited the situation by sending planeloads of arms addressed to the Bosnians. That some of these have been intercepted by the Western enforcers of the arms embargo only heightens the intended demonstration effect.

The fallout from the Bosnian conflict may even contaminate Western Europe. The flood of refugees from the former Yugoslavia helped to fuel an outbreak of neo-Nazi violence in Germany. The influx of Algerians has strained the social fabric in France. Germany, Austria, Italy, and Hungary have acted to tighten immigration restrictions. New rounds of fighting in the Balkans, or new victories for fundamentalists in northern Africa, would send new tides of refugees knocking on the doors of an unreceptive Western Europe, with possibly unsettling effects.

America did not turn its back on Bosnia; from early in the Yugoslav crisis, it has been involved. But it made a deliberate decision not to lead. In 1991 and 1992, the Bush administration opted to play a secondary role to the European Community. Then, in May 1993, the Clinton administration offered its preferred policy—lift and strike—to its allies for discussion but quickly yielded to their demurrals. It fell in behind their proposal to create "safe areas" and to keep the Bosnians disarmed, a policy that reached its terrible, logical conclusion at Srebrenica in July 1995. Then America roused itself to a more assertive role which was welcomed by almost everyone except the Russians. But even this aimed only at reaching the quickest possible settlement, not a just or lasting one.

To oppose well-armed men bent on heartless, aggressive deeds requires courage and determination. These qualities rarely if ever emerge from a collectivity: they require leadership. Boutros Boutros-Ghali cannot provide that leadership. Nor can the governments of France, England, Russia, Germany, or Japan. The world today and for the foreseeable future has one natural leader. If the United States does not accept that role, no one else can substitute. The international community will be formless as a jellyfish—and as brave.

PART FOUR

Leadership through Military Strength

·10·

REMAINING THE SOLE
SUPERPOWER

The bedrock of America's global leadership is military might. Might, of course, is neither the sole component of leadership nor a sufficient one. To its dying day, the Soviet Union kept growing mightier—as measured in tanks and missiles—even while its capacity for leadership ebbed away. Still, brute strength remains the *ultima ratio* of international relations, and many things flow from it.

The sudden implosion of the Soviet Union left the United States as the world's only superpower. It alone has the capacity to exert military force anywhere in the world. While American arms will not always have their way—especially not in limited engagements, as we learned painfully in Vietnam and Somalia—America's unique power affords it unique security. No other power or conceivable coalition could make war on America with any hope of victory. Most nations throughout history would have sorely envied this condition. Had they achieved it, none would have given it up lightly. Neither should we.

Such security, however, does not amount to complete invulnerability. Thousands of nuclear weapons abroad could still blow us to bits. But this threat is a far cry from the era when most of those nuclear weapons were possessed by a rival superpower with which we contended for global supremacy. Neither side intended to use its "nukes" against the other, but neither was prepared to abandon the contest. Thus we lived with the danger that in a crisis the logic of competition could propel the rivals over the nuclear brink. That peril, which fright-

ened my generation, has been lifted, and we can hope that new generations can grow up without it.

The Defense Planning Guidance

In early 1992, the Bush administration enunciated just such a goal.
Actually, the enunciation was only in private—in the form of a draft
of the "defense planning guidance," a classified directive from the
secretary of defense to the chiefs of the armed services. It said: "Our
first objective is to prevent the reemergence of a new rival, either on
the territory of the former Soviet Union or elsewhere, that poses a
threat on the order of that posed formerly by the Soviet Union."[1] This
document was leaked to the *New York Times,* which put it at the top
of page one, as though it were scandalous.[2]

Although it would seem self-evident that American strategy
would aim to prevent the Damoclean sword of superpower rivalry
from being hoisted again, the leaked draft evoked a storm of protest.
Senator Alan Cranston waxed indignant that it aimed to make the
United States "the one, the only main honcho on the world block, the
global Big Enchilada."[3] Senator Joseph Biden allowed that "American hegemony might be a pleasant idea," but he doubted that it would
be "economically, politically or even militarily wise."[4] And George
Stephanopoulos, speaking for Bill Clinton's presidential campaign,
said the draft amounted to "one more attempt . . . to find an excuse
for big [defense] budgets."[5]

On the other end of the political spectrum, Patrick Buchanan
joined in the outcry, branding the document "a formula for endless
American intervention in quarrels and war when no vital interest of
the United States is remotely engaged."[6] Even from within the administration, the memo's authors were, as they say, hung out to dry. The
president said he had not read it. And the press quoted administration officials calling it a "dumb report" that "in no way or shape
represents U.S. policy,"[7] a "document [that is] going down in flames."[8]

Two months later, a severely revised version of the defense guidance was approved by the defense secretary. Where the first draft
spoke of the need to address "those wrongs which threaten not only
our interests, but those of our allies or friends, or which could seriously unsettle international relations," the revised version spoke only
of "those security problems that threaten our own interests."[9] The
revised version also leaned much more to multilateralism. The origi-

nal had declared that when a military response was called for, "we will retain the preeminent responsibility," but the later version averred only that "we [cannot] allow our critical interests to depend solely on international mechanisms."

Above all, the references to forestalling the appearance of any new rival were much attenuated. No longer was this a first objective. Instead, the guidance listed as the third goal of U.S. policy "to preclude any hostile power from dominating a region critical to our interests, and also thereby to strengthen the barriers against the reemergence of a global threat to the interests of the U.S. and our allies."

Former under secretary of defense Paul D. Wolfowitz and his deputy, I. Lewis Libby, the officials chiefly responsible for drafting the guidance, insist that in this last formula the essential idea of the first version was retained. They say that the final version merely purged the original of needlessly provocative rhetoric while keeping its strategic purpose. Yet even if the final guidance lost none of the strategic implications of the early draft, the attentive public came away with the impression that the Pentagon's original capacious strategy had been dropped in favor of a narrow focus on national self-defense. As an unintentionally amusing headline in the *Washington Post* put it: "Pentagon Abandons Goal of Thwarting U.S. Rivals."[10] Wolfowitz and Libby may have won the bureaucratic battles, but they lost the political war. They lost it because the political leadership was reluctant to stand up for the strategy embedded in the guidance.

A Defensible Strategy

The strategy, however, was more than defensible. Having finally been freed from the terrors of the cold war, why on earth would we allow ourselves to slip back into that unhappy state if we can prevent it? Waging a reelection campaign in which he was accused of neglecting domestic problems for the sake of international ones, George Bush was reluctant to be drawn into debate on any issues of defense policy.[11] But it would have been edifying to have heard the critics of the leaked draft explain why America should not seek to prevent the emergence of a new superpower rival.

Costs. One reason might be if the costs were unbearable. But it seems clear that we can preserve military supremacy at a level of expenditure below what we have shouldered for many decades. The necessary level (somewhere around 4 percent of GDP) is equivalent to what West Germany allocated to defense during the cold war. Ironically, since the West German level ran several percentage points below our own, that country's economic robustness was often pointed to as an example of the fruits of *low* defense spending.

Provocation. Some suggest that we should forgo our sole superpower status to avoid provoking other nations to band together against us. This is the normal fate of predominant powers, they warn.[12] But in fact such powers have as often attracted allies and subalterns as opponents. The natural impetus of weaker powers toward stronger is to ingratiate themselves or appease, not to defy. Where hostile coalitions have formed—against Napoleon or Hitler, for example—they have been a response to stark aggression. But America commits no aggression, and American preeminence, contrary to Senator Biden, is not tantamount to "hegemony."

America's hegemonic tendencies, whatever they may have been when the country was young, disappeared as it became a mature power. Within North America, the United States has long been preeminent, but America dictates to neither Canada nor Mexico. Indeed, during the cold war, Mexico, a country as vulnerable to U.S. power as any, often took sides with America's enemy, Cuba—with complete impunity. Japan and Germany emerged as key commercial rivals to America, all the while dependent on America's military protection. If this is hegemony, it is a very benign kind.

Collective Security. Those who opposed preserving our unique superpower status imagine that fine things will happen if we let it go. Some conservatives have suggested that if America had not led the response to Iraqi aggression in 1990, then the states of Europe and Japan, which are far more reliant on Persian Gulf petroleum, would have stirred themselves to repel Saddam Hussein.[13] It is far more likely that they would simply have appeased him, offering a blank check for regional dominance in exchange for a promise to keep the oil flowing.

Some liberals complained that the leaked defense guidance "reject[ed] . . . collective internationalism,"[14] and they quoted Secretary-General Boutros-Ghali's warning that that rejection would spell "the end of the U.N."[15] In truth, the day of collective security, if it is ever to arrive, will be hastened rather than retarded by U.S. preeminence. In the history of the United Nations, collective security actions have been undertaken twice—in Korea and Kuwait. What the episodes have in common is that both times America was the organizer and Americans did most of the fighting.

Clinton's Defense Policy

If President Bush failed to speak out unambiguously in favor of safeguarding America's status as the sole superpower, his successor's approach to defense strategy was still less creditable. The hallmark of Bill Clinton's foreign policy has been its relentless subordination to domestic policy. He has lived up to the statement he made while first campaigning for president that his "vision for security in this new era" is "to take care of our own people and their needs first."[16] The application of this vision to defense policy has meant deep cuts in defense spending.

On the campaign trail, Bill Clinton had advocated a reduction of $60 billion over five years from the amounts proposed by President Bush. But in his first budget presentation, President Clinton sought a reduction twice that size, more than $120 billion. In formulating his first budget, Clinton chose to focus on deficit reduction, but the cuts he proposed in domestic expenditures were offset dollar for dollar by new expenditures. The entire weight of net reductions came out of defense.

As for defense strategy, the Clinton administration announced it had ordered a "bottom up review" of military needs. But the review was conducted only after the president's defense budget cuts had been announced. Its true function was less to assess military requirements than to see what forces could be kept for the money that was left.

A Two-War Strategy. During the cold war, U.S. forces had been configured first and foremost for war against the Soviet Union. Now, the paradigm for defense planning would be the Gulf War, which came, in the inevitable military jargon, to be called a "major regional conflict." The goal of the force structure proposed in the bottom up review was the capacity to fight two such wars.

Why *two*? To avoid creating a temptation for adversaries in one part of the world any time our forces go to war in another. If we find ourselves at war again with North Korea, for example, we would not want Saddam Hussein to know that we have insufficient forces available to repel some new adventure across his borders.

Before the review was completed, however, the Pentagon floated the idea of settling for a smaller force. Its goal would be to win one war while just hanging on in another until forces could be transferred. This plan, however, was harshly criticized by military leaders on the ground that war is rarely predictable enough to allow such delicate planning. The administration backed off, reaffirming its commitment to a two-war capability.

Underfunding. In truth, though, the administration has not budgeted enough to pay for the forces it has proposed, and there are doubts, as well, that those forces, even fully funded, would suffice to ensure success in two wars. The point about underfunding has come not just from the administration's political opponents but from neutral sources. The Congressional Budget Office (CBO) estimated at the beginning of 1995 (before the swearing in of the Republican majority) that the five-year defense plan was underfunded by $53–100 billion. The General Accounting Office (GAO) said the shortfall might run as high as $150 billion.[17] The administration itself acknowledged a funding gap late in 1994 but put the amount at only $49 billion.[18] It announced a budget increase of $25 billion ($15 billion of which would come in the last two years of the five-year period). Then it canceled or delayed some additional weapon systems worth a few billion and revised downward its forecast of the rate of inflation to save another $12 billion.[19] This remedy seems mostly cosmetic.

Even if fully funded, "our forces are either marginal or inadequate to the strategy of defending both Kuwait and South Korea," according to former National Security Adviser Brent Scowcroft.[20] The worry is shared by some Democrats. Congressman Ike Skelton, a senior member of the Armed Services Committee, has warned that in this scenario "we would be stretched paper-thin."[21]

One critical area on which there is wide agreement that current U.S. forces are not up to the two-war scenario is in strategic lift, that is, in the capacity to transport soldiers and equipment to two theaters. The air force's cargo fleet is made up of C-141s, the average age of which is 28.5 years. They have long been slated for replacement by a new plane, the C-17, which has had a troubled history and is only beginning to come into use. General Joseph Hoar, then in charge of U.S. forces in the Middle East, testified to Congress in 1994 that "strategic airlift in this country today is broken. I'm not sure it is workable today for one major regional contingency."[22]

Near Simultaneity. Although the Clinton administration goes through the motions of denying the problem, it has in effect conceded the point. It now says that we have the capacity to fight two regional wars "nearly simultaneously." CIA Director John Deutch, deputy secretary of defense at the time, confessed that "I hide behind the words 'nearly simultaneous.'"[23] The parameters intended by the time frame "nearly simultaneous" are classified, so civilians cannot know how far spaced the two must be for our forces to be able to win them. But undoubtedly once the United States commits itself to one such regional war, it opens a window of vulnerability during which it would be unable to respond effectively in another region.

Criticisms of the Clinton administration's defense budgets go beyond issues tied to the bottom up review. The broader question is whether defense spending has been cut so drastically that vulnerabilities would make themselves painfully evident in a crisis. That happened in 1980 when we suffered a debacle trying to rescue American hostages in Iran, an event widely interpreted as a reflection of deficiencies in military preparedness.

Peace Dividend. Americans have seen little of the "peace dividend" that the end of the cold war was supposed to yield: the savings have not been small but have been sucked into billowing entitlement expenditures almost before anyone could notice. In the four fiscal years since the cold war ended, defense spending was $245 billion dollars lower than had been projected in the last budget request submitted before the cold war ended.[24] The difference for FY 1994 alone exceeded $100 billion. And for FY 1995 the differential will be even greater.

Defense spending, in short, is down nearly one-third in constant dollars and more than one-third as a proportion of gross domestic product. Forces have been reduced accordingly. When the cold war ended, America had 2.1 million men and women under arms. That number is being reduced by a third, to 1.4 million. Similarly, the number of battle force ships is being reduced by 32 percent, and the number of attack and fighter aircraft by 36 percent.[25]

Those forces designed specifically to parry the Soviet Union have been cut much more drastically. Strategic (that is, long-range) nuclear forces, which consumed about 15 percent of defense spending during the cold war, now consume less than 5 percent.[26] American troops in Europe, who used to number 500,000, are now down to 100,000. Other parts of the defense budget, which were less geared to the Soviet threat, have understandably undergone only small reductions. The Marine Corps, for example, has always been designed for rapid response to regional flare-ups rather than for battle between the superpowers. The need for this capability has not diminished proportionately with the cold war.

Nondefense Projects. A growing trend to clutter the defense budget with nondefense items has further squeezed defense spending. It has long been true that Congress distorted some military procurement decisions. A ship here or aircraft there would be kept in production ahead of some weapon of higher value to the military because it was produced in a shipyard or factory located in the district of a strategically situated member of Congress. This is still the case.

That, however, is only the beginning of the current problem. In recent years, programs that have nothing at all to do with defense have been placed in the defense budget. The list includes a Small Business Development Center in Hawaii, boot camps for youthful drug offenders, the development of an electric car, and medical research on breast and prostate cancer, Lyme disease, osteoporosis, and AIDS.[27] Whereas once liberals complained about "pork" in Pentagon budgets, now they themselves insert the pork. Having reached the limit of their ability to shift funds from defense to domestic projects, they burrowed under the so-called budgetary "fire walls" by insinuating domestic projects into the defense budget. As Senator Tom Harkin, the sponsor of a measure that earmarked $210 million within the Defense Department for breast cancer research, put it: "When they asked Willie Sutton why he robbed banks, he said because that's where the money is. Why did I go to the Pentagon? That's where the money is."[28]

Under Clinton, this process has been advanced not just by Congress but also by the executive. Clinton's budgets have included several billion dollars for the conversion of defense industries to civilian purposes, for example, part of the president's "industrial policy." All told, the Congressional Research Service calculates that "non-traditional defense programs" cost about $13 billion a year in FY 1994 and FY 1995, which amounts to 5 percent of the defense budget and more than four times as much as was spent on such things as recently as FY 1990.[29]

Effects of Reduced Spending

The squeeze on funding can reduce our military capabilities in five broad ways:

- reducing the size of our forces
- lowering the caliber and morale of personnel
- diminishing the battle-readiness of our troops
- slowing the rate at which equipment is replaced by more modern equipment
- constraining the research on and development of new equipment

As for the first of these, force sizes are already being reduced by a third. The budget shortfalls described by the GAO and the CBO will, barring further force reductions, take their toll in some or all of the other four ways. As Senator Sam Nunn warned about the FY 1995 defense budget, it "will not be adequate to maintain the current readiness of our forces, provide for their needed modernization and still support the force structure necessary."[30]

Personnel. One secret to the success of America's all-volunteer military force has been the quality of the personnel it has attracted. With the big increases in defense spending in the 1980s came hikes in military pay, benefits, and bonuses. Those changes brought striking improvements in recruitment. The proportion of recruits with high school diplomas rose from 68 percent in 1980 to 94 percent in 1984 to 99 percent in 1992.[31] In the past two years, however, pay increases have been held below the rate of inflation. In addition, funding for housing and other facilities relied on by military families has been cut. And some units whose skills have been in demand for policing missions in places like Iraq, Haiti, and Bosnia have been away from home a greater share of the time than service standards call for.[32] Perhaps as a result, reenlistment rates have fallen, and the military has seen its first slight downturn in the aggregate measures of recruit quality.

Readiness. The issue of readiness has received the most attention because of memories that sharp cuts in defense spending after Vietnam left America with "hollow" forces. That is, the disrepair of equipment and the poor training of personnel yielded a force prone to mishaps and failed missions. In October 1994, National Security Adviser Anthony Lake decried "the Cassandras attacking our readiness."[33] But weeks later the Pentagon acknowledged that, by its own audit, three of twelve army divisions were no longer fully combat ready.[34] This confirmation followed a report by the Defense Science Board Task Force on Readiness in June 1994 that stated: "We observed enough concerns that we are convinced that unless the Department of Defense and the Congress focus on readiness, the armed forces could slip back into a 'hollow' status."[35] In response to such concerns, President Clinton announced in December 1994 that he would restore $25 billion to the defense budget over five years. But most of this money was targeted to the years 2000 and 2001, and the rest was not allocated to maintenance and training.

Modernization. While worries about readiness have evoked a louder public outcry, more of Clinton's economies have come at the expense of modernization. Modernization is the constant process of furnishing fighting personnel with newer equipment. Like all machines and appliances, military hardware wears out. In addition, since all other countries are constantly improving their military technology, we must update ours to retain the technological lead so critical to our military power.

The strategy of the Clinton defense budget has been largely to suspend modernization, allowing our shrinking forces to live off the inventories built up during the previous administrations. Procurement of new weapons was reduced to 17 percent of the defense budget, far below its historical share.[36] In presenting its budget proposal for FY 1996, the Defense Department said that procurement would fall to a level 71 percent below that of 1985.[37] Senator Daniel Inouye voiced the concern of many when he said that "the services . . . are eating their seed corn."[38]

The Clinton administration is not oblivious to the concerns about modernization. It plans to make up the shortfall in procurement in the latter years of its budget projections. But since the Clinton budgets project no real growth in defense spending (they do not even keep up with inflation), deficits in procurement cannot be overcome without offsetting cuts in force size, compensation, readiness, or research. (The Republican alternative budgets are not much different.)

Moreover, the deficit in procurement will be harder to overcome than a deficit in readiness since it takes a long time to bring new weapons into service and many of the major weapons under development in the Reagan buildup have been canceled.[39]

Research and Development. In addition to the lag in current modernization, our ability to modernize our forces in the future is likely to be diminished by cuts in research and development. It is true that we are no longer in a nuclear arms race with the Soviet Union. Nonetheless, we are in a time of rapid technological evolution, centered on advances in information processing. In Operation Desert Storm, for example, we witnessed the burgeoning capability to deliver a weapon precisely on target. One rationale for the substantial reduction in U.S. military manpower is that such reductions will be balanced by improvements in capability. Another is that we can hedge against future threats by keeping up our research. But we are not keeping it up. The research and development budget is shrinking, measured in constant dollars, and is scheduled to reach a level in the late 1990s less than 60 percent of its level in the late 1980s.[40]

In sum, even given the steep reductions in force size, the accounts for personnel, readiness, modernization, and research are all underfunded. Some additional funds could be found by reducing the nondefense expenditures within the defense budget. But unless the sharp decline in defense spending is arrested, problems in any of these areas will be addressed only by exacerbating the problems in the other areas.

The Flaw in Clinton's Defense Plan

The fundamental flaw in the Clinton defense plan is an approach that puts budgetary considerations first. This priority has been encouraged by theories popular in the 1990s that economics has achieved "primacy . . . over security issues"[41] or that "the methods of commerce are displacing military methods."[42] But what, if anything, does this mean? Wealth and power are two goals that individuals and states have pursued since time immemorial. Some humans value one more than the other, but how would one measure in the aggregate which is the more important or sought after? Wealth is pursued by economic means and power by military means. One can, it is true, use wealth to buy weapons, and one can use weapons to seize wealth. But one cannot freely substitute the methods of one for those of the other, as the futility of trying to stop Saddam Hussein by economic sanctions or of trying to run an economy by command bears witness.

The notion that the use of force has lost its utility arose in the 1970s out of America's frustration in Vietnam. It was reinforced by the Soviet failure in Afghanistan and Iraq's failure in Kuwait. Although the use of force has never had much utility for the losing side, it had plenty of utility for Hanoi, for the Afghan Mujahedin, and for America in the Persian Gulf.

Military issues have receded since the cold war because the world is no longer dominated by two superpowers, one of which was highly militaristic, but by one peaceful superpower. Economic issues can enjoy "primacy" over security issues as long as security is ensured. The world of American supremacy is a comparatively secure world. If, however, American power is allowed to wane, security issues may soon be thrust back onto the center of the global stage.

Threat-based Planning

How much power do we need? Secretary of Defense Les Aspin was an advocate of "threat-based" planning.[43] But such an approach underlines our current predicament. What is the threat? Today, we face a variety of possible threats, any of which may or may not materialize. That uncertainty is what led to the "two regional wars" standard.

The problem with threat-based planning, however, is not merely that the threats are hard to predict. With our supreme influence, the first goal of U.S. defense planning should not be to win the next major war but to avert it. Our strategy of deterrence in fact accomplished that goal through the decades when the Soviet Union menaced the peace. Back then, influential voices questioned the logic of deterrence, warning of the catastrophe that nuclear war would bring,[44] but the point of preparing for nuclear war was precisely to prevent it. In the end, our bloodless victory in the cold war gave eloquent answer to those who asked so insistently why we were "wasting" billions on weapons "that would never be used." Today, we should strive not merely to forecast correctly the next threat but to discourage it from emerging. That sound logic lay behind the 1992 defense planning guidance.

Deterring Rivals. As the guidance suggested, we should endeavor to remain the sole superpower and to have no new military rival. To do so, we must keep up our own strength. But also, as it pointed out, we must reassure others. The natural axes of rivalry in Europe between Germany and Russia and in Asia between Japan and China were central to twentieth-century turmoil. During the cold war, these competitions were in abeyance, while (West) Germany and Japan entrusted their security in large measure to the United States. In the aftermath of the cold war, continuing strong American presence can discourage these rivalries from resuming.

As the Clinton administration recommends, we should maintain the capability to wage two major regional wars, but we must be able to do so simultaneously, not "nearly simultaneously." The whole world knows that Saddam Hussein might have come out of his Kuwait adventure more successfully had he pushed immediately into Saudi Arabia rather than giving America time to mobilize. The lesson taken by future aggressors will be to strike quickly, a lesson likely to be reinforced by an American doctrine of *near* simultaneity. Moreover, rogue states like Iran, Libya, and North Korea already cooperate in building their armed forces. It is not hard to imagine that they could coordinate military moves if they knew that the United States was incapable of taking on more than one of them at a time.

Contribution of Allies. Those who find the two-war standard too ambitious complain that it does not account for the likely contributions of our allies. Lawrence Korb asks: "Can we not count on our European allies to provide at least five divisions and five air wings in the event of a Middle East crisis?"[45] The question all but answers itself. In Kuwait in 1991, we received cooperation from our allies. When we bombed Libya in 1986 or resupplied Israel in 1973, however, few of our allies cooperated, and some would not allow us even to refuel or overfly. We can, in short, count on our allies to cooperate with us sometimes, which means that we cannot count on them at all.

Considerations for Planning

China. Among the other chief considerations that should guide our defense planning and budgets is China. Although we should not define China as an enemy and create a self-fulfilling prophecy, we must recognize that China is on a path to rival the United States for economic supremacy early in the next century. And China continues to be ruled by a hard-nosed dictatorial government. While military budgets are decreasing around the globe, China's grows apace, and it is buying up advanced weapons from the former Soviet Union.[46] This regime, which thought nothing of turning its tanks on its own children in Tiananmen Square, will think little of turning them on its neighbors should its interests—or ambitions—so require. Will economic success stimulate an appetite in China for hegemony in East Asia? We cannot predict, but it is a possibility that could rock the world, one that would make huge and unaccustomed demands on American military power.

Technology. Another consideration is the extremely rapid evolution of military technology. With 1.4 million men and women under arms, American forces are much smaller than Russia's or China's and scarcely bigger than India's or North Korea's.[47] Our military supremacy depends on staying ahead of the pack in military technology. Maintaining superiority will require diligence and foresight and generous funding for research and development.

Weapons Proliferation. Even maintaining our lead, however, is scarcely a complete answer to the technological challenges we face. As former defense secretary Aspin put it, knowing that a country trails us in military technology by, say, forty years is cold comfort since forty years ago we built a hydrogen bomb. The spread of weapons of mass destruction puts an important qualification on our military supremacy: even a country far weaker than we are could do us terrible harm. The proliferation of nuclear, chemical, and biological weapons must rank high on any list of emergent post–cold war threats.

According to the Defense Department, at least twenty countries now have or are developing such weapons, and more than a dozen already have operational ballistic missiles that could deliver them.[48] Needless to say, these lists include the world's most irresponsible governments. What can we do about it?

Nonproliferation treaty. The Clinton administration worked hard to secure an indefinite extension of the Nuclear Nonproliferation Treaty. The treaty has several shortcomings. Not all states adhere to it. Some who do, like North Korea, have openly defied its terms. Others who do, like Iraq, have clandestinely evaded it. And the agreement abets certain "peaceful" nuclear projects, notably the use of plutonium as fuel, which are more likely to be covers for bomb making than legitimate energy sources.[49] In short, as Jeane Kirkpatrick puts it, "The problem is that the same governments against whom we most need protection are those most likely to violate treaties."[50]

Still, there is a value to the treaty. Without it there might be a general rush to "go nuclear." Even the most responsible states might feel impelled to join in, for fear of being outclassed by neighbors or potential rivals. Instead, states like Sweden, Brazil, Argentina, and South Africa have turned back from the path of nuclear weapons.

Rogue states. But the problem of rogue states is unanswered. Largely because of it, the Clinton administration announced a "counter-proliferation initiative." Its aims are to improve intelligence about clandestine weapons programs, to disrupt them through trade restrictions, and ultimately to neutralize them on the battlefield.

One rogue state, North Korea, was on a collision course with the United States in 1994 as it prepared to reprocess nuclear fuel that would have given it the ability to build an additional handful of nuclear weapons. Confrontation was averted when Washington and Pyongyang reached an "agreed framework" in October 1994, under which North Korea would close down its existing nuclear program in exchange for which the United States, South Korea, and others would provide two light-water nuclear reactors from which it is more difficult to produce bombs.

Because the framework entails many complicated steps, Under Secretary of Defense Walter Slocombe emphasizes that "punctilious compliance with all the provisions of the agreement is essential."[51] But each time Pyongyang cheats or prevaricates, Washington will ask itself whether this particular violation is worth losing the whole deal over. The United States, then, is bound to accept a lot less than punctilious compliance. In contrast to Slocombe, Assistant Secretary of State Robert Gallucci, who negotiated the deal, implicitly acknowledges as much when he says that one of its "great benefit[s]" is that "it's informal," unlike a treaty. "I don't know whether an 'agreed framework' can be violated or not," he adds, tellingly.[52]

At best, the deal, which rewards North Korea handsomely for its violations of the Nuclear Nonproliferation Treaty, will encourage other rogue regimes to follow suit. And even if it brings a halt to Pyongyang's nuclear weapons drive, it is likely to leave it in possession of the one or two nuclear weapons it probably owns already. This situation underscores the need for defense against nuclear weapons.

Missile defense. Today America has no defense against nuclear weapons because of the 1972 Anti-Ballistic Missile Treaty. It was designed to stabilize the cold war by locking the two superpowers into an embrace of mutual-assured destruction. The proliferation of missiles and weapons of mass destruction is rendering the ABM Treaty obsolete. America and Russia both have reason to protect themselves against nuclear missile attack by third parties. The attacker might be in other respects only a minor military power; yet the threat to deliver just one or a few warheads could serve as an "equalizer"—or so it might hope. Protection against such a threat is technically feasible. When President Reagan spoke in 1983 of a shield against Soviet missiles, skeptics pointed out that even a defense that was 99 percent effective against the Kremlin's 20,000 warheads would allow 200 to get through. But few knowledgeable people doubt that we could devise a defense against one or ten or twenty missiles that would be quite reliable.

The Clinton administration insists that any such threat is still years away. Inspired by the experience with Iraqi Scud attacks, it has given priority instead to developing "theater" defensive weapons that could protect American troops in the field. And it has opened negotiations with Russia to define ways it could develop such weapons without violating the ABM Treaty. But it is not clear that an effective program can be designed around this constraint, nor whether the Russians will cooperate. A better solution would be to get rid of the treaty.

We should, however, hesitate to renounce it unilaterally lest we spook the Russians into reneging on recent agreements to reduce radically our respective offensive arsenals. But we should press hard to open their eyes to the manifest logic of an agreed revision or renunciation that would allow both sides to erect defenses at least against small-scale or accidental attacks.

How Much Defense?

In the end, there is no precise way to calculate our defense needs. The strategist Colin Gray has put it:

> No amount of analytical modeling, computer print-outs, fancy graphics and colored slides can hide completely the fact that for the most part, defense planning is guesswork.

... policy makers and defense planners do not know how much is enough for the future (say, five to ten years out). Moreover, they do not know how to find out how much is enough. . . . they need a robust strategy that allows them to plan against the worst of many possible surprise effects.[53]

One foreign policy specialist recently argued for further defense cuts by quoting Colin Powell as saying, "I would be very surprised if another Iraq occurred."[54] He apparently forgot that Powell, like other high U.S. officials, had been surprised by the first Iraq, too.

Despite the surprise, we were prepared. A panel of former chiefs of staff made the telling point that "of the five major wars involving U.S. forces in the twentieth century, the Persian Gulf War was . . . the only war for which our forces were truly prepared." Ironically, "we were ready for that war only because we had prepared for another conflict with a more formidable adversary, the Soviet Union."[55] Of the other four, we won only two, and in those we took many casualties. In the Gulf War, by contrast, we not only won but suffered few casualties. This was the benefit of having an abundance of military resources.

How much do we need? Enough to prevent, if possible, the emergence of a new rival; to fight, if necessary, two simultaneous regional wars; to lay the groundwork for meeting new threats that may emerge early in the next century; to maintain our lead in military technology. Undoubtedly, this program will cost more, by a few tens of billions per year, than Clinton has proposed to spend or that the Republican-led Congress has approved. We can never calculate exactly how much is the right amount, but we do know—or should—that in defense, it is far better to have too much than too little.

·11·

WHEN TO USE FORCE?

The basic goal of U.S. foreign policy, beyond preserving the existence and freedom of our country, is to prevent another outbreak of large-scale war. If in the nineteenth century a balance of power accomplished that goal, in the twenty-first century it will most likely be accomplished, as I have argued in the preceding chapter, by the maintenance of an *imbalance* of power, that is, through America's position as unrivaled superpower. But merely possessing unmatched strength is not enough: knowing when to use it is the difficult and important part. No formula can answer this question for us. But a key to keeping the peace will be to use our power to discourage aggression.

Criteria for the Use of Force

Various efforts have been made to formulate criteria for the use of force. In 1993, Secretary of State Warren Christopher set forth a list of four conditions.[1] It resembled a list formulated a decade earlier by Secretary of Defense Caspar Weinberger.[2] The two secretaries represented opposite sides of the same Vietnam syndrome. Christopher embodied the tradition of the antiwar liberals, appalled by America's actions in Vietnam and determined not to see them repeated. Weinberger reflected the bitter institutional memory of America's armed forces, dispatched to Vietnam to do a dangerous and dirty job only to have the limb of public support sawed off behind them. They, too, wanted no repetition.

Of course, violence should not be used without compelling moral justification. But neither Christopher's nor Weinberger's list[3] addressed the moral criteria that one finds in the Catholic doctrine of "just war."[4] Rather, they were wholly prudential and seemed driven by the single goal of setting the threshold for force as high as possible. Both, for example, stress the prerequisite of "public support," a requirement that puts the cart before the horse. The American people rarely support military action until the president and his cabinet secretaries make a strong case for it. Their role is to build public support for actions they deem essential to the nation's welfare, not to serve as pollsters. That is the leadership the public expects from them.

Christopher says that we should not go to war without an exit strategy. This criterion might be suitable for minor humanitarian missions, such as in Haiti or Somalia, but not for serious threats to the national interest. We have recently celebrated the fiftieth anniversary of the Allied victory in World War II; yet no exit is in sight either from Germany or from Japan. Does this mean it was a mistake to have fought there?

Weinberger says that force must be a last resort. This point seems to make eminent moral and political sense, but not if it is taken literally. Should we always refrain from using force until every other option has been tried and has failed? By that time, many wrongs would be beyond remedy. It makes far more sense to say that we should *consider* every other course of action. Most of those who opposed Operation Desert Storm argued that we should wait to allow economic sanctions to work. But half a decade after Iraq was defeated and crippled, the economic sanctions are still in place, and they still have not sufficed to compel Saddam Hussein to cease his quest for weapons of mass destruction.

In a world with only one superpower, it is better that it be too inhibited in using force than too free. Nonetheless, great harm can come from either error. A case can be made that until World War I, America erred more often toward a too-ready resort to arms—against the Indians and Mexico, Spain and the Philippines. From the time of World War I, though, when America reached its maturity as a power, the opposite has more often been true. Of the four major wars America has fought since then, three resulted largely from our aversion to using force. American isolationism helped provoke World War II, and the Korean and Persian Gulf Wars occurred because we gave dictators reason to calculate that America would not fight them. Only about the Vietnam War can it be said that we were too incautious about getting into war. And, as the Christopher and Weinberger lists show, the trauma of that episode has strongly reinforced our inhibitions.

Weinberger and Christopher are right to suggest that we ought never to put human life at risk without very careful consideration, but both of them ignore what ought to be the first question, namely, What are the purposes that justify risking life? Of course, no rule can be devised that will spare us from having to assess each situation in its individuality. Still, we cannot evaluate cases except by measuring them against some standards. Necessarily, then, we go back and forth between the general and the specific, each new case must be viewed in light of experience, and in its turn it adds to our experience. Let us review the five cases in which America has used or considered using force since the cold war ended and then consider generalizations for American use of force in this period. Those five cases are Kuwait, Bosnia, Somalia, Rwanda, and Haiti.

The Gulf War

In the first, the American-led coalition won a smashing victory, while absorbing few casualties. The American people reveled in this first post-Vietnam demonstration of the prowess of American arms, and President Bush boasted that we had "kicked the Vietnam syndrome once and for all."[5] Yet some wondered whether this story-book victory might have the reverse effect, that is, whether it would set a standard of optimal circumstance and success that no future military situation could duplicate. *New York Times* columnist Thomas Friedman suggested that the Vietnam syndrome might be replaced by a "Gulf War Syndrome," in which

> the U.S. will engage in military operations abroad only if they take place in a desert with nowhere for the enemy to hide, if the fighting can be guaranteed to last no more than five days, if casualties can be counted on one hand, if both oil and nuclear weapons are at stake, if the enemy is a madman who will not accept any compromise and if the whole operation will be paid for by Germany and Japan.[6]

If the wisdom and necessity of going to war to oust Saddam's forces from Kuwait seem clear in retrospect, they were not so at the time. The opposition was led by the usually hawkish chairman of the

Senate Armed Services Committee, Sam Nunn. "We have an obliga-tion as leaders to distinguish between important interests which are worthy of economic, political [responses] and interests that are vital, that are worth . . . calling . . . on our young men and women in uni-form to sacrifice . . . their lives [for]," he said.[7] Former secretary of defense James Schlesinger warned that U.S. "casualties may be ex-pected to run into several tens of thousands."[8] Former president Jimmy Carter predicted "devastating consequences . . . destabilization of the Middle East."[9] His national security adviser, Zbigniew Brzezinski, foresaw "a global wave of sympathy for Iraq."[10] And former secre-tary of state Cyrus Vance appealed for "adequate time" to allow eco-nomic sanctions to "bring about a peaceful solution of this problem."[11] In the end, President Bush was only barely able to overcome such argu-ments, securing approval for military action by a vote of 52 to 47 in the Senate and 250 to 183 in the House.

Ironically, today the strongest criticism of Bush's actions is not that he was too fast to resort to war but rather too fast to end it. As Saddam Hussein continues to vex the United States, many Americans are asking why, when our armies were moving almost effortlessly through Iraq, they did not go on to oust the tyrant who was the source of the problem.

Nonetheless, we did go to war, and we did win. But why did we fight? Some said that it was for oil. Others emphasized Saddam's drive to acquire nuclear weapons. President Bush mentioned both of these reasons, but he stressed another one: opposing aggression or creating a "new world order."

In his first address after the Iraqi invasion of Kuwait, Bush said, "If history teaches us anything, it is that we must resist aggression or it will destroy our freedom." And he warned that "no one should underestimate our determination to confront aggression."[12] Again and again in the ensuing months, he returned to this theme, telling the United Nations some weeks into the crisis: "The world's key task—now, first and always—must be to demonstrate that aggression will not be tolerated or rewarded."[13]

At first, when Bush spoke about aggression his terms were his-torical. He evoked the experience of the 1930s, and he even likened Saddam to Hitler. But gradually his focus moved toward the future, suggesting that the end of the cold war would allow realization of the vision of collective security incorporated in the UN Charter. "No longer can a dictator count on East-West confrontation to stymie concerted

United Nations action against aggression," he said. Out of the Persian Gulf crisis,

> a new world order . . . can emerge: a new era . . . more secure in the quest for peace. . . . A hundred generations have searched for this elusive path to peace . . . . A world where the rule of law supplants the rule of the jungle . . . . A world where the strong respect the rights of the weak.[14]

Some said that this was empty rhetoric. Senator Edward Kennedy spoke for the skeptics when he said, "The principal reason driving the President's policy of war can be spelled out in three . . . letters: O-I-L."[15] But if oil was the overriding consideration, was war necessary? Saddam, as some opponents of the war pointed out, would have sold us the oil. What else could he do with it? We could have offered him a deal: recognition of his absorption of Kuwait in exchange for an understanding not to use the oil for extortion or to gouge the price or to threaten Saudi Arabia militarily. In all likelihood, he would have leapt at such a deal, for it would have been tantamount to recognizing him as the new regional kingpin. We had no treaty obligations to Kuwait. Why not make such an offer? The essential answer is that we could not countenance Iraq's aggression, for fear of the message it would send about America's role in the world and about what others could hope to get away with.

The degree to which our decisive defeat of Iraq may have deterred others cannot be known. Although the Serbs showed that it did not deter everyone, we can only speculate about what would have ensued had Saddam been allowed to digest Kuwait. How many other ambitious strongmen might have taken inspiration? A prominent Nigerian intellectual told me at the time that he felt gratitude to President Bush. Were it not for Bush's action, he said, "others would have emulated Saddam." "In your region?" I asked. "My own government," he replied.

Bosnia

However effective America's action, aggression raised its head again a year later in the former Yugoslavia. This time the world balked, and President Bush led the balking. Among the Yugoslav conflicts, the issues were clearest in the case of Bosnia and Herzegovina, although even here some questioned calling it a case of aggression. The questions were mostly on two points: whether the war in Bosnia should be seen as an aggressive war or a civil war since most of the Serb attackers were Bosnian Serbs, and whether Bosnia is a bona fide state. Both questions are easily answered.

Although the majority of Serb fighters in Bosnia are residents of Bosnia, the war was initiated by Belgrade. Boris Jovic, vice president of the ruling Serbian Socialist Party, confessed to a BBC interviewer:

> We knew that when Bosnia was recognized, we'd be seen as aggressors because our army was there. So Milosevic and I talked it over, and we realized we'd have to pull a fast one. We transferred all the Bosnian Serbs in our Yugoslav army to their forces [that is, the Bosnian Serb militias] and promised to pay all their costs.[16]

Moreover, Serbia has remained involved intimately in the fighting. General Ratko Mladic, commander of the Bosnian Serb forces, was appointed to that position by Serbian President Slobodan Milosevic (after having commanded Croatian Serb forces in their 1991 war against Croatia).[17] In 1995, Milosevic appointed a new commander of the Croatian Serb forces, General Mile Mrksic, the assistant chief of the general staff of the Yugoslav army. As commander of Yugoslavia's Special Forces, Mrksic had helped lead the 1994 Bosnian Serb attack on Gorazde.[18]

Throughout the war, Serbia has provided arms, fuel, spare parts, and training to Bosnian Serb fighters. When Bosnian Serb forces besieged the largely Muslim town of Srebrenica in 1993, they relied in part on Yugoslav army artillery fired across the border from within Serbia.[19] In 1995, when Serb forces captured the "safe havens" of Srebrenica and Zepa, the attackers included the Serbian government tanks and paramilitary units.[20] According to U.S. officials, the salaries of many officers in the Bosnian and Croatian Serb forces are paid by the Yugoslav army, and wounded Bosnian Serb fighters are evacuated by helicopter to Serbia.[21] Moreover, the *New York Times* reported in June 1995 that the Bosnian Serbs' air defense "remains electronically linked to the Yugoslav army's computers and radars,"[22] a point implicitly confirmed by the chairman of the Joint Chiefs of Staff, General John Shalikashvili.[23]

By any standard, this depth of participation on the part of Serbia (or "Yugoslavia") constitutes aggression. The fact that the fighting in Bosnia is also a civil war changes nothing. In a great many wars, foreign forces are able to find domestic accomplices. The large contingents of Soviet citizens that fought alongside Hitler against their own repressive government scarcely made the war in the USSR a civil war.

As for the issue of whether Bosnia and Herzegovina is a bona fide state, skeptics usually raise two points. One is that the boundaries were drawn artificially by the Yugoslav dictator Tito. The other is that neither Bosnians nor even the Bosnian Muslims constitute a nation. But these objections apply no less forcefully to many, perhaps most, member states of the United Nations, states whose borders were drawn by colonialists and often do not coincide with ethnic boundaries. These exact points were made, and quite accurately, by Saddam Hussein about Kuwait. But in the eyes of international law, a state is bona fide once it is admitted into the United Nations and gains diplomatic recognition from other states, regardless of how it came into existence. Bosnia met these tests.

Somalia

In contrast to Bosnia, the battles within Somalia were entirely internal, and the issues raised by Somalia's tragedy were solely humanitarian, not legal or geopolitical. The combination of natural disaster (drought) with man-made disaster (the collapse of all governmental authority before the predations of bandits and warlords) had taken some 300,000 Somali lives. The Red Cross deemed another million and a half in jeopardy.

When President Bush dispatched American forces to Somalia in November 1992, he was motivated, said the *Washington Post,* by "a growing conviction that many thousands more people would starve to death within weeks in the absence of strong action" and by the reassurance of "a Pentagon calculation that the military risks would be minimal."[24]

Bush pledged that the troops would be home by the time he left office, but when Clinton was inaugurated they were still there. Soon their mission expanded from providing food to "nation building." The impetus for that task came from UN Secretary-General Boutros Boutros-Ghali. It had been staunchly resisted by the Bush administration, but the Clinton administration, although reluctant, had gone along. UN Ambassador Madeleine Albright said that we "aimed at nothing less than the restoration of an entire country as a proud, functioning, and viable member of the community of nations."[25] Such hopes turned to ashes when a company of U.S. Army Rangers was decimated in the streets of Mogadishu while trying to capture Mohammed Farah Aideed, the warlord who had blocked any national reconciliation and had waged guerrilla war against foreign peacekeepers.

Rwanda

Part of the fallout from America's debacle in Somalia was a great reluctance to be drawn into Africa's next calamity, Rwanda, which turned out to be even more ghastly. Estimates of the death toll go as high as 750,000 and even "upward of a million,"[26] although most observers put the number at around 500,000.[27] The vast majority of victims were Tutsis, most slaughtered in cold blood and often gruesomely by Hutu extremists. Before the killing began, the Tutsi population of Rwanda numbered only a little over a million, which suggests that nearly half or perhaps even a majority of Rwanda's Tutsis were killed. The scope of the killing, together with the fact that the predators targeted women and children as much as men, marks this case as the clearest instance of genocide since Hitler's attempt to wipe out the Jews.

The U.S. response was feeble. When the bloodletting began on April 6, 1994, a UN force was already in place in Rwanda from previous conflicts. When ten of its members, Belgians, were killed trying to protect the moderate Hutu prime minister, the incident precipitated a hasty withdrawal of most of the UN force. The Canadian commander, General Romeo Dallaire, however, insisted that with 1,800 properly equipped men he could have stopped the slaughter.[28] In the United Nations, the United States encouraged reducing the force.

After a month, a plan was agreed on for the interposition of an African force furnished with American equipment, especially armored personnel carriers that would have allowed it to move around the country in relative safety. But the U.S. government dragged its feet in delivering the vehicles until the rampage was largely over. It also refused requests to jam the poisonous radio stations, which stoked the genocide by broadcasting general appeals for the murder of Tutsis as well as specific orders to organized bands of killers. Mostly, America limited itself to aiding the refugees who fled Rwanda. The *New York Times* reported that President Clinton had instructed members of his administration not to characterize the events in Rwanda as "genocide" lest it feed pressures for sterner action.[29] Under the terms of the

Convention on Genocide, America and other signatories would "undertake to prevent" genocide. About Rwanda, the administration would concede only that "acts of genocide may have occurred."[30]

Haiti

In contrast to its great reticence of speech and action toward Rwanda, the Clinton administration acted with great vigor toward Haiti. It dispatched an invasion force that restored the duly elected President Jean Bertrand Aristide to office. American forces were able to occupy the island without bloodshed because former president Jimmy Carter charmed military strongman Raoul Cedras into an eleventh-hour capitulation. Oddly, this invasion was sanctioned by the UN Security Council but not by the U.S. Congress.

The Security Council authorized the invasion in the only terms allowed under the UN Charter, namely, by declaring that the Haitian regime constituted "a threat to peace and security."[31] This rationale, of course, was manifest nonsense. The Haitian regime was ugly, brutal, venal, and illegal, but it constituted not the least threat to anyone outside Haiti. In attaining this Security Council resolution, therefore, Washington promoted the view that the charter is infinitely malleable and that it says whatever the Security Council says it says. This position cannot but weaken international law, since the charter is its bedrock and the Security Council is so subject to political vicissitudes.

Justification for Force

Self-Defense. With these experiences as background, what can we deduce about when to use force? The easy case is self-defense. But even that motivation is not automatic, except in response to a direct attack on our territory, and that has happened only rarely. Self-defense ought to extend to defending our citizens or soldiers abroad, which may include rescuing them, as we did the medical students in Grenada, or retaliating for attacks against them, as by bombing Libya after terrorist attacks aimed at American soldiers in Germany.

Self-defense can also be anticipatory. A classic example was Israel's preemptive strike in 1967. Although the United States is not likely to have hostile armies gather on its borders as Israel did, the proliferation of weapons of mass destruction may present us with the need for anticipatory self-defense. We have a precedent in our blockade of Cuba in 1962, which was an act of war taken in response to the threat of nuclear missiles. With the prospect of such weapons soon falling into the hands of states of great lawlessness like North Korea and Iran, America may need to take preemptive measures.

Values. Beyond self-defense lie interests and values. Either can justify the use of force, and often the two are entertwined. But where values alone are at stake, we should use force only rarely. The most basic humanitarian mission is saving lives. Sometimes our armed forces can be the most effective agency for aiding the victims of disaster or tragedy, but where Americans are likely to get killed, we ought to be wary. The reason is not that American lives are inherently more valuable than others. Rather, it is that the risks are not borne equally among us. The men and women who volunteer for service in our armed forces know that their ultimate job is to stand in harm's way to keep the rest of us safe. We owe it to them not to risk their lives lightly.

Humanitarian intervention. Still, there is some threshold beyond which the humanitarian stakes are so high that most Americans, including, I believe, most of those in uniform, would be willing to risk some of our own. That threshold has no exact number, but numbers do matter. When there are hundreds of thousands or millions of human lives at peril, and it is within our means to rescue them, then there is a strong case for doing so. Justice matters, too. If half a million are dying in tribal warfare, we have less cause to try to separate them than if one group is the innocent victim of slaughter by another.

By this standard, we had a strong justification for the original American intervention in Somalia to stop mass starvation. But we had much less reason to stay on for nation building, since that was not a humanitarian emergency and the need for nation building is scarcely limited to Somalia. Some would argue that to have exited Somalia without restoring some stable government and civil society would have meant leaving it to slide back to famine. Perhaps, but the famine of 1991–1992 arose from a confluence of causes that might not be repeated even in the absence of nation building. Or it might have been possible to provide military security for food distribution without the deeper involvement and risks that nation building implied. Indeed, looking back on the UN mission, a former assistant secretary of state for Africa, Chester Crocker, concludes that while nation building was a failure, "one could reasonably estimate that upwards of a quarter of a million Somali lives were saved."[32]

Ironically, a still stronger case for humanitarian intervention can be made for Rwanda, where true genocide occurred and great loss of life, while America, stung by its experience in Somalia, remained on the sidelines.

In contrast, it is hard to argue that the circumstance of Haiti crossed the threshold for humanitarian intervention. Large numbers of lives were not in peril. And while it is true that Haitians were miserable under their military rulers, they were probably not more miserable than numerous other peoples suffering misrule or than they themselves have often been.

The invasion aimed to restore democracy to Haiti, and democracy carries a high humanitarian valiance. Still, there were doubts about whether restoring Aristide was tantamount to restoring democracy. Although he was indeed the people's choice, he had, while in office, countenanced the use of violence against political opponents. The larger question about the democratic rationale, however, is whether America should spread democracy by the sword, a question to which I shall return.

Peacekeeping. Another kind of humanitarian mission is peacekeeping. Early in his term, President Clinton declared, "U.N. peacekeeping holds the promise to resolve many of this era's conflicts."[33] But UN peacekeeping has little to do with keeping the peace in the larger sense of the collective security envisioned in the UN Charter. Rather, it consists of policing settlements of usually isolated disputes. After the chastening experience of Somalia, Clinton put more emphasis on American "interests" in such missions. But the emphasis was largely rhetorical, since it made no clear distinction between interests and values.

Instead, the administration drew a distinction between threats that would warrant a unilateral U.S. response and those that would not. "Direct threats to our nation or our people require us to be prepared for a unilateral military response," explained National Security Adviser Anthony Lake, but "a second category of threats justifies only a limited use of force, and generally under international auspices. Peacekeeping would fall under this category."[34]

The problem with delegating to "international auspices" everything other than "direct threats" is that it means subordinating our own judgment about what needs to be done to the judgment of others whose track record is poor. The United Nations drew us deeply into Somalia for the dubious purpose of nation building, for example, while it held us back from taking stronger measures in Bosnia for the vital purpose of resisting aggression. This issue is a more genuine cause for alarm than the one that overshadowed it—whether Americans should fight under foreign command.

We face a larger question about the American role in peacekeeping. America's "comparative advantage" is in fighting, or what might be called peace enforcement or upholding the peace. The two times that the United Nations undertook or authorized war against an aggressor, the United States did most of the fighting. Throughout the cold war, America shielded most of the world from Soviet expansionism. When NATO forces carry out airstrikes in Bosnia, American planes fly most of the missions, and the same is true when a no-fly zone is enforced over Iraqi Kurdistan. This responsibility falls to us not because American armed forces are so numerous (they are not) but because they are so well armed and trained.

Where a mission entails large numbers of lightly armed soldiers to observe or patrol a tenuous peace, then Americans lose their comparative advantage. Indeed, they may acquire a comparative disadvantage if terrorists or provocateurs are afoot who would look upon Americans as targets of special value. It would be foolish to exhaust the American public's willingness to accept casualties in peacekeeping missions that can readily be performed by others and thereby constrain America's unique war-making capacity, which is a pillar of world peace.

Interests. In sum, rarely should we use force for values alone. It should be reserved for situations where our interests are at stake. But what interests? Throughout history, states have often warred over economic interests, although such *casus belli* have grown less common since the seventeenth century.[35] Today, the United States should never use force over economic issues. The only exceptions would be of the most extreme kind, such as when an ally's economy was being truly strangled through boycott or blockade. (I say an ally because it is much less likely that America itself could be subjected to this treatment.)

The interests often worth fighting for are not material interests but security interests. These are things a step or more removed from direct self-defense that may nonetheless impinge on our safety. We generally have a strong security interest, for example, in defending our allies. The fall of an ally could create a vulnerability for us. We also have a stake in upholding our commitments (as well as in carrying out our threats) so that others will be more eager for our friendship and more reluctant to defy us.

Democracy. Many of the purposes for which we must consider the use of force will advance our values as well as our interests. These include purposes that shape the environment of international relations, or what Arnold Wolfers called "milieu goals." One such is the spread of democracy abroad. While democracy embodies our values, it also conduces to our interest (as I shall discuss in the next chapter) since democratic countries tend to be more peaceful and more friendly to America.

We should work hard to encourage democracy. We should be willing to spend money for it. But we should not go to war for it. Although we have spread democracy through military occupation in places like Japan and Germany, we conquered those countries only in self-defense. Based on that model, a strong case existed for trying to remake Iraq, which we occupied in collective self-defense. It is quite another thing, however, to invade countries that have not broken the peace in order to democratize them. This act is impossible to justify under international law. (Hence the fiction we extracted from the Security Council that the Haitian regime constituted "a threat to peace and security.")

Nor is world opinion likely to accept such a role for the United States. It did so in the case of Haiti because the regime was so unlovely, unimportant, and unconnected. Moreover, ulterior motives may have been at work. After condoning our invasion, the Russians then hastened to claim an analogous right to intervene in their environs.[36]

Strong as our interest is in the spread of democracy, we cannot fight over each setback. According to the authoritative Freedom House annual survey, from 1991 through 1994 alone some forty-four countries deteriorated from "free" to "partly free" or "not free" or from "partly free" to "not free." Moreover, in the process of becoming democratic, many countries experience a few false starts, a few lapses back to dictatorship. We cannot send in the marines for each such lapse.

Exceptions may occur, especially where the issue of democracy combines with others to make a compelling interest, say, if Castroite guerrillas overthrew the elected government of Mexico. (If Castroites won a fair election in Mexico, however uncomfortable it made us, it would be wrong to intervene, but the combined weight of a violation of democracy and a hostile ideology might well constitute sufficient cause.) Another exception might be where the status of democracy in one country affected many others. In 1991, for example, the Organization of American States, whose members are all now democratic, pledged in the Santiago Declaration to protect one another against military usurpations. If the other members are prepared to act to uphold this pledge, a good case can be made that we should help out. At stake then would be not just one country's democracy but the entire political tenor of our hemisphere.

Civil war. Another such purpose is the suppression of civil war. The Clinton administration has spoken of using force "to broker settlements of internal conflicts."[37] The humanitarian value in stopping such conflicts is powerful, since they are often terribly brutal. But civil wars are numerous and notoriously difficult to get in the middle of. American intervention is not warranted, except if we have some strong security stake in the outcome as we did, for instance, in the struggles in Central America during the cold war. Of course, we have a general interest in stability, an interest that grows more urgent when a civil war overspills the boundaries of a single state. But it is more feasible to intervene in those few conflicts that reach that point than in all internecine conflicts prophylactically.

Aggression. Among international conflicts, the most dangerous are those that arise from aggression. The international milieu goal most worth fighting for is to resist aggression. Article 2(4) of the UN Charter, which forbids "the threat or use of force against the territorial integrity or political independence of any state," is the most important tenet of international law. To the extent that we can secure respect for it, we can forestall large-scale wars, although policing this rule entails a willingness to engage in smaller conflicts. Still, that commitment does not entail going everywhere or fighting every battle.

Aggressions are not only more dangerous than internecine wars, they are far rarer, constituting a more manageable number of crises to reckon with. Since World War II, the proscription of aggression has been widely accepted as a matter of right, and often efforts have been made to resist aggression. In this period, there have been about twenty-five wars between states, depending on what counts as a "war"(see the appendix to this chapter).[38] Of these, perhaps half to three-quarters involved acts of aggression (depending on what counts as "aggression"), and the United States involved itself to some degree in about half of them. We went to war in the Persian Gulf, Korea, and Vietnam. We armed the Mujahedin in Afghanistan and resupplied Israel by emergency airlift in 1973. In the Falklands conflict, we gave Britain technical support. In Chad, we airlifted arms while France assumed the main burden of helping repel Libyan aggression. We sent planes to India when it was attacked by China in 1962, although our aid was little and late. And in the Sinai, a case of aggression at least on the part of Britain and France (Israel had a stronger claim to self-defense), we even stepped in against our allies. We did not use force, but since they depended on us for their security, our adamant opposition, coupled with threats against the British pound, compelled them to capitulate.

In most cases in which the United States did not react to aggression, the government of the victim state had itself behaved so badly as to make U.S. assistance to it unthinkable: the Indian intervention in the Pakistani civil war of 1971 that issued in the creation of Bangladesh; the Vietnamese conquest of Cambodia in 1978–1979; and Iraq's invasion of Iran in 1980. In two other cases, which probably qualify as aggressions although not as clearly, the United States remained uninvolved for similar reasons: the Chinese invasion of Vietnam and the Tanzanian occupation of Uganda, both in 1979.

In one case of clear aggression, the Soviet invasion of Hungary in 1956, the United States failed to react because it was afraid of escalation to world war. In two other cases of clear aggression, the United States also failed to react, but without any such reason: the Arab states' attack on Israel in 1948 and Serbia's attack on Bosnia. In two other cases that some considered to be aggression, the United States was itself the aggressor: the invasion of Grenada in 1983 and of Panama in 1989.[39]

One of the ironies of the cold war was that while it engendered much conflict, including by various proxies of the superpowers, it also acted as a constraint. Local actors had to be mindful of impinging on the interests of the superpowers, and since the cold war was global, those interests were nearly ubiquitous.

The end of the cold war creates the possibility of strengthening the law against aggression. Russia is likely to be considerably more cooperative with the Western democracies than the Soviet Union was, even though Russian foreign policy has become more recalcitrant than it was during the initial democratic euphoria of the Soviet collapse. If nothing else, Russia lacks the strategic reach to support miscreant clients in the same way. (And, too, the United States can obey the law more punctiliously than before. Even some who question the legal grounds for America's invasion of Grenada went along with it because Grenada had made itself a Soviet outpost, and in the cold war, the United States was in a state of continuous self-defense against the Soviet Union.)

Conversely, the cold war's end could lead to an increase in aggression through a weakening of superpower constraints. Although America's sharp action against Iraq forestalled that tendency, our inaction against Serbia may negate the effects of the Persian Gulf War. Some take the view that the cold war's end allows the United States to be more indifferent to aggression. But this attitude could easily lead to a proliferation of regional wars that might grow quite dangerous. Moreover, it would squander an opportunity to strengthen the peace for the long term.

Resistance to Aggression

The lesson of World War II was that aggression, if tolerated, spreads. When that lesson has been invoked in regard to Bosnia, some have replied by pointing out that Milosevic is not Hitler and Serbia is not Germany. But successful aggression not only emboldens the aggressor, it also invites emulation. The aggression of World War II did not begin in Czechoslovakia or Austria or even the Rhineland; it did not begin with Germany at all. It began with Japan in Manchuria and Italy in Abyssinia. Both places were insignificant, but the breakdown of the law against aggression was very significant, opening the floodgates for all that followed.

Some say that the appetite for war among the major powers has been permanently soured by the bitter lessons of World Wars I and II, thereby making the threat of general war irrelevant. This is a pleasant thought, but it assumes the very best about the future of Russia, it blithely ignores the looming power of China, about whose appetites we still know little, and it fails to account for the spread of technology, which will enable numerous smaller and less mature powers to wield the same destructive force that great powers wielded fifty or eighty years ago.

That aggression is wrong is now universally acknowledged in the abstract. But this consensus must be undergirded by a practice of resistance to aggression, as in the Persian Gulf. Although America will bear much of the burden, as the norm against aggression solidifies, others may more readily help enforce it. I do not contend that the decision to take up arms against aggression should be automatic. Sometimes it will be unnecessary. (In 1967, Israel defended itself quite devastatingly.) Sometimes it will be too dangerous. (Helping Hungary in 1956 might have meant world war.) Sometimes the prospect of success will be too poor. (We probably could not have saved Tibet from China.) Sometimes the victim will be too repugnant. (Could we have come to the rescue of Khomeini's Iran?) Nevertheless, the presumption should be that America will oppose aggression. Where the use of force is precluded, we should act as vigorously as we can by means of diplomacy, economics, propaganda, and covert action.

Collective Security and American Power

The greatest impediment to drawing a line against aggression is that the very idea is tied to the notion of collective security. This notion contains both a profound insight and a profound flaw. The insight is that peace is indivisible. War in one place will affect people in other places. The world is a seamless web woven ever tighter with each advance in the methods of communication and transportation. The general level of global lawfulness and peacefulness affects everybody. The flaw is the belief that peace can be safeguarded through collective action and collegial decision making. Experience has shown that collegial decision making rarely results in any action, collective or otherwise, and can never substitute for the galvanizing effect of a single, decisive leader.

Until the Covenant of the League of Nations was adopted at Versailles, waging war was no violation of international law. The covenant, explains Ian Brownlie, "introduced a new concept into international law: a distinction between legal and illegal wars."[40] Thus, aggression presumptively meant going to war in disregard of the league's system of resolving disputes. Over the next years, efforts were made to define *aggression* more precisely, but these proved futile. More important, so did collective security, although the problem was not from a weakness of definition but rather a weakness of spine. Everyone understood that Japan had committed aggression in Manchuria and Italy in Abyssinia, but none found the courage to resist it.

When the United Nations was formed, its charter included a proscription of aggression in Article 2(4), although the term *aggres-*

sion was not used. And it too set forth a mechanism for collective security, which also in the main has not worked.[41] Commenting on the failure of the United Nations in Bosnia, the British scholar Rosalyn Higgins observed:

> Collective security guarantees are at the heart of the United Nations' role in the maintenance and restoration of peace. It was not the intention of the Charter that collective security should only be available to an attacked state if others felt that they had a direct interest in assisting; if it could be guaranteed that assistance would entail no harm to their soldiers; and if the political and military outcome was clear from the outset.[42]

Although the point is eloquently stated, experience has shown that most states are unwilling to take on the burdens of disinterested collective security. Churchill foresaw this reluctance. "States, he argued, were not equally concerned with international security. They tended to be preoccupied with their own problems or, at best, with problems of their particular regions. It would make more sense, therefore, to have several regional organizations . . . and above these a supreme council," writes Holsti.[43] To this day, regional bodies like the Organization of American States, the Organization of African Unity, and NATO hold more promise for the development of collective security than the United Nations has shown.

Nonetheless, the United States wanted to create a United Nations, and others went along not because they placed similar hopes in the United Nations but because they placed hopes in the United States. British Secretary of State Anthony Eden put it: "Only by encouraging the formation of some World Organization are we likely to induce the Americans . . . to agree to accept any European commitments designed to range America . . . against a hostile Germany or against any European breaker of the peace."[44] Eden got it just right. Insofar as the charter's principles of peace have been upheld, it has been more through American power than through collective security, but America has preferred to wield its power in the name of the principles in the charter.

In theory, upholding the law against aggression is the *raison d'être* of the United Nations, but experience has taught us (or should have) not to rely on the United Nations. When the United States led in repulsing aggression in Kuwait and Korea, we secured Security Council endorsement, and that was beneficial. In future crises, where we can get such endorsements so much the better. But where we cannot, it should little deter us. The UN Charter includes no requirement for Security Council permission to take up arms against aggression. Article 51 asserts that "nothing in the . . . Charter shall impair the inherent right of individual or collective self-defense if an armed attack occurs against a Member of the United Nations." Where we cannot get UN support, we can always seek the support of other states individually. But as long as we are the world's unique superpower, leadership in upholding the peace will fall largely to us.

APPENDIX 11A
INTERSTATE WARS SINCE WORLD WAR II

Palestine: 1948–1949
Korean: 1950–1953
Russo-Hungarian: 1956
Sinai: 1956
Sino-Indian: 1962
Vietnam: 1965–1975
Second Kashmir: 1965
Six Day: 1967
Football (El Salvador versus Honduras): 1969
Bangladesh: 1971–1974
Yom Kippur: 1973
Turco-Cypriot: 1974
Vietnam-Cambodian: 1975–1979
Ugandan-Tanzanian: 1978–1979
Sino-Vietnamese: 1979
Russo-Afghan: 1979–1989
Iran-Iraq: 1980–1988
Falklands: 1982
Lebanon: 1982
Grenada: 1983
Chad-Libya: 1987
Panama: 1989
Persian Gulf: 1990–1991
Croatia-Bosnia-Serbia: 1991–
Armenia-Azerbaijan: 1992–

PART FIVE

Political and Economic Leadership

·12·

FOSTERING DEMOCRACY

While military might is the bedrock of our security, peaceful political leadership is essential to the pursuit of both our values and our interests. Our most important political goal is encouraging the spread of democracy.

The Nature of Democracies

The spread of democracy serves our interests in the most powerful ways. Democracies are more peaceful, and they are more friendly to America. The more democracy spreads, the less likely we are to have to use our military might.

Generally Peaceful. Democracies virtually never go to war with each other. The exceptions to this rule are trivial. The conservative writers Paul Gottfried and Patrick J. Buchanan have made much of Britain's declaration of war against Finland in 1941.[1] But Finland was then allied to Nazi Germany, and Britain acted under extreme pressure from its ally, the Soviet Union. Even then, the declaration was rhetorical. Nary a shot was fired between Britain and Finland. The strongest example that I know of two democracies' fighting was Lebanon's participation in the Arab League's war against newborn Israel in 1948. But within the councils of the league, Lebanon had argued against the attack, and it kept its participation in the war to a minimum.[2]

These exceptions are so strained that they only underscore how robust the rule is. Indeed, it has been said that the proposition that democracies do not war on one another is "as close as anything we have to an empirical law in international relations."[3] Nonetheless, some argue that the fact that democracies do not fight *each other* does not mean that they are more peaceful in general. "This is a much more controversial proposition . . . for which there is little systematic evidence," according to political scientist Bruce Russett.[4] While Russett's argument rests on several social scientific studies, it flies in the face of common sense.

Russett says that those who claim that democracies are more peaceful "would have us believe that the United States was regularly on the defensive, rarely on the offensive, during the cold war."[5] And so it was! The point is not that the United States was never on the offensive in any particular episode of the cold war, but that the cold war as a whole was a one-sided creation of the Soviet Union, while the United States all along wanted peace. "Revisionist" historians doubted this interpretation, but it was conclusively verified when the Soviet Union under Gorbachev turned to peace: the cold war ended instantly. This outcome points up the weakness of much social science theorizing, based on quantitative analysis: it counts a conflict equally for both sides, while in substance, the roles of the two sides may not be equivalent at all.

Of the twenty-five interstate conflicts since World War II,[6] only India's attack on Pakistan in 1971, the French and British attacks on Egypt in Suez, and perhaps the American invasions of Grenada and Panama were offensives on the part of democracies. Israel's 1982 attack on the Palestine Liberation Organization in Lebanon and Turkey's invasion of Cyprus, both by democratic governments, were reactive.[7] The other nineteen wars, most of which deserve to be called aggressions, were launched by dictators. Moreover, in the cases where democracies initiated war, they were responding to some egregious behavior on the part of the government they attacked, be it that of Yahya Khan, Gamel Abdel Nasser, Bernard Coard, Manuel Noriega, the PLO, or the Greek junta. In contrast, many of the wars initiated by dictators—North Korea's attack on South Korea, Iraq's on Kuwait, the USSR's on Hungary or Afghanistan, Libya's on Chad, and others— were unprovoked acts of rapacity.

It is true that the European democracies were once greedy colonial powers who fought to conquer and keep their possessions. But the era of Western colonialism ended after World War II, sealed by America's strong opposition to it, and no new Western aggressiveness has replaced it. Indeed, in this century, the democracies have several times helped to cause wars by being so pacific that dictators were tempted to overreach.

Even if it were only true, as Russett and others would have it, that democracies are more peaceful toward other democracies, that fact alone establishes that spreading democracy will make the world more peaceful. Most of the investigations of this subject cover a period beginning long ago and continuing through the early 1980s. For most of this time, democracies accounted for only a small fraction of states, and therefore the peace among democracies had only modest effect on the total incidence of war. But as democracies grow more numerous—constituting a majority of states today, by some measures—the fact of their peacefulness toward one another grows increasingly important.

Friendly to America. In addition to being more peaceful, democracies are also more friendly to America. We have gone to war with dictators of the Left and the Right, but no democracy has ever been our enemy. On the other side of the ledger, our allies have usually been democracies. When we fought in the Persian Gulf, thirty-odd states joined our coalition. A handful were regional states with a direct stake in the outcome. Of the rest, nearly three-quarters were fellow democracies.[8]

To take another measure of friendliness, democracies more often side with the United States in the United Nations. Every year the Department of State produces a report showing how often the other member states voted the same way as America on issues before the General Assembly. I have compared these percentages with the member states' ratings on Freedom House's annual survey of freedom. In 1994, the most recent year available, the average "free" country voted with the United States 61 percent of the time, the average "partly free" country 45 percent of the time, and the average "not free" country 37 percent.

Philosophical Basis. Not only does the spread of democracy serve our interests, it also fulfills our deepest values. Democracy contributes to many things we hold dear: peace, economic opportunity, and civil rights. But our own democracy does not rest on empirical data about the benefits of democracy. Rather, it rests on philosophical postulates about human dignity. The Declaration of Independence puts it that "all men are created equal and endowed . . . with unalienable rights," that governments exist to secure these rights, and that their just power is derived from the consent of the governed. From those assertions, it follows that people everywhere are as needful of and entitled to democracy as we are.

Universality. Sometimes it is argued, however, that democracy is not a universal value, that the people of this or that undemocratic country do not want democracy. In preparation for the UN Human Rights Conference in Vienna in 1993, the caucus of Asian states, led by a coalition of dictatorships—from Communist to clericalist to capitalist—produced a manifesto implying that Asian peoples do not want human rights.[9] Aside from the self-contradiction of invoking the people's will (why, except on democratic premises, should it matter what the people want?), this argument fails both empirically and logically.

It fails empirically because few dictators have ever dared submit to a popular test. Those that have have usually had a bad surprise. In 1988, General Pinochet in Chile put his continuance in office to a vote, formulating the proposition in a way calculated to win a mandate. But the people voted no. In 1989, Poland's Communist rulers contrived an election to allow some popular participation while preserving their own power. Part of the fix was that the full slate of top Communists ran without opposition, but even they were defeated when the mass of voters crossed out their names. And in 1977, Indira Gandhi's martial law regime was ousted in a sudden election she called to legitimate it.

The argument that some peoples do not want democracy fails logically, as well, because if the people want dictatorship, democracy will never stand in their way. They can vote for dictatorship. If the people want democracy, however, dictatorship very often has stood in their way. About no nation is it said that although it really wants to live under dictatorship, unfortunately it is saddled with democracy. Of many, the converse can be said.

Stronger than the claim that some peoples "don't want" democracy is the argument that some might not succeed at sustaining it. Democracy, so the argument goes, rests on various social, economic, or cultural prerequisites. Societies that are non-Western, that are very poor, that have high rates of illiteracy, or that have patriarchal traditions are not suited, or at least not ready, for democracy. After World War II, when Africa was decolonized, each newly independent state began with a democratic constitution, but within a generation, virtually every one lapsed into dictatorship. What could one expect, it was asked, from societies with no middle class and few educated people, from societies lacking democratic traditions?

This argument has some truth, but only some. It begs the question of how democratic traditions can be acquired except by practicing democracy. While democracy originated in the West, growing out of the ideas of the Enlightenment and English parliamentarism, not all democracies are Western. And while democracy correlates with economic development, literacy, and the like, the correlation is far from perfect. Neither Japan nor South Korea is Western; neither India nor Botswana is rich. Yet all are democratic. And this is just the tip of the iceberg. In its 1995 survey (covering 1994), Freedom House rated seventy-six countries as "free." Fully half are in the third world. To be sure, some of these are tiny island states in the Pacific or in the Caribbean where they were heavily influenced by former British rule. To be sure, some may be fragile democracies and may not be back on the "free" list next year. Nonetheless, the numbers are too overwhelming to be discounted.

In fact, these numbers may understate the case. In addition to its seventy-six "free" countries, Freedom House found another thirty-eight that it ranked as only "partly free" but that it categorized as democratic polities. These might be called flawed or imperfect democracies because they suffered from weak governmental institutions or domestic conflict, but their governments were chosen in bona fide, competitive elections. Thirty out of these thirty-eight were also in the third world. Despite all the obstacles, democracy is having a big influence on the nonrich, non-Western world.

Transplanted Democracy. Why do some people find this influence surprising? All across the non-Western world, people cannot get enough of Western technology, Western economics, Western entertainment, Western consumer goods, Western fashions. Then why not Western political institutions, too? Those who say that democracy cannot be transplanted to alien cultural soil speak as if culture were something so deep as to be virtually immutable. But what is more basic to a nation's culture than its religion? And yet there are few places where the dominant religion is indigenous. Christianity was born in Palestine. Today it prevails in more than a hundred countries, of which, ironically, Palestine is not one. Buddhism originated in India, but India is not one of the thirteen predominantly Buddhist countries. Islam originated in Arabia. Today it flourishes in more than forty countries from Africa to the Pacific. If religious ideas can take root far from their native soil, then why not political ideas, too?

The same skepticism that we hear today about democracy's prospects in various parts of the world could be heard a few decades ago about places where we now take democracy almost for granted. During World War II, the State Department's leading expert on Japan told President Truman that, in planning to remold that country, "the best we can hope for is a constitutional monarchy, experience having shown that democracy in Japan would never work."[10] The great historian Arnold Toynbee commented after Italy succumbed to fascism that "it [is] an open question whether this political plant [democracy] can really strike permanent root anywhere except in its native soil."[11]

Toynbee seemed to be suggesting a point that many made a few decades ago, sometimes obliquely: that Catholic countries, steeped in hierarchy, were inhospitable to democracy. But then came Vatican II, which shifted the weight of the church from the side of established authority to the side of change. According to Samuel Huntington, partly as a result of Vatican II "roughly three quarters of the countries that transited to democracy between 1974 and 1979 were Catholic countries."[12] Today, most of the world's predominantly Catholic countries are democracies. This statistic again illustrates the spurious immutability of culture.

A further weakness in arguments of cultural determinism is that we understand little about the effect of culture on politics or economics. Huntington has reminded us that a few decades ago all predominantly Confucian societies were poor, and social scientists argued that something in the behaviors inspired by Confucianism made or kept them poor.[13] Since then, Confucian societies have grown rich at a faster pace than Christian or Muslim societies have ever done. Now social scientists are busy trying to understand what it is in Confucianism that conduces to the generation of wealth.

Those skeptical about the further spread of democracy often cloak themselves in the garb of historical realism and dismiss the advocates of democratization as naïve enthusiasts. But it is the skeptics who are ahistorical. Two hundred and twenty years ago, the United States became the first democracy in the modern world. The white, male electorate, restricted in some states to property owners, amounted to fewer than 1 million people out of a world population of roughly 800 million, or less than one-tenth of 1 percent. Today, some 40 to 60 percent of the countries of the world (depending on whether only Freedom House's 76 "free" countries or its 114 "democratic" polities are counted), with from 20 to 55 percent of global population, have democratically elected governments. Although the 220-year trend line is not smooth, it has traced a fairly steady rise. What reason could there be to suppose that now suddenly the curve will flatten as if held back by a glass ceiling?

Waves of Democracy. Huntington's fine book, *The Third Wave,* gives the skeptics ammunition. He says that the current trend of democratization, which began in 1974, is the third of its kind. The first wave of democratization, he says, began with the American and French Revolutions and lasted until the democratic collapses in Europe in the 1920s and 1930s. The second wave came with the decolonization that followed in the wake of World War II and lasted only until the 1960s. Each of the first two waves has been followed by an ebb tide. And indeed, since the great euphoria after the breakup of the Soviet empire, several momentarily democratic states have already returned to dictatorship.

One thing that is unsatisfying about Huntington's wave metaphor, however, is that the waves are so uneven. The first one lasted about 150 years and the second, 20 years. How long will the third wave last? If it, too, lasts 150 years, that will bring us to the year 2125. By then all the world may be democratic. (Or mankind may have incinerated itself, may have moved to another planet, or may have discovered some new political system better than democracy.) Moreover, the metaphor implies a lack of general progress. Waves rise and fall. But each of the two democratic reverses that followed Huntington's waves was brief, and neither one wiped out all the gains. So perhaps global democracy proceeds by taking several steps forward and then one step back. The trend is still unidirectional.

Huntington, however, offers one statistic that seems to weigh against this conclusion. He says that the proportion of states that were democratic in 1990 (45 percent) was no greater than the proportion in 1922. That is no progress! But wait: based on the looser Freedom House definition ("democratic" polities rather than "free" countries), which is the one that corresponds with Huntington's statistic of 45 percent democracies in 1990, the proportion of states that were democratic had risen to 60 percent by 1994. In other words, the third wave was still rising.

Even aside from this increase, the apparent equivalence between 1922 and 1990 is spurious. In 1922 there were only 64 states; in 1990 there were 165. But the number of peoples had not grown appreciably. The difference was that in 1922 most peoples lived in colonies, and they were not counted as states. The 64 states of that time were mostly the advanced countries. Of those, the proportion that were democratic rose from 45 percent in 1922 to two-thirds in 1990, a significant gain. The additional 101 states counted in 1990 were mostly former imperial possessions. Only a minority, albeit a substantial one, were democratic in 1990, but since virtually none of those were democratic in 1922, that gain was also significant. In short, there was progress all around, but that progress was obscured by asking what percentage of *states* were democratic. Asking the question this way counts a people subjected to a *domestic* dictator as living in a nondemocracy, but a people subjected to a *foreign* dictator did not count at all. By this way of counting, when the Soviet Union absorbed the Baltic states in 1940, the *percentage* of democracies increased! (Instead of four separate dictatorships, that is, there was now just one.)

The United States as Agent of Democracy

If it is true, as I believe I have demonstrated, that the further spread of democracy is both desirable and possible, can the United States be the agency of its growth? Since democracy means self-rule, it seems intuitively plausible that each nation must achieve democracy for itself, that democracy cannot be imposed from without. But such intuition is wrong. Countries have often spread democracy to others, or at least encouraged its development.

The eminent political sociologist, Seymour Martin Lipset, points out that the single strongest correlate of democracy is having been a British colony.[14] That correlation applies not because the territories that Britain happened to colonize were predisposed to democracy, but because British tutelage imparted certain ideas and certain features of government that comported with democracy. Still, the main engine of the remarkable spread of democracy across the globe over the past two centuries has been the United States.

Early Role. Through the nineteenth century, America's role was mostly as a model, inspiring the French Revolution, the constitutions of the Latin American republics, and the programs of British reform movements and workingmen's clubs. Much of the political drama in nineteenth-century Europe revolved around struggles to combat or nurture the virus of democracy that sprang from America.

In the twentieth century, America emerged as the world's mightiest power, and its role in spreading democracy became more direct. In the settlement of World War I, it was America that insisted on the principle of self-determination and on democratic governments. In the years that followed, most of these new democratic regimes collapsed, but in the decades since, most of those countries have become democratic again, building on their earlier experiences. After World War II, America's insistence on self-determination extended to the former colonial world. Again, newly created states were endowed with democratic structures, and again many did not endure. But democracy did endure in the countries America occupied.

Cold War Role. In the cold war against Soviet communism, America found that its national security was entwined with the democratic cause. America had identified itself with that cause before, as when President Wilson declared that we were entering World War I to "make the world safe for democracy." But our competition with the Soviet Union, for whom ideological struggle was second nature, spurred America to much greater ideological intensity. Washington employed propaganda, covert action, foreign aid, and even sometimes military action in waging a fight against its rival and for democracy. American influence was instrumental in bringing about democratization in Latin America; southern, central, and eastern Europe; and several countries in East Asia.

Today's Role

Today, America can and should continue to be an engine of democracy. Although we had success at imposing democracy through military occupations, we cannot, as I have argued in the previous chapter, seek to spread democracy by the sword. If, however, we are drawn into occupying a country by dint of its own aggression, as was the case with Iraq, we would be wise to try to democratize it. The late Turgut Ozal, former president of Turkey, said that he had urged the

United States to do just that in 1991 but was told by Secretary of State Baker that Iraq was incapable of democracy. Ozal, who knew Iraq far better than Baker did, disagreed with that judgment.[15] The United States could have ousted Saddam, pulled together an interim governing coalition of Iraqi dissidents, supervised an open election, and still withdrawn within a year. Even if democracy had not taken hold firmly, there are degrees of democracy and undemocracy (as we see, for example, in the former Soviet republics), and the result might have been something imperfect but considerably more palatable than Saddam's continued rule.

Nonetheless, this situation was rare, and the main work of promoting democracy is peaceful. It consists of private and public diplomacy, overseas broadcasting, education and training, assistance to democratic forces, and other forms of material aid.

Diplomacy. Although external forces can succeed at promoting democracy, ultimately of course, it is indigenous people who must create and sustain it. The role of outsiders is to support and assist democrats and to swell their numbers. Sometimes it is also to persuade existing rulers to yield or relax power. The United States is by far the most influential country in the world. When our leaders speak out about the virtues of democracy and when we demonstrate our earnestness by calibrating democracy into the degree of friendliness we show to regimes and by embracing worthy dissidents, we strengthen those working to democratize their countries. We cannot easily bend other governments to our will, but pressure from Washington weighs heavily on most.

Foreign Aid. Because of the astonishingly rapid increase in the number of democracies in the past twenty years (from 1974 to 1994 the number of Freedom House's "free" countries has gone from 41 to 76, while the number of "democratic" polities has increased even more, from around 45 to 114), the greatest task today lies in helping fledgling democracies to solidify. Despite the perennial unpopularity of foreign aid, this goal is well worth spending money on, if we can spend it effectively.

Unfortunately, the unpopularity of foreign aid is due not only to niggardliness but also to the failure of much of our aid. *Congressional Quarterly* said of the Agency for International Development: "Members of Congress and numerous panels and commissions have pointed to the foreign aid organization as an example of how not to run a government agency."[16] The problem, however, lies deeper than the shortcomings of an agency: it lies in the very notion of "development." Development is a hazy concept whose only clear kernel of meaning is economic growth.

The Clinton administration has compounded the murkiness by replacing the concept of development with "sustainable development." First popularized by the World Commission on Environment and Development, "sustainable development" is an idea at odds with growth. As environmentalists see it, the countries that are already affluent have depleted "nonrenewable" resources. The poor countries will have to find a nobler, and slower, path to affluence that is kinder to the earth. "The planetary ecosystem could not stand," said the commission, "to bring developing countries' energy use up to industrialized country levels." Instead, we must discover a new "energy pathway."[17] But will we help democracy solidify in the newly democratic states by instructing them on the virtues of solar panels and windmills? Or by telling them not to raise their living standards until new technologies have been perfected?

Developing countries would rather learn how to achieve economic growth. The economists Herbert Stein and Murray Foss have illustrated how rare economic growth has been in history: if the civilized world had enjoyed growth at the paltry rate of 1 percent per annum from the time of the Roman Empire, we would each of us be billionaires today.[18] What we do know about growth is that what we thought we knew about it a generation ago was exactly wrong. Then, the prevailing view among "development economists" was that an active public sector was the key to growth. Now, we have substantial evidence that the opposite is true. Although we still have much to learn, the general rule of encouraging the private sector and restraining the public sector is one we can pass along with confidence.

Beyond offering advice, can we use our public sector to aid the private sectors of developing countries? It seems counterintuitive. To be sure, a private sector cannot be created by government. But government can and must create an appropriate framework, especially a legal framework of property rights, contract enforcement, and the like. Moreover, in countries where the economy has been owned by the government, or has been highly regulated, government action is necessary to privatize or deregulate. U.S. foreign aid can provide the technical assistance necessary to carry out such measures. In some cases, too, stand-by funds can provide the backing needed for currency stabilization, as worked so successfully in Poland. In the political realm, technical assistance may also be useful in organizing elections and in setting up functioning parliaments, courts, local governments, and the like.

Probably the most important help we have to offer is in sharing our institutional know-how. In societies in transition, leadership falls disproportionately on the young. In addition to energy and courage, they have the advantage of not having to unlearn old ways. Still, new ways have to be learned or invented, and often, these cannot be learned at home. Through study missions and internships in America, the emergent young leaders can learn how the institutions of our democracy function. Then they can take the lead in adapting these lessons to their own societies.

Broadcasting. For societies still laboring under the weight of dictatorship, probably the most valuable thing we can do to spur them toward democracy is broadcasting. After the iron curtain disappeared, we learned that Western broadcasting to the Soviet bloc had been even more effective than we had dared hope. Lech Walesa said of Radio Free Europe that "its contribution was enormous."[19] Vaclav Havel said the Voice of America was "the most listened-to Czechoslovak radio station."[20]

RFE and VOA perform somewhat different functions. VOA's specialty is news about America as well as world news. RFE concentrates on providing domestic news to each of the countries to which it broadcasts. Side by side, they made a potent combination. People living under dictators benefit from learning about the world outside and about democratic practices exemplified by America, and they need to know the truth about developments in their own countries that their censored media will not report. The emergence of free domestic media in Eastern Europe has eliminated the need for RFE in some countries although not in those, like the former Soviet Union and Yugoslavia, where democratic institutions are still shallow at best.

There is also a crying need to duplicate the RFE model in Asia and the Middle East. VOA already broadcasts to those places. But in countries like China, Burma, Vietnam, Laos, North Korea, Iran, Iraq, Libya, and Syria, a Radio Free Asia or a Radio Free Middle East could play an even more constructively subversive role by broadcasting uncensored domestic news and providing a platform for a range of suppressed opinions. In 1992, a joint presidential-congressional commission, of which I was a member, concluded that Radio Free Asia could be run for the modest sum of $35–39 million a year plus a similar amount in start-up costs.[21]

In time, as satellite dishes grow smaller and cheaper, direct-broadcast television may supplant the role of short-wave radio in evading the censors of closed societies. Already the regimes of Iran and China have imposed criminal penalties against private ownership of dishes. But for at least another decade or two, radio will remain crucial.

The National Endowment for Democracy. Another effective instrument for spurring the growth of democracy in countries still in the thrall of dictatorship is the National Endowment for Democracy and its companion institutes.[22] The theory behind the NED is that democracy does not come about as a result of circumstances but that it is created by democrats. The work of the NED is to find these democrats—in opposition, underground, or exile—and to support their activities with small grants. The NED's funds come from the U.S. Treasury, but the endowment itself is incorporated as an independent organization. The main reason for this arrangement is that the recipients of NED grants might be painted as unpatriotic in their own countries if they accepted money directly from the U.S. government. Having the funds awarded independently by an autonomous endowment provides a modicum of buffer.

Areas of Strategic Interest

The priority targets for America's efforts to foster democracy are not hard to identify. They are the areas of greatest strategic interest to us in the coming years: Russia, China, and the Islamic world.

Russia. Although Russia cannot be the world power that the Soviet Union was, it possesses the world's largest arsenal. These weapons make Russia a source of danger, if only from the possible dispersion of its lethal instruments abroad. For several years already, Russian democracy has teetered at the brink, but so far it has not fallen off. Instead, its elected president and elected parliament seem to muddle along, despite the terrible setback of the ghastly, unnecessary war in Chechnya. The Heritage Foundation, which is usually skeptical toward foreign aid, has commented: "The crisis of Russian democracy is deep. . . .without U.S. aid, however, it will only get worse."[23]

Two kinds of criticism have been made against American aid to

Russia thus far. First, with budget problems here at home, we cannot afford to spend much in Russia. Second, much of the aid has been wasted, either pilfered by corrupt Russian officials or squandered on high-flying Western consultants who fill Moscow's priciest hotels and kindle local resentment. The first criticism is foolish. Given what it may cost us in dollars and pain if Russia goes bad, almost any level of aid is justified if it will help solidify democracy. But the second criticism is more telling: sending money is pointless if it fails to reach its intended useful destination.

Unfortunately, we have no ready gauge of the effectiveness with which aid is used. The task of transforming Russia is immense, and there is little precedent to guide it. Necessarily, Russian reformers and their foreign backers will learn only through trial and error. Preventing aid from being embezzled or siphoned is of course essential, but among the very things we want to help Russia develop are a criminal justice system that effectively constrains corruption and modern practices of management and accounting. We face a chicken-and-egg dilemma: shall we give no aid until those things exist?

The U.S. Agency for International Development has invested heavily in the privatization of Russian industry through the distribution of vouchers. This vast and complex operation could not have been carried out without outside technical help. AID boasts that as a result of its efforts, 70 percent of industry in Russia is now privately owned. Critics point out, however, that possession of shares has not placed meaningful ownership in the hands of citizens: laws on property, a stock market, and other institutions are still weak or absent. In these areas, too, aid can help. Although the voucher program is only a mixed success, it is a step in the direction of meaningful privatization.

Mixed successes are probably the best we can hope for in Russia, but they are worth the price. We ought to continue offering technical support in overhauling economic and governmental institutions, in combating crime, and in dismantling weapons. We should bear in mind, too, that the essential political problem is that the genuine democrats are too few and too weak. Small grants to underwrite pro-democracy parties, civic groups, clubs, publications, and the like can be very important. The NED and its allied organizations can give this kind of help more effectively than AID and the apolitical contractors on whom it relies. Some of the aid funds for Russia therefore ought to be shifted accordingly.

Diplomatically, we should continue, as both the Bush and the

Clinton administrations have done, to stroke Russia. But we should draw a line at allowing our relations with other nations to be hostage to Russia's pleasure, such as on the issue of NATO expansion. That, Russians should know, is out of bounds. Also out of bounds is Russia's backing of Serbian aggression, a throwback to pan-Slav mischief incompatible with a role of legitimate international leadership.

One of the best ways we can hedge against things going bad in Russia is to aid Ukraine. With a population of more than 50 million and a history entwined with Russia's, Ukraine is the heart of the "near abroad." If Ukraine remains independent, the reconstitution of the USSR—the avenue of resurgent Russian imperialism—is blocked. The Russian army's difficulties in Chechnya, with a population of less than 1 million, suggest that it could not in the foreseeable future retake Ukraine by force. But Ukraine could fall into its lap, as Belarus has done, as a result of its own political and economic failures. After several years of immobility, Ukraine began a series of far-reaching reforms following the election of Leonid Kuchma as president in July 1994. We should give the Ukrainian reformers all the help we can.

China. If China continues to grow rich without growing free, it will pose a mortal threat to world peace in the twenty-first century. Encouragingly, the events in Beijing's Tiananmen Square and in eighty other cities in 1989, although they ended tragically, demonstrated that a large part, probably the majority, of urban Chinese yearn for democracy. Moreover, that sentiment seems to have strong, though silent, sympathy within the Communist Party itself. At a minimum, the strength of Communist commitment has eroded. As sinologist Andrew Nathan puts it: "The people who operate the control network no longer have faith in the ideology."[24] The combined effect of ideological erosion within the establishment and a popular yearning for democracy means that "democratic reform will always present itself as a possible tactic to factions seeking to improve their power positions," says Nathan.[25]

On May 26, 1994, President Clinton moved to "delink" trade from human rights in America's relations with China rather than impose sanctions.[26] Since he had made explicit public threats that China had defied, this decision humiliated America and damaged its credibility. Nonetheless, there was a strong case against trade sanctions on the grounds that China's flourishing commerce worked to weaken the tight control of its regime. For that reason, many Chinese dissidents opposed trade sanctions. A far more effective tool for democratizing China would be Radio Free Asia. This institution could in itself begin the process of building a democratic China by serving as a forum where a variety of views could contend. And it could set a model for free journalism in China, employing some of the open-minded Chinese journalists who found themselves in exile as a result of their honest reportage.

The Islamic World. In the Islamic world democracy has made fewest inroads. And it is there, too, that a vibrant antidemocratic ideology is still on the rise. This ideology is sometimes referred to as fundamentalism, but a better term is *Islamism,* or political or radical Islam. What is distinct about the bearers of this ideology is not that they observe religious laws strictly but that they put politics at the center. True, Islam does not recognize a distinction between the religious and the governmental spheres, but nowhere does the Koran instruct believers to blow up airplanes. However strictly one wishes to follow scriptural injunctions, believers have a choice between focusing on the spiritual and focusing on the political. And political inferences are not self-revealing: they necessarily require interpretation if they are to be applied to the contemporary world.

Even if the near-term prospects for democracy in the Islamic world are weak, we still have compelling cause to support moderate and humane versions of Islam against the radicals. Nowhere are the differences between the varying degrees of antidemocratic practices more dramatic. Some regimes in Islamic countries, though autocratic, tolerate a modicum of dissenting opinion and the practice of non-Islamic religions, do not kill and torture their peaceful opponents, do not sponsor terrorism, and do not define the West or America as their sworn enemy. We have a large interest in seeing those kinds of attitudes prevail over their bloodthirsty opposites.

In 1994, National Security Adviser Anthony Lake spelled out a policy of "dual containment" toward the mutual enemies Iran and Iraq.[27] But the truth was that our policy toward Iraq went beyond containment: we aimed for the ouster of Saddam Hussein.[28] In contrast, in the case of Iran we stressed, as Under Secretary of State Peter Tarnoff put it, that we "are not seeking to overthrow the government of Iran."[29] Assistant Secretary Robert Pelletreau went so far as to declare that Washington regarded the Iranian regime as "permanent,"[30] and the State Department went out of its way to anathematize the

Iranian People's Mujahadeen, one opposition group aiming for the violent overthrow of the regime.[31] These acts and comments were undoubtedly signals calculated to warm relations with the "moderates" whom Washington supposed were in power in Tehran. Apparently, those efforts were in vain, for in 1995 the Clinton administration toughened its stance. Spurred by the possibility that Congress would impose comprehensive sanctions, the administration imposed a ban on the purchase of Iranian oil.

Still, the search for moderates among Islamic extremists was not abandoned. It merely changed venue. U.S. diplomats opened a dialogue with representatives of Algeria's Islamic Salvation Front (FIS), with an eye to improving relations with Islamic movements throughout the region. This quest did not begin with the Clinton administration. It was the Reagan administration that sold arms to Tehran in exchange for hostages. Reagan never could acknowledge that he had done so, since such dealings were a betrayal of everything his presidency stood for, much as if Lincoln had secretly trafficked in slaves.

Yet Reagan, too, was not the first to chase the mirage of moderates. The practice began long before the advent of Islamism. It used to focus on Communist regimes. President Truman confided to Secretary of State Edward Stettinius after Potsdam that he was concerned about Stalin's health since Stalin's passing might lead to a takeover by the hard-liners.[32] In a sense, Stalin was a "moderate" among the Bolsheviks as compared with Trotsky, his "radical" rival. This point only illustrates how small our stake is in the tactical differences that separate factions within movements whose underlying goal is to destroy us. Perhaps the "moderates" will be more effective enemies.

Just as it was futile to seek reconciliation with the Communists (until, under Gorbachev, they sued for peace), so it is with the Islamists. Their core commitments are to theocracy at home and anti-Westernism abroad. Wherever they get the chance, they persecute mercilessly the very people in their societies with whom we have the most cause for empathy. As for their attitude toward us, we can do little to win them over, since, as Bernard Lewis has shown, their "hatred . . . becomes a rejection of Western civilization as such, not only what it does but what it is, and the principles and values that it practices and professes."[33]

While Islam is one of the world's great faiths that may endure in perpetuity, Islamism is a fad that could pass as quickly as the fads of pan-Arabism or Arab socialism. Our goal should be to help it to an early grave before it hurts too many more people or seriously damages world peace. We can do three things:

- First, through broadcasting, cultural exchanges, and the NED we should nurture voices of liberalism and democracy within the Islamic world. These voices need not be secular. A way must be found to reconcile democracy and Islam, just as ways have been found to reconcile democracy with Catholicism and Confucianism.
- Second, through diplomacy, economic and military aid, and intelligence activities, we should help pro-Western regimes that are besieged by Islamists. Although these regimes are not democratic, the Islamists who would replace them would be even less so. Turkey, the Islamic world's sole democracy, deserves our special favor.
- Third, we should work to bring down the theocracy in Iran. For decades we were beset by Communist movements all over the world, but when the heart of the Communist octopus stopped beating in Moscow, all the tentacles withered. To be sure, the Islamist movements are made up of indigenous people and thrive on native grievances. The same was said, just as truthfully, about the Communist movements. But Iran supports them, and it is their model. It is also a country with more assets than any of the others where Islamists bid for power. If Islamist rule collapses in Tehran, the movement everywhere will lose its potency.

Conclusion. These are the three threats that may roil our peace in the years ahead: a Russia that reverts to dictatorship and bellicosity or that yields to anarchy spewing forth a vast arsenal; a China still hardened by Communist politics but enriched by capitalist economics that seeks its era of dominance; an Islamic world ruled in large part by fanatics who hate the West, trading oil revenues for weapons of mass destruction. These are threats, as I have argued in chapter 10, against which we should keep up our military might and preparedness. But far better than having to address them militarily would be to defuse them through political means. The best balm we have is the spread of democracy.

·13·

FREE TRADE

Just as America can foster a more peaceful and hospitable global environment through promoting the spread of democracy, it can further these goals as well by renewing its lagging leadership of the quest for free trade. Although the degree to which economic frustration is a "root cause" of all manner of other social discontents or destructive ambitions[1] is easy to overstate, the general improvement in living conditions undoubtedly makes many human conflicts more tractable. And no one doubts that free trade, although it may harm particular individuals or companies, conduces to worldwide prosperity.

Professional economists are as near to unanimous on this point as on anything. And the belief is corroborated by the world's experience since World War II. The United States led in crafting international economic institutions, including the General Agreement on Tariffs and Trade (GATT), which sponsored a progressive lowering of trade barriers. Over forty-odd years, average tariffs were reduced from about 45 percent to about 3 percent. From 1950 through 1975, the volume of world trade expanded by 500 percent. World economic growth proceeded at a rate just under 5 percent. "Trade between nations had never been so free," said Anne Krueger, president of the American Economic Association, and "world GNP [grew] at rates never before realized over such a long period of time."[2]

In this period, Western Europe and Japan rebuilt their devastated economies and infrastructure. At the same time, the United States enjoyed a quarter-century (from 1948 to 1973) of its most rapid growth. And, too, a part of the third world—at least those few countries that perceived the advantage of focusing their economies on foreign trade—began the ascent from poverty.

New Trade Barriers

As the 1970s wore on into the 1980s, however, these felicitous trends abated. The growth of trade slowed as did the growth of the world economy. The progressive liberalization of trade stalled.

Although tariffs on the whole did not increase, new forms of impediments to trade came into more common use. These included measures against "dumping," and others that penalized imports that were said to have been unduly subsidized by their home governments. "Voluntary" agreements were extracted by stronger countries from weaker ones to limit their exports of various products or to buy more imports. In the eyes of economists, such measures are even more harmful than tariffs because they create greater inefficiencies, because they are inherently discriminatory against third parties, and because their economic costs are harder to measure and assess.

Fear of Japanese Economic Strength

Instead of continuing its historic role as the champion of free trade, the United States joined in the barrier building. The impetus behind this effort came mostly from the new "yellow peril" panic. A few generations earlier, white Americans, especially in the West, were seized with the fear that low-wage Asian immigrants would take all the jobs. This time, the notion reappeared with the wrinkle that the Asians would take our jobs without even setting foot in the United States. They would simply send over their low-cost goods and drive all American manufacturers out of business.

John Connally, the former secretary of commerce, first elevated the new yellow peril to a national political issue. He declared during his campaign for the 1980 Republican presidential nomination that unless the Japanese changed their trading practices, they should "sit on the docks of Yokohama in their own Toyotas, watching their own television sets."[3] The thought was by no means restricted to one party. Walter Mondale, the 1984 Democratic presidential candidate (and later ambassador to Japan), warned that "our kids" would have nothing "to do [except] sweep up around the Japanese computers."[4] Nor was the rhetoric restricted to politicians. Journalist Theodore White warned that the Japanese were "dismantling American industry."[5] Columnist William Pfaff said that America's relationship with Japan had taken on a "colonial quality,"[6] with America as the colony. And a host of other writers penned popular books making similar points.[7]

Such views were scarcely unrepresentative. A 1989 Gallup poll asked Americans to identify the world's top economic power; twice as many named Japan as named the United States.[8] And a 1990 survey of the general public and of opinion leaders, conducted by the Chicago Council on Foreign Relations, found that "both [groups] believe the economic power of Japan will be a more critical threat to American vital interests in the next few years than will Soviet military power."[9]

The Japan scare was not made up out of whole cloth. Neither, of course, was the earlier alarm: there really were a large number of immigrants from Asia willing to work for low wages. But like the old scare, the new one was vastly exaggerated and inspired a variety of responses that were foolish or ugly. Japan, and in its train several smaller Pacific Rim states, did enjoy a burst of astonishingly rapid growth. The growth was fueled by exports, especially to the vast American market. Japanese and other Asian manufacturers developed a mastery in the production of electrical appliances and automobiles that enabled them to turn out better goods than American companies, often at lower prices. And, moreover, in a variety of industries, American businesses found it impossible to penetrate the Japanese market. As analysts compared Japan's rate of growth with America's in the 1960s and 1970s, they could readily see, by extrapolation, that the Japanese economy would overtake ours perhaps before the end of the century. Indeed by the late 1980s, some claimed that in a sense Japan was already ahead. "Japan has, as I predicted it would, become the undisputed world economic champion," crowed Clyde Prestowitz in 1989.[10]

The new yellow-peril scare evoked three destructive responses. One was protectionism. If American firms were succumbing to competition from imports, then those imports should be blocked or reduced to protect American jobs. The second was Japan bashing, which consisted both of obloquy—especially the charge that Japan had gained its advantage through unsavory practices—and of efforts to coerce Japan into purchasing additional quantities of various American products and restraining its own commerce. The third was mimicry, expressed in a spate of proposals that America transform its methods of trade and its broader economic institutions to resemble the Japanese model more closely.

Protectionism

Protectionist measures did not consist in the main of increases in tariffs. In part, they consisted of legislation empowering the U.S. trade representative to designate countries as unfair traders. Countries thus named were then asked to reach "voluntary" agreements to limit their exports to America. To encourage them to acquiesce, we threatened punitive duties, although such duties normally would violate America's obligations under GATT. In addition, protectionist measures included "antidumping" provisions and "countervailing" duties. Dumping is the practice of selling goods below cost for the purpose of driving competitors from the marketplace so that the dumper can gain a monopoly and then charge exorbitant prices. Countervailing duties are intended to stymie the efforts of a foreign government to secure an inflated market share for its industries by subsidizing its exports.

One wonders how many foreign companies would be so bold as to try to gain control over the American market by selling under cost. Assuming that they could gain their objective and then boost prices to make up the initial loss, how long could they keep new competitors out? The risk would seem all the more daunting in the teeth of the antidumping laws. And yet, hundreds of foreign companies have been penalized for dumping. By 1990, nearly 10 percent of imports were covered by antidumping orders.[11]

What can explain this? The concept of dumping has become badly distorted. Any domestic manufacturer undersold by a foreign competitor can bring a charge of dumping, and, under the Trade Act of 1974, the burden of proof rests to a considerable extent on the accused. The foreign firm may be found guilty if it sold at a price even slightly below an estimate of its costs, without any proof that its aim was to corner the market, or even if it sold above cost but below the price it charged somewhere else. A seller may have a number of innocuous reasons for offering goods below cost, such as selling off perishable or out-of-season goods. Such reasons would imply no monopolistic purpose and, in domestic commerce, would violate none of America's restraint-of-trade laws. Indeed, if an importer violated these laws, he could be taken to court just like anyone doing business in the United States. As a result of the explosion of antidumping measures and other administrative restraints, the proportion of American imports that fell under restrictions other than tariffs rose from 12 percent in 1980 to 21 percent in 1984.

Japan Bashing

Japan bashing affected both imports and exports. In a string of hard-nosed negotiations in the 1980s, America extracted Tokyo's pledge to limit its export of automobiles to the United States to 1.68 million per year and to encourage its industries to purchase 20 percent of their semiconductors from America, among other concessions. No sooner had the Uruguay Round of GATT negotiations been completed, and the World Trade Organization come into existence, than U.S. Trade Representative Mickey Kantor announced new threats against Japan. One of the signal features of the WTO is its enhanced machinery for resolving disputes, but it was ignored by Kantor. Instead, he threatened to impose a punitive duty of 100 percent on luxury automobiles from Japan unless the Japanese agreed to buy a fixed number of auto parts from America and to provide dealerships in Japan for American cars. Japan refused these demands, and after a tense confrontation Washington backed down.

Mimicry

As for mimicry, the American government has not yet explicitly adopted any measures imitative of the Japanese economic system. But the Clinton administration, despite its leadership in behalf of the North American Free Trade Agreement (NAFTA) and GATT, has moved toward "managed trade," or at least to a much deeper involvement by government, including the president himself, in securing purchases of American goods. This is a step in the direction of "strategic trade," a concept forcefully advocated by some foreign policy specialists and a small number of dissident economists, including Laura D'Andrea Tyson, whom Clinton appointed as head of the Council of Economic Advisers.[12]

The strategic trade economists argue that free trade is only "optimal" in a setting of "perfect competition." Because of such reasons as economies of scale and the high research costs involved in advanced industries, contemporary international trade, they say, does not fit the model of perfect competition. The reality of "imperfect competition" creates the possibility that free trade will not be optimal. Instead, government can intervene in the import and export markets to maximize its nation's benefit. Put more concretely, the argument holds that the governments of Japan and the other fast-growing Pacific states helped to nurture "strategic" industries, to promote exports, and to discourage imports. This tactic, it is claimed, has been the key to their success.

The advocates of strategic trade believe that the American government should identify industries or technologies that will lead or dominate commercial life in the years ahead. It should then lend the weight of public resources to strengthening those selected and should help them seize the advantage in export markets. In addition, according to some strategic trade advocates, the shift of the American economy from manufactures to services is worrisome because jobs in manufacturing tend to pay more or because manufacturing has greater implications for the nation's economic, technological, or military well-being.[13] Therefore, they advocate protecting domestic manufacturing against foreign competition.

The most respected economist who advocated strategic trade was Paul Krugman of Stanford University. But several years of empirical and analytical investigation led Krugman to reverse his position substantially. While he still believes that government intervention could, in theory, yield results superior to those of free trade, he concludes that in practice such intervention is likely to have the opposite effect.[14] Not only has Krugman broken with the strategic trade advocates, but he has become one of their most devastating critics. He has challenged the very notion of national "competitiveness" that underlies their thesis. "The idea that a country's economic fortunes are largely determined by its success on world markets . . . is flatly wrong," he says.[15] Yet despite the defection of Krugman, some strategic traders soldier on.

The protectionist reaction to the so-called yellow peril has already done harm to the American economy. Strategic trade would do a great deal of additional harm. And Japan bashing may in the long run prove the most damaging of all, for it will injure not only our economy but also our security.

The Cost of Protectionism

During the debate about ratification of NAFTA, the yellow peril turned into the "brown peril." Treaty opponents like Ross Perot argued that American jobs would flow to Mexico so fast that a "giant sucking sound" would be heard. Outside of automotives and high-technology areas, it is not Japan that the protectionists fear but poor countries whose low-wage labor may enable their factories to produce many goods more cheaply than American firms can do. Ironically, as Jagdish Bhagwati and Vivek Dehejia have reminded us, for several postwar decades, it was the poor countries who erected barriers against imports on the grounds that their industries needed to be shielded against competition from the advanced countries.[16] This theory was so widely accepted that it even enjoyed the imprimatur of the United Nations.[17] After leading these countries to stagnation or even deeper poverty, the theory has finally been abandoned by most of the third world only to be adopted now by some advanced countries.

While protectionism may save some jobs and businesses, it does so at considerable cost to the total U.S. economy. The "voluntary" agreement of Japan to limit its car exports to America is estimated to have increased the cost of each new Japanese car purchased here by $2,400 and of American-made cars by $750 to $1,000.[18] Barriers to the import of clothing and textiles are estimated by the U.S. International Trade Commission to cost the American economy $18 billion a year.[19] According to one estimate, every job saved in the auto industry through protection costs the American people $105,000,[20] and in other industries the cost ranges from $42,000 per job in textiles to $1 million in carbon steel.[21] Ironically, although the mantra of the strategic trade advocates is that the government should "pick winners" (that is, promote industries that will shape the future), those who support industrial protection are in effect encouraging the government to back losers, propping up industries that cannot compete in open markets.

While protection aids some, it damages others. Anne Krueger points out, for example, that "most jobs associated with automobiles are in industries servicing them."[22] Trade barriers that drive up the price of cars reduce the number of cars in use. Therefore, while preserving some jobs making cars, we reduce the number of other jobs in related industries. Some items whose prices have been driven up by import restrictions, such as steel, are important components of products that may be exported. Because the components are more expensive, the finished products will be too. Therefore, American exporters will sell fewer of them and hence employ fewer people. Thus, for example, because sugar is a key ingredient in so many foods, it is estimated that the number of manufacturing jobs destroyed by the sugar import quota exceeds the total number of American sugar growers.[23]

Consequences of Protectionism

What if the foreign exporters against whom we are closing our markets persuade their governments to retaliate? Then the loss of sales incurred by our export industries would compound the damage caused by our own barriers. Indeed, the U.S. enthusiasm for imposing nontariff barriers like antidumping duties has helped stimulate their growth worldwide. Of course, our government could try to forestall retaliation by warning the other government that if it retaliates against American goods, then we would take further measures against its goods. Such would be the path to a trade war that would cause still deeper economic damage, with possibly dangerous diplomatic consequences, as well.

Even if things do not get that far out of hand, the American turn toward protectionism is especially consequential because of America's role over the past sixty years as the leading promoter of free trade. If we encourage the practice of closing markets, no one else is likely to resist the trend.

Argument against Strategic Trade

While import barriers constitute a time-honored form of government intervention in the economy, the apostles of strategic trade propose new forms of intervention that go far beyond American traditions. As Clyde Prestowitz put it, "It will not suffice to recast U.S. international economic policy; the United States must develop a wholly new economic strategy in which international competitiveness is a natural extension of the revitalization of the domestic economy."[24] The aim would be to "optimize the structure of the U.S. economy."

What it means to optimize the structure of the economy is not clear, and not all strategic trade advocates would be of one mind. Still, most propound "industrial policy," that is, government subsidies to various industries. In addition, Prestowitz advocates creating "a national health care program," which he says would "contain costs and free resources."[25] Fred Bergsten, too, proposes to "cut health care costs" to "improve the competitive performance of the American economy."[26] But how can those costs be cut except by government takeover or control of health care, a large slice of the U.S. economy?

Prestowitz has other novel ideas, like employing "the world's greatest educational institution, the U.S. Army, in an emergency adult education effort."[27] The goal would be a worthy one, to eliminate functional illiteracy, but using the military to tackle domestic social and economic problems smacks of statism. It lends credence to Henry Nau's observation that "managed trade is a backdoor to a managed economy."[28]

What is wrong with managed or strategic trade is the same thing that is wrong with a managed economy. A free economy produces inequities and waste. For that reason, socialism has been so alluring to so many. We can make more "rational" choices, say the socialists, and hypothetically that is right. But the idea fails because no government, no single center, can possibly command enough information about the infinity of individual economic preferences to enable its judgments to be more rational than the results yielded by markets. So, too, with that part of the economy that consists of foreign trade. Hypothetically, if the government knew everything, it could make the best choices, but since it cannot have such knowledge, it is better to allow choices to be determined in the marketplace.

Moreover, if the government managed trade, its decisions would not reflect even the best information at its disposal. Rather, they would reflect politics. Various interests would fight for government interventions of benefit to themselves. Our system works that way and was meant to work that way. A rare exception is the Federal Reserve Board, which is structured deliberately to insulate decisions about monetary policy and interest rates from politics. This separation generates a tension with the political process manifested by episodic and awkward invitations from presidents to Federal Reserve chairmen for private tête-à-têtes and by occasional calls in Congress for lifting the Fed's independence. If the government were to involve itself more heavily in subsidizing industries and exports and protecting domestic producers, such power would inevitably be subjected to the political process. Otherwise, it would derogate from the democratic nature of our system, and Americans would never stand for it.

This example highlights the point that what works for other countries may not work for us.[29] The Japanese, for example, have by tradition a powerful bureaucracy independent of the democratic process. They also have a tradition of obedience, which may facilitate government-business partnership, that Americans do not share. Indeed, the reason that many Americans go into business is to be their own boss.

The differences are not just cultural but also situational. Countries trying to catch up economically, such as the "tigers" of the Pacific Rim, have models to emulate. Broadly speaking, they would like their economies eventually to resemble America's or Germany's or Japan's. Knowing where they are going may make it feasible for government to make some technological and industrial choices. But what is our model? Because America is the most advanced country, we are peering out into an unknown future. How could our bureaucrats foretell its needs? What alternative is there to the trial and error of the marketplace?[30]

If we want to benefit from the lessons of the Asian model, it is not government intervention in the economy that we should imitate. The real keys to Asian success have been low budget deficits and inflation, high savings and investment, and education and self-discipline. As Paul Krugman puts it, "If there is a secret to Asian growth, it is simply deferred gratification."[31] Now, there is an area in which we have something to learn.

Japan's Economic Problems

If all these arguments against trying to mimic Japan are somewhat abstract, one is quite empirical. Just as Clyde Prestowitz crowned Japan the "undisputed world economic champion," the trends began to change. The Japanese real estate market collapsed, as did the stock market, which has lost more than half its value since 1990. Japanese economic growth slowed in the 1980s to a rate only slightly ahead of America's, and in the 1990s, Japan sank into a recession deeper and longer than the one America suffered in 1991–1992.

In contrast, the American economy has shown many signs of health. America has regained its place as the world's largest exporter. In the past several years, U.S. manufacturing has registered robust gains in productivity. And the share of new U.S. patents given to American inventors has climbed during the 1990s after declining the two previous decades.[32]

As for "competitiveness," the Japanese government surveyed 110 critical technologies in 1991, concluding that America led in 43, Japan in 33, and other countries in the rest.[33] In 1992, America regained the lead in the production of semiconductors that it had lost to Japan in the mid-1980s. And in the *World Competitiveness Report,* published by a Swiss research institute, the United States regained the overall lead over Japan.[34] In short, the trends that led to the yellow-peril scare have abated or reversed. The long-term effectiveness of Japan's way of doing business is less than was imagined. And America's ability to adapt to a more challenging economic environment is greater than was believed. We could make as compelling a case that the Japanese need to adopt more of our ways as that we need to adopt theirs.

Although Japan-the-juggernaut has given way to Japan-the-leaky ship, Japan bashing remains in style. The Clinton administration has taken a stentorian tone toward Japan, issuing demands and threats that the Japanese have resisted, casting bilateral relations in their darkest light in decades. Instead of seeking changes in specific Japanese practices that the United States believes are deleterious, Washington has simply demanded that Japan import given amounts of American products. Echoing the double-talk that so poisoned domestic debate over affirmative action, Deputy Secretary of the Treasury Roger Altman declared that "the United States is not seeking targets," rather "goals" and "measurable results."[35] But when Japanese purchases of U.S. semiconductors dipped below the agreed "goal," USTR Mickey Kantor demanded that the Japanese government take action.

To many, it is obvious that the Japanese have unfairly restricted American access to their markets. But to economists, the issue is not so clear. Most of them, says Jagdish Bhagwati, "remain . . . skeptical of [such] claims."[36] Japanese culture and American are at opposite ends of the spectrum of openness. While America is a nation of immigrants, Japan is insular, not even accepting as "Japanese" those of Korean stock who have resided in Japan for several generations. Some of the trade barriers that foreign exporters experience in Japan may have nothing to do with collusion by business or government but merely with the preference of Japanese consumers for native products. This preference violates no trade rule.

The World Trade Organization has procedures, as GATT did, for impartially adjudicating complaints to determine whether an exporter's frustrations are the result of innocent or tortious conduct. Instead of relying on these mechanisms, Washington has flatly demanded that Tokyo command its citizens and companies to purchase American goods.

Such a demand is bound to chafe the Japanese. And, too, they have reason to resent the hypocrisy that leads us to demand that they open their markets to such products as American beef, while at home we protect our own beef producers against foreign competition. Assistant Secretary of State Winston Lord, an Asia specialist, was reported to have written privately to Secretary of State Christopher in 1994 warning that American actions on trade among other issues "risk corroding our positive image in the region."[37]

The administration's line was that security relations with Japan were "solid" and could be sealed off from economic issues. This view was either disingenuous or self-delusional. No doubt the administration hoped that it could attack Japan on the economic front without damaging other interests. But it must have realized it was risking a serious strain. It was willing to take this risk, apparently on the grounds that, as Deputy Secretary Altman put it, there was "a diminished need for a bulwark against Soviet expansionism."[38]

Security Interests

Although Soviet expansionism has faded, that decline is counterbalanced by an increased need for a bulwark against China and for help in dealing with North Korea's nuclear program. Indeed, if it is true, as many believe, including most Japan bashers, that Asia's economic growth is making it the new cockpit of world politics, then the importance of Japan to American security interests will grow larger, not smaller.

Our relationship cannot but be damaged by playing hardball with Japan and treating it like an enemy. Even if tensions with Japanese leaders can be papered over, Japan is a democracy, and the ill will we create with the Japanese public cannot easily be reversed. Public opinion polls taken by the Gallup organization and *Yomiuri Shimbun* and by Louis Harris and *Asahi Shimbun* show that at least since the election of Bill Clinton, majorities or pluralities of Japanese think relations between the two nations are not good.[39] Ultimately, leaders of democratic countries reflect popular sentiments. Columnist Jim Hoagland shrewdly observed that Japanese Trade Minister Ryutaro Hashimoto may have strengthened his prospects of becoming prime minister by facing down Mickey Kantor's threat of punitive duties on luxury cars. If Hashimoto triumphs, says Hoagland, "he will be the first postwar Japanese prime minister whose power will stem from his determination to defy the United States rather than his ability to work smoothly with Washington."[40]

More than our relations with Japan will suffer from our Japan bashing. Jagdish Bhagwati has commented that our "trade threats create the impression, now worldwide, that America believes in the law of the jungle rather than the rule of law."[41] Indeed, Secretary of Commerce Ron Brown virtually proclaimed as much when he said: "I don't want a level playing field. . . . I want it tilted toward us."[42] Perhaps because they were offended by such attitudes, other nations tended to side with Japan against us, even though we claimed we were trying to open the Japanese market to everyone.

NAFTA, GATT, and the WTO

While Clinton has mishandled relations with Japan, he deserves credit for securing passage of NAFTA and the agreements concluded in the Uruguay Round of GATT. He had to beat back opposition within his own party from the likes of House Majority Leader Dick Gephardt, who proclaimed he was concerned about "job losses—whether they be net or gross."[43]

In palliating Democratic opposition, Clinton insisted on adding provisions on labor standards and environmental issues to NAFTA and putting them on the agenda for the next GATT (or now, the World Trade Organization) negotiations. But poor countries cannot be expected to match the standards of the developed countries in these realms. Congressman Gephardt warned that "environmental protection can be seriously damaged in the quest for economic growth."[44] But it is equally true that growth can be damaged in the quest for environmental protection. The developed countries set about repairing their environments after they achieved affluence. The less-developed countries do not want to slow their ascent from poverty for the sake of the environment. Who are we to stand in their way?

While both the NAFTA and the GATT ratifications served to put the American body politic back on the track of free trade, the two agreements are in tension with each other. The rules of GATT specifically allow "free trade areas," such as NAFTA or the European Community, but these are exceptions to the fundamental GATT principle that each nation apply trade rules equally to all others. Instead of a global regime of open trade, some prognosticators see the emergence of three trading blocs: the Americas, Europe, and Asia. Such a division would leave out some of the poorest countries, mostly in Africa, and weaken their prospects for growth. And it could breed new political or military tensions between the blocs.

A happier prospect is the continued development of the WTO.

In addition to creating the WTO and cutting tariffs around the world by about one-third, the Uruguay Round Agreement extended the basic barrier-reducing principles of GATT to foreign investment, service industries, and agriculture,[45] and it added protections of intellectual property rights. It also strengthened procedures for settling disputes.

Dispute resolution is especially important. The best argument that could be made for the kind of threats America has brandished against Japan is that by threatening to close off our open market, we could compel the other side to open its closed market. The problem with this method (even if this is a fair description of the situation between the two countries) is that it is, as Frank Lavin has pointed out, the trade equivalent of the mutual assured destruction (MAD) doctrine.[46] The threat may work if our bluff is not called, but we will do ourselves damage if we have to carry it out. And it engenders resentment. The WTO, in contrast, will provide a mechanism to open closed markets without the risk or the acrimony. For that reason it is so regrettable that in the first months after the new system went into effect, the United States ignored the WTO and reverted to big-stick tactics against Japan.

Oddly, some conservatives have raised objection to the WTO on the grounds that it would impinge on American sovereignty and that it would prove as noisome as that other international organization, the United Nations. The first point is vacuous. Every treaty we sign reduces our freedom of action if we obey it, as do all contracts. The WTO will be no different. The second objection is stronger insofar as the United Nations has brought us unforeseen problems. But the WTO is simply the extension of GATT and its secretariat, which have been around as long as the United Nations and have shown none of its irksome characteristics.

American Leadership in Free Trade

We ought to see the WTO as an ideal arena for resuming American leadership in behalf of free trade. A natural agenda exists in extending the WTO principles to industries still not covered, negotiating additional rounds of tariff reductions or elimination, strengthening protections of intellectual property, making the dispute procedures work effectively, and bringing in new members who are willing to play by the rules.

A key to exercising effective leadership in the WTO will be to reverse the foolish trends within our own trade policies that arose from the yellow-peril scare. Even within the rules of the WTO, nations have a lot of leeway in creating or dismantling barriers. We ought to set an example of liberal trading practices. Liberalization will mean lower prices for American consumers, and economists in substantial majority agree that it is economically wise. It will bring other benefits as well.

Alfred E. Eckes, the former chairman of the U.S. International Trade Commission, argues that with the cold war over, America can "stop trading access to the American market for foreign policy favors."[47] But in addition to its faulty economics, this argument is wrong politically. In foreign policy, economic concessions are a cheap coin. The other main currency is blood. The world remains dangerous, and peace and security must be top priorities. If they can be advanced at the expense of economics, it is a wise exchange.

The protectionists and free traders usually begin with the premise that economics have become supreme.[48] But this notion is senseless. Most people devote much of their attention and energy to making or managing money. As soon as a loved one dies or is in danger, however, the true order of life's priorities is starkly revealed. This story has been told thousands of times. And no wise person puts his pocketbook ahead of health care, life insurance, and other forms of protection. So it is with nations. Economics can be supreme as long as security is assured. But as long as security is uncertain, economics are secondary.

Keeping our markets open may be the best method we have for aiding developing countries and countries newly liberated from communism. And it will strengthen our ties with allies and earn us good will with others. The good will is important because, as I have explained in chapters 10 and 11, America has a unique role to play in protecting peace and security through its military strength. Most nations will be glad that we do so, but still many will resent and envy our supreme power. We can soften such sentiments if in the economic realm we are cooperative and not bullying.

If there were a cost to pay to advance these foreign policy goals, it would be worth paying. But in fact, liberalizing our trade practices benefits us economically at the same time that it benefits us politically. As such, it is as close an approximation as there is to what economists say cannot exist: a free lunch.

·14·

CONCLUSION

Since the cold war ended, Americans have felt tempted to reduce their international engagement. Full-blown isolationism appeals to few of us, despite the oratorical powers of Patrick Buchanan. But the call to put the world's troubles at arm's length, to lay down burdens, and, as Congressman Barney Frank put it, to "be nicer to ourselves," is seductive both to liberals and to conservatives.[1]

In 1995, President Clinton accused the new Republican congressional majority of isolationism, and he was right insofar as it slashed foreign programs while treating many domestic entitlements more gingerly and needlessly cutting taxes and insofar as the House voted to dismantle important foreign policy instruments, such as the U.S. Information Agency. But who was Clinton to talk? The plan pushed by Senator Jesse Helms to abolish foreign policy agencies originated with Clinton's own secretary of state. And a large part of the isolationism of which Clinton accused the Republicans consisted of restraints on U.S. involvement with the United Nations, an involvement swelled by Clinton's own isolationist wish to deflect responsibilities for global security so that he might concentrate on "our own problems."

The voice that beckons us home is singing a siren song, for we cannot go home again. We can close bases and bring some American soldiers back to the states. But we cannot return to being just another country among countries. That role has not been available to us for eighty years, and it is less available now than ever before. We emerged

206

from World War I with the potential to be the world's strongest power, but we allowed the potential to waste, and the balance of power became unsettled. We emerged from World War II sharing supremacy with the Soviet Union; had we abdicated, as we were tempted to do, the results would have been even more disastrous. Now we have emerged from the cold war as the lone superpower, carrying a weight in world affairs unmatched in history except perhaps by the Roman or British Empires at their height. If we refuse to exercise the leadership that accrues naturally from our position, world politics will remain in volatile disequilibrium. It will be impossible for any other power, certainly any democratic power, to find the confidence to lead from under our shadow.

The Tragedy of Bosnia

Bosnia illustrates this point tragically. The war in the Balkans was the great test of leaving leadership to Europe and the United Nations. That conflict, however, revealed the sad decay of the United Nations from an organization whose ideal was to unite nations against an aggressor to achieve collective security into one where nations unite behind the aggressor to achieve peace at any price. That was the plain meaning of the public complaints by Yasushi Akashi, the highest UN representative in Bosnia, that NATO airstrikes to protect UN-declared "safe areas" would discourage the Muslims from giving up.[2]

The Bosnia debacle also revealed the weakness of the other great democracies, which allowed themselves to be held hostage by Serbia. They absorbed one humiliation after another, while stoically enduring the suffering of others. They could not fight without the United States. They could not even withdraw, so we were informed, without our coming to extricate them.

Our Unique Opportunity

Even if we could return to the status of a nation like any other, why would we want to? Owen Harries says that America's "dirty little secret" is that it enjoys its status as superpower. What is dirty about it? And why should it be a secret? The Pax Americana, if you want to call it that, is unlike the Pax Romana or Pax Britannica in that it consists only of influence, not of empire. While our power may sometimes have been overbearing or oppressive, we have used it to liberate, not to conquer. We do not guard our status by keeping others down: some of our competitors are countries we have nurtured. Americans have every reason to feel proud and to keep our country strong, safe, and successful.

How shall we do that? We look out into a future that we cannot predict. The configuration of global politics is amorphous. We strain to perceive the threats that might confront us. In this book, I have offered some unoriginal thoughts about where threats may come from: Russia, China, radical Islam, and the proliferation of weapons of mass destruction. I have urged specific military, political, and economic policies designed to prepare for them or fend them off. But we do not know which of these threats will materialize, or in what form, or what other ones may appear that we do not foresee.

For that reason, it is tempting to wait to deal with threats only when they become clear and present dangers. History shows that we are very effective at doing that. We entered World War I late and won it. We entered World War II late and won it. We entered the cold war late and won it. Each time, though, that lateness had costs. I am optimistic that should we have to do it again, we will win again, if we preserve military strength and preparedness. But the cornerstone of our policy should not be to win the next war but to prevent it.

American Influence

The story that lies ahead of us is not already written, nor will it be determined by abstract "forces." It will be created by men and women. And because America is the most influential nation, it will be created by Americans more than by others. To imagine we are omnipotent would be folly: we have influence, not control. But to imagine we are impotent would be folly, too. America has already had a huge influence on the world. Today, the majority of the world's rulers have been elected by their subjects. This change is enormous, brought about within two hundred years, in large measure by American influence.

The world is also progressing toward universal free enterprise. This blessing, too, is brought about in part by American influence. Through promoting democracy and free trade, we can help sustain these two beneficent trends. The more difficult goal is peace. It is beyond even America's mighty influence to put an end to war. Nonetheless, with the advent of weapons of mass destruction we cannot accept the inevitability of another general war nor even of large-scale regional wars. We must try to prevent them by strengthening the norm against aggression as well as by encouraging democracy and prosperity.

Isolationists are fond of saying that we should lead by example. And so we should. The example that will impress the world even more than our domestic institutions is our behavior in the international arena. We should be strong, generous, and lawful. We should be a good friend and a bad enemy. We should comport ourselves with honor, a virtue held in contempt since Vietnam. Honor means behaving righteously ourselves, and it requires keeping our promises and threats. There is no honor in using our power to extort trade concessions. Nor is there honor in proclaiming safe havens that are not safe—nor in accepting human rights violations in China, nuclear weapons in North Korea, or Serbian aircraft in the skies over Bosnia after having said that we would accept none of these things. To act in these honorless ways makes America small. It diminishes our influence and makes the world more dangerous and unpredictable.

Strengthening our sense of honor will also help us with our domestic problems. Isolationists claim that we cannot afford the money costs of weapons or aid or other foreign expenditures. President Clinton said he could not afford to pay much attention to Bosnia because he was busy solving domestic problems. But our domestic problems do not arise from a lack of money or of presidential attention: they arise more from weakness of character. This is true not only for social problems but for economic ones, too. Because of the rising rates of divorce and illegitimacy, fewer Americans live in intact families, and this trend is a major cause of poverty. The weakness of the family is a major cause of the deterioration of schools and of crime, not to mention unhappiness. Another cause of crime is a criminal justice system that fails to hold people accountable for their behavior. Spending all we earn and more, and saving very little, is behind our trade deficit and sluggish economic growth, although we would rather blame the Japanese.

The amelioration of these problems lies in persuading or inducing people to behave more responsibly. Although government action can help, its effectiveness will depend on fostering responsibility. We are unlikely to learn to behave collectively more responsibly here at home while turning our back on responsibilities abroad. Far from there being a trade-off between addressing our domestic problems and conducting an active foreign policy, the two go hand in hand.

We should shoulder international responsibilities not just because this is the moral thing to do but because, as is usually the case with following the moral path, it is also in our best interests.

The American leader who first recognized that we could no longer separate our fate from the state of peace and freedom in the world was President Wilson. The contrast I have drawn between Wilson's outlook and President Washington's is in one sense unfair: the two lived at different times. Washington's cautious, isolationist approach may well have suited an infant nation far removed from the cockpit of world politics. But some 120 years later, Wilson saw not only that the world had grown smaller but that we had become the power most capable of influencing it. Much in Wilson's thought has not stood the test of time. The hopes he invested in international organization and in disarmament were misplaced. Self-determination of nations has turned out to be a more mischievous principle than he imagined, democracy more perishable. And yet Wilson's central insight—that America must labor to uphold the peace rather than await outside events passively—has been confirmed and reconfirmed. It was confirmed, in the breach, when America's rejection of Wilson in favor of isolationism brought on World War II. It was reconfirmed when the Wilsonian policy of "containment" brought us through the terrible perils of the cold war to victory.

The trends that Wilson recognized nearly eighty years ago have advanced much further. The world is ever more closely interknit, and America carries so much weight that if we disengage, turmoil is certain, and that turmoil will eventually catch up with us. Where ambitious tyrants rise, even if we choose to ignore them, they will covet our wealth and fear our power. If we leave them alone, they will still not leave us alone. We were surprised when Japan attacked us, surprised when Hitler declared war on us, surprised when Stalin broke our wartime partnership and initiated the cold war. We have trouble grasping how much such forces see us as an obstacle to their goals. Although we did not set out to be the sole superpower, it is what we have become, and we have no safe or peaceful way to retreat from this position. The wiser course is to make the most of it, not in aggrandizement, but in pursuit of our own security and world peace.

Chronological Highlights
of the Wars
# of Yugoslavia's Dissolution

1987

DECEMBER: Slobodan Milosevic engineers the ouster of his former patron, Ivan Stambolic, from the presidency of Serbia, using the claim that Stambolic was too indulgent toward the Albanian population of Kosovo.

1989

MARCH: At Milosevic's instance, legal changes in Yugoslavia vitiate the autonomous status of Kosovo and Vojvodina.

JUNE: At a mass rally of Serbs in Kosovo, Milosevic threatens intercommunal violence.

1990

APRIL: Pro-independence forces win free election in Slovenia. Led by Franjo Tudjman, nationalists win first free election in Croatia.

JULY: The Croatian Assembly adopts a variety of nationalist measures. Croatian Serbs declare autonomy from Croatia.

NOVEMBER: In first free elections in Bosnia and Herzegovina, vote splits along ethnic lines.

DECEMBER: Serb voters elect Milosevic president.

1991

MARCH: Serbian leader Milosevic and Croatian leader Franjo Tudjman meet and reportedly agree to divide Bosnia and Herzegovina between them.

MAY: Serbia blocks the scheduled rotation of offices that would have made the Croat, Stipe Mesic, head of the Yugoslav presidency. Croatia and Slovenia threaten to secede.

JUNE: Secretary of State James Baker travels to Belgrade for meetings with leaders of all the Yugoslav republics, urging them to remain united. Nonetheless Croatia and Slovenia soon declare independence while signaling their willingness to negotiate. Yugoslav forces attack Slovenia prompting the EC to dispatch a mediating mission. Its leader, Jacques Poos of Luxembourg, declares: "This is the hour of Europe, not of the Americans."

JULY: Fighting ends in Slovenia, but conflicts increase in Croatia.

AUGUST: Fighting further intensifies in Croatia with the Yugoslav army taking on a more active role on the side of the Serbs.

SEPTEMBER: The UN Security Council votes to embargo all arms deliveries to Yugoslavia.

DECEMBER: The EC announces that it will recognize Slovenia and Croatia in one month and will do the same for any other republic of the former Yugoslavia that meets constitutional and human rights criteria set by its Badinter Commission. Macedonia and Bosnia and Herzegovina apply for recognition. The Badinter Commission requires that Bosnia and Herzegovina hold a referendum. Germany decides not to wait for its fellow EC members and proceeds to recognize Croatia and Slovenia. Serbs in Croatia declare themselves the Republic of Serbian Krajina.

1992

JANUARY: Cease-fire takes hold in Croatia. UN observers arrive, to be followed (two months later) by peacekeeping forces.

FEBRUARY: Referendum in Bosnia and Herzegovina yields overwhelming vote for independence, but Serbian population mostly boycotts the vote.

MARCH: Irregular Bosnian Serb forces begin attacks against non-Serb civilians and the Bosnian government.

APRIL: The United States recognizes Bosnia and Herzegovina and also Croatia and Slovenia. The EC, which had already recognized the latter two, recognizes Bosnia and Herzegovina, as well.

MAY: The United States and the EC withdraw their ambassadors from Belgrade. The United Nations adopts economic sanctions against Yugoslavia. Croatia, Slovenia, and Bosnia and Herzegovina are admitted into the United Nations. The UN Security Council imposes economic sanctions on Yugoslavia.

JULY: President Bush, dismissing appeals for American action in Bosnia, likens the conflict there to a "hiccup."

AUGUST: U.S. and UN officials raise alarms about reports of atrocities by Serbs and the existence of concentration camps. The United Nations and the Conference on Security and Cooperation in Europe appoint special officers to investigate human rights abuses. The Security Council authorizes the use of "all necessary measures" to ensure delivery of humanitarian aid in Bosnia.

OCTOBER: The UN Security Council votes to impose a "no-fly" zone over Bosnia but does not authorize any means of enforcement.

NOVEMBER: UN Human Rights Commission Special Rapporteur Tadeusz Mazowiecki issues a report saying that Serbian "ethnic cleansing" in defiance of Security Council resolutions is undermining the authority of the United Nations.

DECEMBER: Secretary of State Lawrence Eagleburger proposes exempting Bosnia from the UN arms embargo, but no action follows. Also, at an international conference, Eagleburger calls for war crimes prosecutions and names a list of suspects starting with Serbian president Milosevic and Bosnian Serb leader Radovan Karadzic.

1993

JANUARY: Hakija Turajlic, deputy prime minister of Bosnia, is executed by Serbian fighters while the French UN forces under whose "protection" he was traveling look on passively. UN representative Cyrus Vance and EC representative David Owen propose a settlement (that they had adumbrated in October) based on dividing Bosnia into ten provinces and giving each major ethnic group dominance in three.

FEBRUARY: Secretary of State Warren Christopher announces the Bosnia policy of the new administration. It avoids any forceful action, brushes aside the Vance-Owen plan to divide Bosnia and Herzegovina into ethnic cantons, but embraces the "Vance-Owen negotiations" and pledges to support them with "the weight of American diplomacy." The UN Security Council authorizes the creation of a tribunal to prosecute war crimes.

MARCH: The UN Security Council authorizes the use of force to enforce no-fly zone. The United States initiates airlifts of humanitarian supplies to Bosnian civilians.

APRIL: The "parliament" of the Bosnian Serbs rejects the Vance-Owen plan, which had been accepted readily by the Bosnian Croats and grudgingly by the Bosnian government under U.S. pressure. Full-scale fighting breaks out between Bosnian government forces and Bosnian Croats, creating a triangular war.

MAY: The Clinton administration announces its decision to embark on a policy of "lift and strike," moving to lift the arms embargo on Bosnia and to undertake airstrikes against the Serbs. Christopher travels to Europe to seek the concurrence of allies, but Britain and France reject this policy, and Washington backs down. Instead, it embraces the Joint Action Program proposed by Russians and West Europeans to create "safe areas" for Muslims in Bosnia. These are declared by the UN Security Council.

AUGUST: As the siege of Sarajevo tightens, America says it will not tolerate the city's strangulation, and NATO threatens airstrikes. The Serbs pull back slightly from two peaks overlooking the city, and the threat is withdrawn.

1994

FEBRUARY: A shell lands in an outdoor market in Sarajevo, killing sixty-eight and wounding hundreds. NATO demands that Serbian heavy weapons be withdrawn from within 20 kilometers of the city and announces a ten-day deadline. The United Nations succeeds in diluting this ultimatum so that all Serbian weapons need not be withdrawn but merely placed under UN observation.

MARCH: Through American mediation, Muslims and Croats in Bosnia agree to stop fighting each other, to join their territories, and to affiliate in some way with Bosnia.

APRIL: Serbian forces turn their attention to another "safe area," Gorazde, shelling it and violating its perimeter. Defense Secretary William Perry declares that America will do nothing to stop Gorazde from being overrun but is quickly contradicted by National Security Adviser Anthony Lake. NATO delivers a new ultimatum to the Serb forces demanding relaxation of the siege of Gorazde. This ultimatum, too, is diluted, but it succeeds in staying the Serbs from conquering the city.

June: In a reversal of policy, America joins with Europeans in endorsing a settlement based on territorial division, granting Serbs de facto sovereignty over 49 percent of Bosnia and Herzegovina while reserving 51 percent for the coalition of Muslims and Croats. This becomes known as the "contact group" plan, and all Bosnian parties are told they have until the end of July to "take it or leave it." The Croats and the Muslims accede, but the Serbs refuse.

AUGUST: Yugoslavia announces severance of ties with Bosnian Serbs. The next month it agrees to international monitoring of its border with Bosnia to ensure that war materiel does not continue to flow to the Bosnian Serbs. But officials of the United Nations and Western governments and journalists continue to report frequent violations of this putative embargo.

1995

MAY: In response to increasing Serbian attacks on Sarajevo and on UN peacekeepers, NATO bombs some Bosnian Serb ammunition dumps. The Serbs retaliate by taking hostage nearly 400 UN peacekeepers, and the bombardment is halted. Croatian government forces, in a surprise offensive, recapture western Slavonia, one of the sectors held by Croatian Serbs.

JUNE: The Bosnian Serbs release UN hostages, receiving in exchange a secret pledge that no further NATO attacks will occur.

JULY: Bosnian forces overrun the "safe areas" of Srebrenica and Zepa, while the United Nations and NATO refrain from any intervention to stop them. An estimated 5,000–10,000 Muslim POWs are subjected to mass extermination. The Senate votes by more than two-thirds to lift the arms embargo on Bosnia.

AUGUST: In a lightning offensive, the army of Croatia rolls through most remaining areas held by the Croatian Serbs since 1991, recapturing all except eastern Slavonia along the border with Serbia. The Serb residents of the recaptured territories flee en masse to Serbia or Serb-held sections of Bosnia. In response to Serbian artillery attacks killing dozens in downtown Sarajevo, NATO undertakes its first significant airstrikes against the Serbs. These continue over a few weeks. The House votes by more than two-thirds to lift arms embargo on Bosnia.

SEPTEMBER: In negotiations mediated by U.S. Assistant Secretary of State Richard Holbrooke in Geneva, all three parties to the Bosnian struggle formally agree to a framework for a settlement dividing Bosnia and Herzegovina along the 51-49 percent formula. This formula now approximates the division of control on the ground, since in the preceding weeks a combined Muslim-Croat offensive has wrested significant swaths of territory from Serb control.

OCTOBER: A cease-fire takes effect throughout Bosnia and Herzegovina. Although numerous previous cease-fires had been announced during the course of the war, this one is the first that is generally obeyed.

NOVEMBER: Meeting in Dayton, Ohio, the presidents of Serbia, Croatia, and Bosnia and Herzegovina agree to a settlement based on a territorial division. Bosnia and Herzegovina will retain its legal international personality, but in practice it will be divided into two "entities," one Serbian and the other Croat and Muslim.

DECEMBER: The Dayton agreements are formally signed in Paris. American and other members of a 60,000-person international peacekeeping force, under the auspices of NATO, begin to take up positions between the Serbian and the Muslim-Croat sections.

NOTES

Chapter 1: Introduction

1. Elaine Sciolino, "Despite Heat, Christopher Has 'The Time of My Life,'" *New York Times,* June 1, 1993.
2. Saul Friedman, "Some Change in the Air; 'Confusing Times' on World Stage," *Newsday,* May 30, 1993.
3. Quoted in Norman J. Ornstein and Mark Schmitt, "Post–Cold War Politics," *Foreign Policy,* no. 79 (Summer 1990), p. 179.

Chapter 2: The Return of Isolationism

1. In some views, the American military remained superior to the Soviet; American commanders testified that they would not wish to exchange forces with those of the USSR. But the American advantage lay in the sophistication and flexibility of its military apparatus. In raw firepower, the Soviets were unmatched.
2. Harris Wofford, "The Democratic Challenge," *Foreign Policy,* no. 86 (Spring 1992), p. 102.
3. This was a speech about the importance of promoting democracy delivered in Milwaukee on October 1, 1992.
4. Daniel Williams and Ann Devroy, "Defining Clinton's Foreign Policy," *Washington Post,* September 20, 1993.
5. Carroll J. Doherty, "Foreign Policy: Is Congress Still Keeping Watch?" *Congressional Quarterly,* August 21, 1993, p. 2267.
6. National Opinion Research Center survey conducted February–April, 1993. It has asked a similar question and recorded similar responses for many years, going back to 1947.

7. Cited in "America's Role in the World," *The Polling Report,* January 24, 1994, p.6.

8. The *Times Mirror* Center, "America's Place in the World," November 1993.

9. John E. Rielly, ed., *American Public Opinion and U.S. Foreign Policy* (Chicago: Chicago Council on Foreign Relations, 1995), p. 6.

10. Ibid., p. 14.

11. Norman Ornstein and Mark Schmitt, "Post–Cold War Politics," *Foreign Policy,* no. 79 (Summer 1990), p. 180. Similar results were obtained in an October 1993 Harris poll, which asked respondents to estimate the proportion of federal spending devoted to foreign aid. The median estimate was 20 percent. See the *Harris Poll 1993,* no. 55, November 1, 1993.

12. William G. Hyland, "Foreign Affairs at 70," *Foreign Affairs,* vol. 71, no. 4 (Fall 1992), p. 184.

13. William G. Hyland, "The Case for Pragmatism," *Foreign Affairs,* vol. 71, no. 1 (America and the World 1991–1992), p. 52.

14. Ibid.

15. Charles William Maynes, "America without the Cold War," *Foreign Policy,* no. 78 (Spring 1990), p. 18.

16. Owen Harries, "Fourteen Points for Realists," *The National Interest,* no. 30 (Winter 1992–1993), pp. 110–12.

17. Theodore C. Sorenson, "America's First Post–Cold War President," *Foreign Affairs,* vol. 71, no. 4 (Fall 1992), p. 22.

18. Zbigniew Brzezinski, "Selective Global Commitment," *Foreign Affairs,* vol. 70, no. 4 (Fall 1991), pp. 19–20.

19. James Schlesinger, "Quest for a Post–Cold War Foreign Policy," *Foreign Affairs,* vol. 72, no. 1 (America and the World 1992–1993), p. 28.

20. William G. Hyland, "America's New Course," *Foreign Affairs,* vol. 69, no. 2 (Spring 1980), p. 3.

21. George Bush, "Inaugural Address," *Weekly Compilation of Presidential Documents,* week ending Friday, January 27, 1989, p. 100.

22. "National Security, Redefined," *New York Times,* November 10, 1992.

23. "Looking Homeward: Regional Views of Foreign Policy," *Foreign Policy,* no. 88 (Fall 1992), p. 38.

24. Carnegie Endowment for International Peace National Commission on America and the New World, *Changing Our Ways* (Washington, D.C.: Carnegie Endowment for International Peace, 1992), p. 18.

25. Owen Harries, "Drift and Mastery, Bush-Style," *The National Interest,* no. 23 (Spring 1991), p. 5.

26. Owen Harries and Michael Lind, "Realism and Its Rivals," *The National Interest,* no. 34 (Winter 1993–1994), p. 111.

27. "National Security, Redefined," *New York Times,* November 10, 1992.

28. Carnegie Endowment, *Changing Our Ways* , pp. 54, 13.

29. Janne E. Nolan et al., "The Imperatives for Cooperation," in Janne Nolan, ed., *Global Engagement: Cooperation and Security in the 21st Century* (Washington, D.C.: Brookings Institution, 1994), p. 5.

30. Charles Krauthammer, "The Lonely Superpower," *New Republic,* July 29, 1991, p. 26.

31. Harries, "Drift and Mastery, Bush-Style," p. 5.

32. Hyland, "America's New Course," p. 4.

33. Morton H. Halperin and David J. Scheffer with Patricia L. Small, *Self-Determination in the New World Order* (Washington, D.C.: Carnegie Endowment for International Peace, 1992).

34. Michael Lind, "National Disinterest," *The National Interest,* no. 24 (Summer 1991), p. 110.

35. As of February 1995, 119 of the 230 Republicans in the House, and 20 of 52 in the Senate, had been sworn in since 1990.

36. Ann Devroy, "Veto Aimed at Foreign Policy Bill," *Washington Post,* May 24, 1995.

37. *NBC Nightly News,* May 6, 1993.

38. Warren Christopher, "American Leadership at Stake," Statement before the Subcommittee on Foreign Operations of the Senate Foreign Relations Committee, May 18, 1995, *U.S. Department of State Dispatch,* vol. 6, no. 21 (May 22, 1995), p. 411.

39. Warren Christopher, "A Foreign Affairs Budget That Promotes U.S. Interests," Statement before the Subcommittee on Foreign Operations of the Senate Appropriations Committee, March 2, 1994, *U.S. Department of State Dispatch,* vol. 5, no. 11 (March 14, 1994), pp. 139–40.

40. Paul M. Weyrich, "A Populist Policy," *The National Interest,* no. 21 (Fall 1990), pp. 54–55.

41. Henry Cabot Lodge, "Foreign Relations of the United States, 1921–1924," *Foreign Affairs,* vol. 2, no. 4 (June 15, 1924), p. 535.

CHAPTER 3: THE NEW GREAT DEBATE

1. Arnold Wolfers, *Discord and Collaboration* (Baltimore: Johns Hopkins University Press, 1962), p. 73.

2. Thomas Jefferson, *Second Inaugural Address,* March 4, 1805. U.S. Congress, House of Representatives, Committee on House Administration, *Inaugural Addresses of the Presidents of the United States from George Washington to Harry S. Truman,* 82d Cong., 2d sess., House doc. no. 540, 1952, p. 15.

3. David C. Hendrickson, "The Renovation of Foreign Policy," *Foreign Affairs,* vol. 71, no. 2 (Spring 1992), p. 63.

4. William E. Borah, *Bedrock: Views on Basic National Problems* (Washington, D.C.: National Home Library Foundation, 1936), pp. 52–53.

5. Henry Cabot Lodge, "Foreign Relations of the United States, 1921–1924," *Foreign Affairs,* vol. 2, no. 4 (June 15, 1924), p. 538.

6. "X" [George Kennan], "The Sources of Soviet Conduct," *Foreign Affairs,* vol. 25 (July 1947), p. 576.

7. Carnegie Endowment for International Peace National Commission on America and the New World, *Changing Our Ways* (Washington, D.C.: Carnegie Endowment for International Peace, 1992), p. 1.

8. Realism is a school of thought about international relations whose leading figures are Hans Morgenthau, George Kennan, Walter Lippmann, Reinhold Niebuhr, E. H. Carr, and Henry Kissinger. Its core idea is that international relations consist of the interplay of states driven by innate interests that are usually determined by geography and that any policy that deviates from this, or appears to, is either illusory or misconceived. For a fuller explication and critique, see my *Exporting Democracy: Fulfilling America's Destiny* (Washington, D.C.: AEI Press, 1991), chap. 3.

9. Martin Gilbert, *Winston S. Churchill,* vol. 4, *The Stricken World, 1916–1922* (Boston: Houghton Mifflin, 1975), p. 229.

10. Quoted in ibid., p. 228.

11. Jeffrey Sachs, "The Reformers' Tragedy," *New York Times,* January 23, 1994.

12. Nicholas D. Kristof, "The Rise of China," *Foreign Affairs,* vol. 72, no. 5 (November–December 1993), pp. 59, 65.

13. "War Games, Money Games," *New York Times,* February 19, 1992.

14. Quoted in Jim Wolfe, "Iraqi Army's Ruin Makes Drawdown Safer: Powell," *Navy Times,* April 15, 1991, p. 24.

15. Lee H. Hamilton, "A Democrat Looks at Foreign Policy," *Foreign Affairs,* vol. 71, no. 3 (Summer 1992), p. 39.

16. Robert J. Samuelson, "War and Remembrance," *Washington Post,* January 12, 1994.

17. Saddam does not yet have the means to deliver a nuclear weapon, except perhaps by terrorist infiltration, but the technology of missiles is proliferating even faster than that of bombs, so the possibility that he, or others like him, could within a few years possess both the weapon and the means of delivery is not far-fetched.

18. Edward C. Luck, "Making Peace," *Foreign Policy,* no. 89 (Winter 1992–1993), p. 140.

19. See Samuel P. Huntington, "The Clash of Civilizations?" *Foreign Affairs,* vol. 72, no. 3 (Summer 1993), pp. 22–49.

20. Carnegie Endowment, *Changing Our Ways,* p. 12.

21. John Kifner, "Boost for U.S. Stand—Iraq's Leader Issues Call for Holy War," *New York Times,* August 11, 1990.

22. See, for example, Council on Competitiveness, *The Competitiveness Index* (Washington, D.C., 1988), Appendix II; Barry P. Bosworth and Robert Z. Lawrence, "America in the World Economy," *Brookings Review,* no.

7 (Winter 1988–1989), p. 43; Herbert Block, *The Planetary Product in 1980: A Creative Pause?* (Washington, D.C.: U.S. Department of State, Bureau of Public Affairs, 1981), pp. 74–77.

23. According to the authoritative annual "Survey of Freedom" conducted by Freedom House, there were 114 democracies as of the end of 1994 out of a total of 191 independent states. See Adrian Karatnycky, "Democracies on the Rise, Democracies at Risk," *Freedom Review,* vol. 26, no. 1 (January–February 1995), p. 5.

24. George F. Kennan, *American Diplomacy, 1900–1950* (New York: Mentor Books, 1952), p. 82.

25. Hans J. Morgenthau, *In Defense of the National Interest* (New York: Knopf, 1951), p. 3.

26. Glenn H. Snyder and Paul Diesing, *Conflict among Nations* (Princeton: Princeton University Press, 1977), p. 498.

CHAPTER 4: CAN WE AFFORD TO LEAD?

1. Congressman Dan Glickman, quoted in Gregory J. Bowens, "Panel Reportedly Cut Request for Satellite, Technology," *Congressional Quarterly,* June 12, 1993, p. 1493.

2. *Budget of the United States, FY 1996: Historical Tables* (Washington, D.C.: Government Printing Office, 1995), table 15.6, p. 241.

3. Program on International Policy Attitudes, *Americans and Foreign Aid: A Study of American Public Attitudes,* March 1, 1995, Washington, D.C., pp. 6–7. The average response to these two questions was even more off target than the median, 18 percent as the estimated current amount and 8 percent as the preferred "appropriate" level. The study was reported in Barbara Crossette, "Foreign Aid Budget: Quick, How Much? Wrong," *New York Times,* February 27, 1995.

4. *Historical Tables,* table 8.3.

5. Bipartisan Commission on Entitlement and Tax Reform, *Final Report to the President,* Washington, D.C., January 1995, pp. 97–99.

6. These and other figures in this paragraph from *Historical Tables,* table 8.3.

7. Commission, *Final Report,* pp. 121–23.

8. Ibid., pp. 17–20.

9. For a fuller account of this issue, see John H. Makin and Norman J. Ornstein, *Debt and Taxes* (New York: Times Books, 1994), pp. 151–55.

10. U.S. Congress, House of Representatives, Committee on Ways and Means, *1994 Annual Report of the Board of Trustees of the Federal Old-Age and Survivors Insurance and Disability Insurance Trust Funds,* 103d Congress, 2d session, House doc. 103–231, April 12, 1994, table II.F18, p. 119.

11. *Historical Tables,* tables 8.4 and 15.5.

12. All these figures come from *Historical Tables,* table 15.5.

13. Bruce M. Russett, *What Price Vigilance? The Burdens of National Defense* (New Haven: Yale University Press, 1970), p. 128.

14. Paul Kennedy, *The Rise and Fall of the Great Powers* (New York: Random House, 1987).

15. See, for example, Herbert Stein, "America Is Rich Enough to Be Strong," *AEI Economist,* February 1988, p. 3; Samuel Huntington, "The U.S.—Decline or Renewal?" *Foreign Affairs,* vol. 67, no. 7 (Winter 1988–1989), pp. 76–96; and my *Exporting Democracy: Fulfilling America's Destiny* (Washington, D.C.: AEI Press, 1991), chap. 5.

16. Herbert Stein and Murray Foss, *An Illustrated Guide to the American Economy* (Washington, D.C.: AEI Press, 1992), pp. 14–15.

17. James E. Payne and Anandi P. Sahu, "Defense Spending and Economic Growth: An Evaluation of the Overall Impact," in Payne and Sahu, eds., *Defense Spending and Economic Growth* (Boulder, Colo.: Westview Press, 1993), p. 14.

18. Gordon Adams and David Gold, "The Economics of Military Spending: Is the Military Dollar Really Different," in Christian Schmidt and Frank Blackaby, eds., *Peace, Defense and Economic Analysis* (New York: St. Martin's Press, 1987), p. 266.

19. Emile Benoit, *Defense and Economic Growth in Developing Countries* (Lexington, Mass.: D.C. Heath and Co., 1973), p. 2.

20. Ibid., pp. 21–23.

21. Robert D. Hormats, "The Roots of American Power," *Foreign Affairs,* vol. 70 no. 3 (Summer 1991), p. 139.

Chapter 5: Can Others Share the Burdens?

1. William Pfaff, "Redefining World Power," *Foreign Affairs,* vol. 71, no. 1 (America and the World 1991–1992), p. 34.

2. Richard Nixon, "Remarks to Midwestern News Media Executives Attending a Briefing on Domestic Policy in Kansas City, Missouri. July 6, 1971," *Public Papers of the Presidents,* pp. 806–7.

3. For a fuller refutation of the theory of American decline, see my *Exporting Democracy: Fulfilling America's Destiny* (Washington, D.C.: AEI Press, 1991), chap. 5, "Is America in Decline?"

4. See chap. 3, note 22.

5. Pfaff, "Redefining World Power," p. 38.

6. Herbert Stein and Murray Foss, *An Illustrated Guide to the American Economy* (Washington, D.C.: AEI Press, 1992), p. 9.

7. The 1994 *Europa World Yearbook* gives the 1992 per capita income in the United States as $23,120 and in Taiwan as $10,202.

8. See Heinz Gollwitzer, *Europe in the Age of Imperialism* (New York: W.W. Norton, 1979), p. 79.

9. See, for example, Martin Gilbert, *The First World War: A Complete*

History (New York: Henry Holt and Co., 1994), pp. 25–26.

10. *Encyclopaedia of the Social Sciences* (New York: Macmillan, 1937), vol. 6, pp. 135–36.

11. Rene Albrecht-Carrie, *A Diplomatic History of Europe since the Congress of Vienna*, rev. ed. (New York: Harper & Row, 1973), p. 460.

12. Ibid., p. 488.

13. Dennis Mack Smith, *Mussolini: A Biography* (New York: Vintage Books, 1983), p. 198.

14. Joachim von Ribbentrop, *The Ribbentrop Memoirs* (London: Weidenfeld and Nicolson, 1954), p. 41.

15. See, for example, John Wheeler-Bennett, *The Nemesis of Power: The German Army in Politics—1918–1945* (London: Macmillan, 1953), p. 352; or Maurice Beaumont, *The Origins of the Second World War* (New Haven: Yale University Press, 1978), p. 188.

16. Quoted in Martin Gilbert, *Churchill: A Life* (New York: Henry Holt and Co., 1991), p. 595. See also Margaret Thatcher, *The Downing Street Years* (New York: HarperCollins, 1993), p. 824.

17. Adam Ulam, *Stalin: The Man and His Era* (Boston: Beacon Press, 1973, 1987), p. 540.

18. Letter from President Charles de Gaulle to President Lyndon Baines Johnson, March 7, 1966, reprinted in various compendiums.

19. "French Memorandum Delivered to the Fourteen Representatives of the Governments of the Atlantic Alliance," reprinted in *The Dynamics of World Power: A Documentary History of United States Foreign Policy 1945–1973*, general editor, Arthur M. Schlesinger, Jr., vol. I, *Western Europe*, ed. Robert Dallek (New York: Chelsea House, 1973), p. 836.

20. John L. Hess, "France Stresses Atom Deterrent," *New York Times*, January 30, 1968.

21. James L. Stokesbury, *A Short History of the Korean War* (New York: William Morrow, 1988), p. 36.

22. Foreign Minister Maurice Couve de Murville, quoted in Henry Tanner, "Impact of Vietnam on Europe Grows," *New York Times,* February 25, 1968.

23. See, for example, Edward A. Kolodziej, *French International Policy under de Gaulle and Pompidou* (Ithaca: Cornell University Press, 1974), chap. 10; or Henry Kissinger, *Years of Upheaval* (Boston: Little, Brown and Company, 1982), chap. 16.

24. "New Strains on U.S.-Europe Alliance," *U.S. News and World Report,* November 12, 1973, p. 32.

25. Ibid.

26. On the once-controversial subject of Soviet support for international terrorists, see Michael Dobbs, "Russian Says Soviets Aided Terrorists," *Washington Post,* May 26, 1992.

27. White House spokesman Larry Speakes, quoted in Bernard Weinraub,

"Italy Said to Free 2 P.L.O. Aides; U.S. Issues a Warrant for One; Hostages Tell of a 'Death List,'" *New York Times,* October 13, 1985.

28. Quoted in John Tagliabue, "Bonn Rules Out Trade Sanctions against Libyans," *New York Times,* January 4, 1986.

29. Quoted in E.J. Dionne, Jr., "West Europe Generally Critical of U.S.," *New York Times,* April 16, 1986.

30. Neil A. Lewis, "U.S. Jets Hit 'Terrorist Centers' in Libya; Reagan Warns of New Attacks If Needed; One Plane Missing in Raids on 5 Targets," *New York Times,* April 15, 1986.

31. See Bernard D. Nossiter, "U.S. Finds Itself Virtually Isolated in U.N. over the Nicaraguan Crisis," *New York Times,* March 29, 1983; and Raymond Bonner, "Behind Nicaraguan Buildup: Soviet-Bloc Aid Cited," *New York Times,* April 27, 1983.

32. Philip Webster, "Thatcher Comes off the Fence," *Times* (London), October 31, 1983.

33. Quoted in Timothy Garton Ash, *In Europe's Name: Germany and the Divided Continent* (New York: Random House, 1994), p. 289.

34. Paul C. Warnke to Joshua Muravchik, Washington, D.C., October 31, 1995.

35. Ellen Lentz, "West Germany Worried over Neutron Bomb Prospect," *New York Times,* July 24, 1977.

36. For an account of Carter's decision making on this issue, see Zbigniew Brzezinski, *Power and Principle* (New York: Farrar, Straus, Giroux, 1983), pp. 301–6.

37. Interview with Richard Perle, Washington, D.C., December 28, 1994.

38. Strobe Talbott, *Deadly Gambits: The Reagan Administration and the Stalemate in Nuclear Arms Control* (New York: Knopf, 1984), pp. 40–41.

39. See Jeffrey Herf, *War by Other Means* (New York: Free Press, 1991), p. 137.

40. Ibid., pp. 125–26.

41. Quoted in Rick Atkinson, *Crusade: The Untold Story of the Persian Gulf War* (New York: Houghton Mifflin, 1993), p. 83.

42. See, for example, Michael Wines, "Iraq's Nuclear Quest: Tentacles in Four Continents," *New York Times,* December 23, 1990; and also Michael Ledeen, "Iraq's German Connection," *Commentary,* April 1991, pp. 27–30.

43. See, for example, Elaine Sciolino, "U.S. Hopes to Broaden Ban on Arms Sales to Iran," *New York Times,* November 18, 1992; Steve Coll, "Technology from West Floods Iran," *Washington Post,* November 10, 1992; and R. Jeffrey Smith, "U.S. Seeks to Halt Western Export of 'Dual-Use' Technology to Iran," *Washington Post,* November 10, 1992.

44. Youssef M. Ibrahim, "Iraq Said to Sell Oil in Secret Plan to Skirt U.N. Ban," *New York Times,* February 16, 1995.

45. See, for example, "Poor Relations," "One Wall Replaces Another,"

and "Better Than Aid," all in the *Economist,* May 1, 1993, pp. 54–56; "Guilt by Association," *Economist,* July 11, 1992, pp. 25–27; and "A New Iron Curtain," *World Press Review,* August 1993, p. 40.

CHAPTER 6: CAN WE TURN THE WORLD OVER TO THE UN?

1. Jeane Kirkpatrick, "United Nations Doublespeak Disappears," *Los Angeles Times,* September 2, 1990.

2. Morton Kondracke, "Javier of the U.N.," *New Republic,* August 13, 1990, p. 20.

3. "National Security Strategy of the United States," The White House, January 1993 (USGPO, 1993), p. 7.

4. Final Report of the U. S. Commission on Improving the Effectiveness of the United Nations, September 1993, p. 10.

5. Boutros Boutros-Ghali, "Empowering the United Nations," *Foreign Affairs,* vol. 71, no. 5 (Winter 1992–1993), pp. 89–90.

6. United Nations, *Report of the Secretary General on the Work of the Organization,* A/50/60, S/1995/1, January 1, 1995, p. 4.

7. Kondracke, "Javier," p. 21.

8. Boutros-Ghali, "Empowering the United Nations," p. 89.

9. Boutros Boutros-Ghali, *An Agenda for Peace,* Report of the Secretary-General pursuant to the statement adopted by the Summit Meeting of the Security Council on January 31, 1992, paragraph 44.

10. Ibid., paragraph 29.

11. Warren Strobel, "Peacekeepers Do Everything Everywhere," *Washington Times,* July 19, 1992.

12. Bill Clinton, Address to the Los Angeles World Affairs Council, August 13, 1992, prepared text, p. 7.

13. Madeleine K. Albright, "Address to the Council on Foreign Relations," June 11, 1993, press release USUN 96-(93), p. 2.

14. President Bill Clinton, Address to the General Assembly of the United Nations, September 27, 1993.

15. "'It's Self-Evident That We . . . Can't Solve All the Problems,'" *Washington Post,* October 17, 1993.

16. Jim Hoagland, "The Blame Game," *Washington Post,* October 21, 1993.

17. United Nations, Security Council, Resolution 814, March 26, 1993.

18. Daniel Williams, "U.S. Troops to Remain in Somalia," *Washington Post,* August 11, 1993.

19. Madeleine K. Albright, "Yes, There Is a Reason to Be in Somalia," *New York Times,* August 10, 1993.

20. David C. Morrison, "Wanted: Peacekeeping Policy," *National Journal,* November 27, 1993, p. 2859.

21. *The Clinton Administration's Policy on Reforming Multilateral Peace Operations*, May 1994, Executive summary, p. 1.

22. Madeleine K. Albright, Statement before the Subcommittee on Appropriations for Foreign Operations, Export Financing and Related Programs of the House Committee on Appropriations, May 5, 1994, p. 2.

23. Elaine Sciolino, "New U.S. Peacekeeping Policy De-emphasizes Role of the U.N.," *New York Times*, May 6, 1994.

24. Madeleine K. Albright, "The United States and the United Nations: Confrontation or Consensus?" Address to the Council on Foreign Relations, Washington, D.C., January 26, 1995, p. 5.

25. Boutros Boutros-Ghali, "Supplement to an Agenda for Peace: Position Paper of the Secretary-General on the Occasion of the Fiftieth Anniversary of the United Nations," A/50/60, S/1995/1, paragraph 6.

26. Ibid., paragraph 43.

27. Ibid., paragraph 77.

28. Ibid., paragraph 45.

29. Albright, "Yes, There Is a Reason to Be in Somalia."

30. Keith B. Richburg, "7 Peace Keepers Killed in Somalia," *Washington Post*, September 6, 1993.

31. Thomas E. Ricks, "Disappointment in Somalia: Out of It in Africa," *Wall Street Journal*, December 9, 1994.

32. Quoted in Jeane Kirkpatrick, "Clinton Has No Business Heeding U.N. Mandates," *New York Post*, October 11, 1993.

33. U.S. Congress, Senate, Subcommittee on Coalition Defense and Reinforcing Forces of the Committee on Armed Services, *Hearings on FY 1995 Defense Authorization*, May 12, 1994, Reuters transcripts, story number t7921, p. 18.

34. William Drozdiak, "No Rescue for Rwanda," *Washington Post*, June 18, 1994.

35. Anthony Parsons, "The United Nations in the Post–Cold War Era," *International Relations*, vol. 2, no. 3, p. 189.

36. For example, in 1994 the human rights organization, Freedom House, which each year assesses the degree of freedom in each country, listed the twenty worst regimes. Of the twenty, six were currently members of the Human Rights Commission: Angola, China, Cuba, Libya, Sudan, and Syria.

37. Henry A. Kissinger, "Recipe for Chaos," *Washington Post*, September 8, 1993.

38. Parsons, "The United Nations," p. 190.

39. Ibid.

40. Ibid., p. 191.

41. President Bill Clinton, Address to the General Assembly of the United Nations, September 27, 1993, *The Reuter Transcript Report*, p. 13.

42. Boutros-Ghali, "Empowering the United Nations," p. 91.

43. Boutros-Ghali, *An Agenda for Peace,* paragraph 5, and also "Supplement to *An Agenda for Peace,*" paragraph 1.

44. Quoted in Ian Nish, *Japan's Struggle with Internationalism: Japan, China and the League of Nations* (London: Kegan Paul International, 1993), p. 239.

45. Cited in Peter J. Beck, "The League of Nations and the Great Powers, 1936–1940: A British Perspective," Paper presented to the Woodrow Wilson House seventy-fifth anniversary symposium on the League of Nations, Washington, D.C., March 1994, p. 16.

46. Innis Claude, *Swords into Plowshares,* 4th ed. (New York: Random House, 1971), pp. 60, 66.

47. Boutros-Ghali, *An Agenda for Peace,* paragraph 86.

48. Richard L. Armitage, "Bend the U.N. to Our Will," *New York Times,* February 24, 1994.

49. Claude, *Swords into Plowshares,* p. 445.

CHAPTER 7: "THE HOUR OF EUROPE"

1. Quoted in Misha Glenny, *The Fall of Yugoslavia* (New York: Penguin Books, 1993), p. 35.

2. David Gompert, "How to Defeat Serbia," *Foreign Affairs,* vol. 73 no. 4 (July–August 1994), p. 35.

3. Glenny, *The Fall,* p. 149.

4. "European Community Wants a United, Democratic Yugoslavia," *The Reuter Library Report,* April 4, 1991.

5. Noel Malcolm, *Bosnia: A Short History* (London: Macmillan, 1994), p. 218.

6. Leonard J. Cohen, *Broken Bonds: The Disintegration of Yugoslavia* (Boulder, Colo.: Westview, 1993), p. 199. See also *Foreign Broadcast Information Service,* Eastern Europe, June 3, 1991, p. 43.

7. Deputy Assistant Secretary of State James Dobbins before the Senate Subcommittee on European Affairs, February 21, 1991. Cited in Paula Franklin Lytle, "U.S. Policy toward the Demise of Yugoslavia: The 'Virus of Nationalism,'" *East European Politics and Societies,* vol. 6, no. 3 (Fall 1992), p. 309.

8. Lytle, ibid., p. 310.

9. U.S. Department of State, Office of the Assistant Secretary, "U.S. Policy toward Yugoslavia," Statement by Margaret Tutwiler, spokesperson, May 24, 1991, pp. 3, 2.

10. Ibid., pp. 1, 2.

11. "Europe: The Road to War," *Economist,* July 6, 1991, p. 45.

12. Cohen, *Broken Bonds,* p. 218.

13. David Binder, "U.S. Voices Regret on Yugoslav Crisis," *New York*

Times, June 27, 1991.

14. David Binder, "Europeans Warn on Yugoslav Split; U.S. Deplores Move," *New York Times,* June 25, 1991.

15. John Tagliabue, "Yugoslav Army Uses Force in Breakaway Republic; Slovenia Reports 100 Wounded or Killed," *New York Times,* June 28, 1991.

16. Quoted in Lytle, "U.S. Policy toward the Demise of Yugoslavia," p. 311.

17. See, for example, Gompert, "How to Defeat Serbia," p. 35.

18. "Europe: The Road to War," p. 45.

19. Interview with Kenneth Juster, Washington, D.C., August 5, 1994.

20. Tanjug, June 1, 1991, reprinted in *Foreign Broadcast Information Service,* Eastern Europe, June 3, 1991, p. 43. Galvin has no recollection of saying anything like this, which he says would have been beyond his authority (telephone interview, October 6, 1994.) Nonetheless, the words attributed to him did accurately reflect NATO policy and also reflected what Tanjug's masters wanted its readers and listeners to hear.

21. *Economist,* April 25, 1992, p. 56.

22. Gompert, "How to Defeat Serbia," p. 41.

23. Interview with George Kenney, Washington, D.C., July 19, 1994; interview with Kenneth Juster, Washington, D.C., August 5, 1994.

24. "The Future of the Balkans: An Interview with David Owen," *Foreign Affairs,* vol. 72, no. 2 (Spring 1993), p. 6.

25. Alan Philps, "Moscow Defiant on Euro Plan to Defuse Crisis," *London Daily Telegraph,* June 20, 1991.

26. "Crisis in Yugoslavia; EC Dashes into Its Own Backyard," *Financial Times,* July 1, 1991.

27. *Wall Street Journal Europe,* July 1, 1991.

28. Rosalyn Higgins, "The New United Nations and Former Yugoslavia," *International Affairs,* vol. 69, no. 3 (July 1993), p. 473.

29. Quoted in Peter W. Rodman, "Bosnian Quagmire," *National Review,* June 26, 1995, p. 27.

30. Gompert, "How to Defeat Serbia," p. 35.

31. John M. Goshko and David Hoffman, "West Considering Yugoslav Arms Embargo, Aid Cutoff," *Washington Post,* July 4, 1991.

32. William Drozdiak, "Lack of an Armed Option Limits EC's Yugoslav Peace Initiative," *Washington Post,* September 5, 1991.

33. "Men of Blood," *Economist,* August 17, 1991, p. 43.

34. "Into the Dark," *Economist,* September 21, 1994, p. 57.

35. James B. Steinberg asserts that "we all know in retrospect that Milosevic and the JNA [Yugoslav army] were not blind to the advantages of this arms embargo." But he does not explain how we know it. See his "Turning Points in Bosnia and the West" in Zalmay M. Khalilzad, ed., *Lessons from Bosnia,* Conference proceedings, CF-113-AF, Rand Corporation, 1993, p. 6.

36. Misha Glenny reports "the dispatch of hundreds of thousands of

pieces of weaponry mainly to the two militant Serb regions of [Bosnia and Herzegovina]" in 1990. Although not all details of this operation are known, it is clear that the army was involved. Glenny, *The Fall of Yugoslavia*, pp. 150–51.

37. Christopher Wilson, "Serbia Rejects EC's Yugoslavia Plan, Conference May be Suspended," *The Reuter Library Report*, November 5, 1991.

38. *Recognition of the Yugoslav Successor States*, Position paper of the German Foreign Ministry, Bonn, March 10, 1993, Official translation, German Information Center, vol. 16, no. 10, p. 2.

39. Wolfgang Krieger, "Toward a Gaullist Germany? Some Lessons from the Yugoslav Crisis," *World Policy Journal*, vol. 11, no. 1 (Spring 1994), p. 32.

40. John Newhouse, "The Diplomatic Round: Dodging the Problem," *New Yorker*, August 24, 1992, p. 63.

41. "Wreckognition," *Economist*, January 18, 1992, p. 48.

42. Steinberg, "Turning Points in Bosnia and the West," p. 7.

43. "Recognizing Facts and Fantasies," *Economist*, December 7, 1991, p. 58.

44. Quoted in James E. Goodby, "Peacekeeping in the New Europe," *Washington Quarterly*, vol. 15, no. 2 (Spring 1992), p. 161.

45. "Turning Point in Yugoslavia," *Economist*, January 11, 1992, p. 43.

46. Ralph Johnson, deputy assistant secretary of state for European and Canadian affairs, Hearings of the Senate Committee on Foreign Relations, October 17, 1991; cited in Lytle, "The Virus of Nationalism," p. 312.

47. Lytle, "U.S. Policy toward the Demise of Yugoslavia," p. 314.

48. Goodby, "Peacekeeping," p. 162.

CHAPTER 8: AGGRESSION AND INDIFFERENCE

1. Paul Lewis, "U.N. Rules Out a Force to Halt Bosnia Fighting," *New York Times*, May 14, 1992.

2. Paul Lewis, "U.N. Chief Opposes Bosnia Peace Force," *New York Times*, April 25, 1992.

3. David Binder, "U.S., Frustrated, Backs Off from the Crisis in Yugoslavia," *New York Times*, May 4, 1992.

4. *New York Times*, May 25, 1992; cited in Paula Franklin Lytle, "U.S. Policy toward the Demise of Yugoslavia: The'Virus of Nationalism,'" *East European Politics and Societies*, vol. 6, no. 3 (Fall 1992), p. 314.

5. "The Lilliputian Is Still Wriggling," *Economist*, June 6, 1992, p. 52.

6. "Operation Balkan Storm?" *Economist*, May 30, 1992, p. 12.

7. Cited in Lytle, "U.S. Policy toward the Demise of Yugoslavia," p. 314n.

8. Ibid., p. 315.

9. Press conference in Munich, Germany, July 8, 1992; quoted in Lytle, "U.S. Policy and the Demise of Yugoslavia," p. 316.

10. John F. Burns, "In Sarajevo, the Cavalry Seems Far Away," *New*

York Times, August 9, 1992.

11. Gompert, "How to Defeat Serbia," p. 38.

12. Interview with Stephen Walker, Washington, D.C., August 10, 1994.

13. Elaine Sciolino, "In Bosnia, Peace at Any Price Is Getting More Expensive," *New York Times,* January 10, 1993.

14. Interview with Marshall Freeman Harris, who in February 1993 was the State Department desk officer for Bosnia, Washington, D.C., July 21, 1994.

15. "Bosnia's Serbs against the World," *Economist,* May 8, 1993, p. 53.

16. R.W. Apple, Jr., May 5, 1993.

17. R.W. Apple, Jr., "Clinton Pushes a Bosnia Plan of Arms Supplies and Bombing," *New York Times,* May 7, 1993.

18. UN Security Council Resolution 836 (1993).

19. Interview with Harris.

20. Warren Christopher, "New Steps toward Conflict Resolution in the Former Yugoslavia," Opening statement at a news conference, Washington, D.C., February 10, 1993, *U.S. Department of State Dispatch,* vol. 4, no 7, February 15, 1993, p. 81.

21. Quoted in Steven A. Holmes, "Backing Away Again, Christopher Says Bosnia Is Not a Vital Interest," *New York Times,* June 4, 1993.

22. Quoted in Sabrina Petra Ramet, "The Yugoslav Crisis and the West: Avoiding 'Vietnam' and Blundering into 'Abyssinia,'" *European Politics and Societies,* vol. 8, no. 1 (Winter 1994), p. 212.

23. Quoted in Paul Lewis, "Owen, in Shift, Backs New Bosnia Plan," *New York Times,* June 18, 1993.

24. Quoted in Thomas L. Friedman, "President Softens Opposition by U.S. to Divided Bosnia," *New York Times,* June 18, 1993.

25. John F. Burns, "All Alone: Bosnia Loses Any Hope of Being Saved," *New York Times,* July 25, 1993.

26. Interview with Walker.

27. Daniel Williams, "'Outraged' by Shelling, Clinton Says: 'We Rule Out Nothing,'" *Washington Post,* February 6, 1994.

28. Ibid.

29. Elaine Sciolino, "Clinton Rules Out a Quick Response to Bosnia Attack," *New York Times,* February 7, 1994.

30. Roger Cohen, "NATO Gives Serbs a 10-Day Deadline to Withdraw Guns," *New York Times,* February 10, 1994.

31. John Pomfret, "U.N., NATO in Dispute over Bosnia," *Washington Post,* February 14, 1994.

32. Barton Gellman and Daniel Williams, "U.S. Eases Stance on Serb Guns," *Washington Post,* February 16, 1994.

33. John Pomfret, "Deadline Passes without Attack," *Washington Post,* February 21, 1994.

34. Roger Cohen, "On Hilltop outside Sarajevo, A Serbian Battery Defies U.N.," *New York Times,* February 22, 1994.

35. John Pomfret, "NATO Blocks Serbs' Effort to Take Guns," *Washington Post*, May 3, 1994.

36. Quoted in Michael R. Gordon, "U.S. Rules Out Military Force against Serbs," *New York Times*, April 4, 1994.

37. Quoted in Elaine Sciolino, "White House Says Force Is a Choice in Aiding Bosnians," *New York Times*, April 8, 1994.

38. Michael R. Gordon, "The Bluff That Failed," *New York Times*, April 19, 1994.

39. Rick Atkinson, "NATO Has Plan for Massive Airstrikes against Bosnian Serb Forces," *Washington Post*, April 25, 1994.

40. William Drozdiak, "U.S., Allies Agree on Map for Partition of Bosnia, Add Incentives, Sanctions," *Washington Post*, June 30, 1994.

41. Warren Christopher, "The Middle East Peace and Other Vital Interests," Statement before the House Committee on Foreign Affairs, July 28, 1994, p. 4.

42. Daniel Williams, "U.S. Seeks New Deadline for Serb Acceptance of Bosnian Peace Plan," *Washington Post*, July 30, 1994.

43. Chuck Sudetic, "Bosnian Serbs Reject Plan for 3d Time, Defying Russia," *New York Times*, August 2, 1994.

44. Jonathan C. Randal, "Civilian Inspectors to Verify Blockade of Bosnian Serbs," *Washington Post*, September 16, 1994.

45. Frederick Cuny, "Milosevic Outwits the West Again," *Washington Post*, October 5, 1994.

46. Quoted in Nicholas Doughty, "Perry Doubts Serbia Sealed Bosnia Border," *Washington Post*, October 1, 1994.

47. John Pomfret, "Serbs Free Nearly All Hostages," *Washington Post*, June 14, 1995.

48. John Pomfret, "U.N. Rejects NATO Request to Bomb Serb Airfield after 'No-Fly' Violations," *Washington Post*, June 22, 1995.

49. Stephen Engelberg, Tim Weiner, Raymond Bonner, and Jane Perlez, "Srebrenica: The Days of Slaughter," *New York Times*, October 29, 1995.

CHAPTER 9: THE LESSONS OF BOSNIA

1. "Powerless Are the Peace-Makers," *Economist*, November 9, 1991, p. 48.

2. "The Frost Hardens in Bosnia," *Economist*, November 20, 1993, p. 51.

3. Laura Silber and Carol J. Williams, "U.N. Begins Trial Lifting of Yugoslavia Sanctions," *Los Angeles Times*, October 6, 1994.

4. "The Relief of Sarajevo," *Economist*, July 4, 1992, p. 43.

5. United Nations, Department of Public Information, *The United Nations and the Situation in the Former Yugoslavia*, Reference paper, March 15, 1994, p. 14.

6. John F. Burns, "Top Bosnian Aide Is Slain by Serb," *New York Times*, January 9, 1993.

7. Michael R. Gordon, "Policy's Limits in Bosnia," *New York Times*,

March 4, 1993.

8. "Victory for War," *Economist,* December 26, 1992–January 8, 1993, p. 61.

9. "America Drops In," *Economist,* February 27, 1993, p. 51.

10. "Serbs Say Air Strikes Would Hit U.N. Troops as Well," *Washington Times,* January 12, 1994.

11. Kurt Schork, "Bosnian Serbs Threaten U.N. with 'All Out' War," *Reuters,* November 23, 1994.

12. The British historian Norman Stone collected some of these grandiose tales and checked them carefully, and devastatingly, against the historical record. See Norman Stone, "Shooting Down the Myth of Serbia's Mighty Guerrillas," *Times* (London), August 16, 1992.

13. Elaine Sciolino, "Bosnia Threatened with U.N. Pullout, 2 U.S. Reports Say," *New York Times,* July 10, 1993.

14. Jonathan C. Randal, "Divided Bosnian Leadership Delays Talks on Partition," *Washington Post,* June 26, 1993.

15. Interview with Stephen Walker, former State Department official, Washington, D.C., August 10, 1994.

16. "Pass the Parcel," *Economist,* December 4, 1993, p. 55.

17. John M. Goshko, "U.S. Endorses NATO Role in U.N. Plan for Bosnia," *Washington Post,* February 1, 1994.

18. Quoted in John Pomfret, "Two U.N. Officials Accuse U.S. of Prolonging War in Bosnia," *Washington Post,* April 30, 1994.

19. Ibid.

20. For a cogent argument that the embargo violates the charter not only in spirit, see letter from Max M. Kampelman to Senator Carl Levin, July 27, 1994. I have a copy of this letter, which has been circulated, and copies can be had, I presume, from the sender or receiver or from the Action Council for Peace in the Balkans, Washington, D.C., of which Kampelman is an officer.

21. Resolution 727, January 8, 1992, point 6.

22. Interview with Kenneth I. Juster, Washington, D.C., August 5, 1994.

23. Quoted in Pat Towell, "Senate Retreats from Mandate to Arm Bosnian Muslims," *Congressional Quarterly,* July 2, 1994, p. 1812.

24. See, for example, Roger Cohen, "Balkan Moral Order Upset As Victim Becomes Victor," *New York Times,* November 6, 1994.

25. Catherine Bertini, "Foreword," World Food Programme, *Situation Report No. 5,* September 1993, p. 1.

26. All of the foregoing numbers are from DCI Interagency Task Force, "Bosnia by the Numbers," March 1, 1994, unclassified, CL BY 715914, DECL OADR.

27. Quoted in William Drozdiak, "European's Balkan Stance Attests to Rising German Influence," *Washington Post,* December 18, 1991.

28. See "Recognition of the Yugoslav Successor States," Position paper

of the German Foreign Ministry, official translation, *Statements and Speeches,* vol. 16, no. 10, German Information Center, New York, 1993.

29. John Newhouse, "The Diplomatic Round: Dodging the Problem," *New Yorker,* August 24, 1994, p. 66..

30. Alan Riding, "Kohl Urges Arming of Bosnian Muslims," *New York Times,* June 23, 1993.

31. "Pass the Parcel," *Economist,* December 4, 1993, p. 55.

32. Alan Riding, "Its Competitors Distracted, France Gets to Be a Power," *New York Times,* June 27, 1993.

33. Barbara Crossette, "Baker Puts Pressure on Europeans for U.N. Penalties against Serbs," *New York Times,* May 25, 1992.

34. "The Lilliputian Is Still Wriggling," *Economist,* June 6, 1992, p. 53.

35. Newhouse, "The Diplomatic Round," p. 68.

36. See, for example, Elaine Sciolino, "Who Can Make Peace in Bosnia?" *New York Times,* January 28, 1994; and Thomas W. Lippman and John M. Goshko, "Gap Remains in U.S.-France Dispute," *Washington Post,* January 28, 1994.

37. Quoted in Joel Brand, "U.N. Denounces Serb Firing of 4 Missiles," *Washington Post,* November 5, 1994.

38. John F. Burns, "Britain Warns Sarajevo: Expect No Military Help," *New York Times,* July 18, 1992.

39. Elaine Sciolino, "Bosnia's Serbs Smirk, and Keep Shooting," *New York Times,* May 9, 1993.

40. David Gompert, "How to Defeat Serbia," *Foreign Affairs,* vol. 73, no. 4 (July–August 1994), p. 38.

41. On Owen, see Noel Malcolm, "Lord Fraud," *New Republic,* June 14, 1993, pp. 19–20. On Rose, see my "Yellow Rose," *New Republic,* December 5, 1994, pp. 24–25.

42. William E. Schmidt, "Thatcher Assails West's Bosnia Policy," *New York Times,* April 15, 1993.

43. Michael R. Gordon, "Clinton Considers a Tougher Policy to Halt the Serbs," *New York Times,* April 17, 1993.

44. James Rupert, "'I Am So Glad to See Them,'" *Washington Post,* February 22, 1994. See also Victoria Clark, "Diplomatic Footwork Worthy of the Bolshoi," *Washington Times,* February 22, 1994.

45. Quoted in Lee Hockstader, "Yeltsin Voices Anger That He Was Not Consulted," *Washington Post,* April 12, 1994.

46. Ibid.

47. Warren Christopher Press Conference, State Department, Washington, D.C., April 11, 1994.

48. "The Future of the Balkans: An Interview with David Owen," *Foreign Affairs,* vol. 72, no. 2 (Spring 1993), p. 6.

49. Mihajlo Mihajlov, "Lessons of Yugoslavia," *Problems of Post-*

Communism (Fall 1994), p. 52.

50. *NBC Nightly News,* May 6, 1993.

51. Daniel Williams, "Ex-Official Accuses U.S. of Being Soft on Serbs," *Washington Post,* February 4, 1994.

52. See Cohen, *Broken Bonds,* p. 215.

53. See James E. Bjork and Allan E. Goodman, *Yugoslavia, 1991–92:Could Diplomacy Have Prevented a Tragedy?* (Washington, D.C.: Institute for the Study of Diplomacy, Georgetown University School of Foreign Service, 1993), p. 6; and "An Inch Deeper into the Balkan Quagmire," *Economist,* July 18, 1992, p. 47.

54. See "United versus Rovers," *Economist,* September 14, 1991, p. 60.

55. "After Bosnia, GATT Is Easy," *Economist,* July 24, 1993, p. 49.

56. Elaine Sciolino, "Mission in Somalia: Secretary Besieged," *New York Times,* October 16, 1993.

57. Jeane Kirkpatrick, "Boutros-Ghali's Power Grab," *Washington Post,* February 1, 1993.

58. David Ottaway and Julia Preston, "U.N. Rejects Airstrikes in Bosnia; Talks Break Up," *Washington Post,* January 20, 1994.

59. Paul Lewis, "U.N. Chief Defends Role on Air Strikes in Bosnia," *New York Times,* January 24, 1994.

60. Anthony Lake, "Bosnia: America's Interests and America's Role," Speech, Johns Hopkins University, April 7, 1994, p. 5.

61. John Pomfret, "In Bosnia, U.N. Troops Finally Go to War," *Washington Post,* May 5, 1994.

62. Julia Preston, "Airstrike Request Rejected in Bosnia," *Washington Post,* February 23, 1994.

63. John Pomfret, "Two U.N. Officials Accuse U.S. of Prolonging War in Bosnia," *Washington Post,* April 30, 1994.

64. Paul Lewis, "U.S. Says U.N. Officials in Balkans Lack Will to Oppose Serbs," *New York Times,* May 2, 1994.

65. Marlise Simons, "U.N. Tribunal Indicts Bosnian Serb Leader and a Commander," *New York Times,* July 26, 1995.

66. Roger Cohen, "British Commander in Bosnia: In a Quagmire and Sniped at from All Sides," *New York Times,* September 25, 1994.

67. Daniel Williams, "Despite Warnings, U.S. General Meets with Serb War Crimes Suspect," *Washington Post,* September 1, 1994.

68. Patrick Bishop, "Lifting the Bosnia Arms Embargo Is a Rendezvous with Catastrophe," *Daily Telegraph,* August 31, 1994.

69. Paul Adams and Bruce Clark, "UN Threat Wins Pledge from Bosnian Moslems," *Financial Times,* September 20, 1994.

70. "Bosnia's Thorny Rose," *U.S. News and World Report,* October 31, 1994, p. 38.

71. Roger Cohen, "At Odds over Bosnia," *New York Times,* October 2, 1994.

72. "U.N. Withdraws Allegation That Serb Bodies Mutilated," *Wash-*

ington Post, October 8, 1994.

73. John Pomfret, "Bosnian Serbs Seeking to Thwart U.S., Allies," *Washington Post,* August 2, 1994.

74. Chuck Sudetic, "Sarajevo Is Hit by Artillery Fire in Worst Attack since February," *New York Times,* November 9, 1994.

75. "Bodies of Serbs Found Mutilated near Sarajevo," *Washington Post,* October 7, 1994.

76. "U.N. Withdraws Allegation That Serb Bodies Mutilated," *Washington Post,* October 8, 1994.

77. Carol J. Williams, "Is U.N. Peacemaker Really an Appeaser?" *Los Angeles Times,* October 27, 1994.

78. Roger Cohen, "U.N. General Opposes More Bosnia Force," *New York Times,* September 29, 1994.

79. Exchange of correspondence among Albert Wohlstetter, Commander Bill Luti, CNO Executive Panel, and Captain J. P. Mitchell, chief of public information, Allied Forces Southern Europe. Copy in author's files.

80. R. W. Apple, Jr., "Diplomacy's Goal in Bosnia Seems Not Bold Action but Avoiding It," *New York Times,* May 23, 1993.

81. "Pass the Parcel," *Economist,* December 4, 1993, p. 54.

82. Daniel Williams, "Meeting on Bosnia Yields 'Lowest Common Denominator' of Agreement," *Washington Post,* August 1, 1994.

83. John M. Goshko, "U.S. Endorses NATO Role in U.N. Plan for Bosnia," *Washington Post,* February 1, 1994.

84. William Claiborne and Daniel Williams, "U.N. Chief Prods NATO on Bosnia Airstrikes," *Washington Post,* February 7, 1994.

85. Thomas W. Lippman and John Lancaster, "Clinton Team Is Committed to Airstrikes," *Washington Post,* April 12, 1994.

86. Ruth Marcus, "NATO Powers Consider Expanding Bosnia Role," *Washington Post,* April 19, 1994.

87. Christoph Bertram, "Irreconcilable Partners," *Washington Post,* November 2, 1994.

88. Vaclav Havel, "A New European Order?" *New York Review of Books,* March 2, 1995, p. 43.

CHAPTER 10: REMAINING THE SOLE SUPERPOWER

1. "Pentagon's New World View," *Washington Post,* May 24, 1992.

2. Patrick E. Tyler, "U.S. Strategy Plan Calls for Insuring No Rivals Develop," *New York Times,* March 8, 1992.

3. Barton Gellman, "Aim of Defense Plan Supported by Bush," *Washington Post,* March 12, 1992.

4. Joseph R. Biden, "How I Learned to Love the New World Order," *Wall Street Journal,* April 23, 1992.

5. Patrick E. Tyler, "Lone Superpower Plan: Ammunition for the Critics," *New York Times,* March 10, 1992.

6. Ibid.

7. Patrick E. Tyler, "Senior U.S. Officials Assail Lone-Superpower Policy," *New York Times,* March 11, 1992.

8. Gellman, "Aim of Defense Plan Supported by Bush."

9. These and the other excerpts cited in this and the next paragraph are from "The Pentagon's New World View," *Washington Post,* May 24, 1992.

10. Barton Gellman, "Pentagon Abandons Goal of Thwarting U.S. Rivals," *Washington Post,* May 24, 1992.

11. For example, later his advisers regretted having passed over lightly Bill Clinton's pledge to open the armed services to avowed homosexuals.

12. See Robert W. Tucker, "Realism and the New Consensus," *The National Interest,* no. 30 (Winter 1992–1993), p. 35; and Owen Harries, "Of Unstable Disposition," *The National Interest,* no. 22 (Winter 1990–1991), p. 103.

13. Owen Harries, "Drift and Mastery, Bush-Style," *The National Interest,* no. 23 (Spring 1991), p. 5.

14. Tyler, "U.S. Strategy Plan Calls for Insuring No Rivals Develop."

15. Biden, "How I Learned to Love the New World Order."

16. Bill Clinton, "A New Covenant for American Security," Speech delivered at Georgetown University, December 12, 1991.

17. General Accounting Office, "Future Years Defense Program. Optimistic Estimates Lead to Billions in Overprogramming," U.S. GAO, Washington, D.C., July 1994, p. 2, cited in Pat Towell, "GOP Faces a Clash of Priorities in Its Bid to Boost Readiness," *Congressional Quarterly,* January 14, 1995, pp. 166, 168.

18. Department of Defense news release, "Modernization Priorities in the FY 1996–01 Budget," December 9, 1994.

19. Ibid.

20. Rowland Evans and Robert Novak, "Lean Days at the Pentagon," *Washington Post,* October 13, 1994.

21. Pat Towell, "Gulf Mission Arms Both Sides in Debate over Downsizing," *Congressional Quarterly,* October 15, 1994, p. 2967. John McCain, a leading Republican spokesman on defense issues, recruited a panel of retired chiefs and deputy chiefs of staff—one from each of the services— to review the proposed force. They concluded that the ground forces provided are insufficient. While they agree with the administration's calculus that one such war would require five divisions, they complain that the total of ten divisions called for is inadequate because not all would be available or readily redeployable from current missions. For this and related points, see General Charles A. Gabriel, General Alfred M. Gray, Admiral Carlisle A. H. Trost, and General Robert W. RisCassi, *A Report on Military Capa-*

bilities and Readiness for U.S. Senator John S. McCain, February 7, 1995.

22. Quoted in Eric Schmitt, "Some Doubt U.S. Ability to Fight Wars on 2 Fronts," *New York Times,* October 17, 1994.

23. Response to questions during panel discussion "U.S. Force Structure: Enough to Meet the Peace," American Enterprise Institute, Washington, D.C., December 7, 1994.

24. I am talking in terms of budget authority for fiscal years 1991 through 1994, comparing the projections in the Department of Defense budget submission of April 1989 with the actual amounts obligated. In a sense, taking April 1989 as a baseline understates the peace dividend. Although the Warsaw Pact had not yet begun to break up, we were already deep into the warming years of *glasnost* and *perestroika,* and therefore the April 1989 budget already reflected a reduced sense of threat as compared with the tenser years of the cold war.

25. Department of Defense, "FY1995, Background Briefing," February 5, 1994, and numbers from "General Purpose Force Levels," p. 8, cited in Office of Senator John McCain, "How Serious Is the Clinton Defense Deficit?" December 1994.

26. Secretary of Defense William J. Perry, "Annual Report to the President and Congress," February 1995, p. 166.

27. Dana Priest, "'Non-Defense' Projects Targeted," *Washington Post,* February 10, 1995; Walter Pincus and Dan Morgan, "Congress Protects Pork in Pentagon Spending," *Washington Post,* March 28, 1995.

28. Priest, "'Non-Defense' Projects."

29. "GOP Targets," *Congressional Quarterly,* January 14, 1995, p. 168.

30. Pat Towell, "Measure Heralds a Tug of War between People, Programs," *Congressional Quarterly,* September 10, 1994, p. 2527.

31. "Recruit Quality over Time," table prepared by the Office of the Assistant Secretary of Defense for Legislative Affairs, Washington, D.C., November 1994. I am grateful to John F. Luddy II for bringing this chart to my attention.

32. See, for example, General John M. Loh, "Adapting U.S. Military Organizations to the New Security Environment," *Strategic Review* (Spring 1994), pp. 11–12. Loh says that the retention rate for AWACS pilots was only 21 percent in 1993 and 34 percent in 1994, and he attributes this to missions that have kept AWACS crews away from home for an average above 160 days a year as compared with a service standard of 120 days.

33. Warren and Anita Manshel Lecture by Anthony Lake, "American Power and American Diplomacy," Harvard University, October 21, 1994.

34. Bradley Graham and John F. Harris, "Army's Combat Readiness Overstated, Perry Admits," *Washington Post,* November 16, 1994.

35. Defense Science Board Task Force on Readiness, *Final Report,* Department of Defense, Office of the Under Secretary of Defense for Acquisi-

tion and Technology, Washington, D.C., June 1994, p. i.

36. William W. Kaufmann, "'Hollow' Forces?" *Brookings Review* (Fall 1994), p. 26.

37. Under Secretary of Defense–Comptroller, "FY1996 DoD Budget Briefing," Washington, D.C., February 6, 1995. (The pages of this document are not numbered; the statistic I have cited appears on a page with the heading, "Defense Recapitalization.")

38. Associated Press, "Senate Defense Bill Called 'Bare-Bones,'" *Washington Post,* July 26, 1994.

39. See Dov S. Zakheim, "A Top-Down Plan for the Pentagon," *Orbis,* vol. 39, no. 2 (Spring 1995), pp. 180–82; and Pat Towell, "Administration Hedges Bets in $1.3 Trillion Program," *Congressional Quarterly,* February 12, 1994, p. 335.

40. Secretary of Defense William J. Perry, "Annual Report to the President and Congress" (Historical Budget Tables), February 1995.

41. C. Fred Bergsten, "The Primacy of Economics," *Foreign Policy,* no. 87 (Summer 1992), p. 6.

42. Edward N. Luttwak, "From Geopolitics to Geo-Economics," *The National Interest,* no. 20 (Summer 1990), p. 17.

43. Some citations from Aspin on the subject may be found in Dov S. Zakheim and Jeffrey M. Ranney, "Matching Defense Strategies to Resources," *International Security,* vol. 18, no. 1 (Summer 1993), pp. 51–52.

44. Jonathan Schell, *The Fate of the Earth* (New York: Alfred A. Knopf, 1982); and "The Pastoral Letter on War and Peace; The Challenge of Peace; God's Promise and Our Response," The National Conference of Catholic Bishops, 1983, reprinted in Jim Castelli, *The Bishops and the Bomb: Waging Peace in a Nuclear Age* (Garden City, N.Y.: Image Books, 1983).

45. Lawrence J. Korb, "Les No More: How the Pentagon Undid the Defense Secretary," *Washington Post,* December 19, 1993.

46. Chong-Pin Lin, "The Power Projection Capabilities of the People's Liberation Army," Paper presented at the sixth annual People's Liberation Army Conference in Coolfont, West Virginia, June 9–11, 1995. See also Nicholas D. Kristof, "The Rise of China," *Foreign Affairs* (November–December 1993), pp. 59–74.

47. U.S. Arms Control and Disarmament Agency, "World Military Expenditures and Arms Transfers, 1993–1994," U.S. Government Printing Office, Washington, D.C., February, 1995, p. 4.

48. "Report on Nonproliferation and Counterproliferation Activities and Programs," Office of the Deputy Secretary of Defense, Washington, D.C., May 1, 1994, p. ES-1.

49. See Albert Wohlstetter and Gregory S. Jones, "A Nuclear Treaty That Breeds Weapons," *Wall Street Journal,* April 4, 1995.

50. "Missile Shield a Must," *New York Post,* February 28, 1995.

51. Walter B. Slocombe, "Resolution of the North Korean Issue," Remarks (as written) to the American Enterprise Institute Conference on Peace on the Korean Peninsula, March 13, 1995, p. 10.

52. Comments during question-and-answer session at the American Enterprise Institute Conference on Peace on the Korean Peninsula, March 13, 1995.

53. Colin S. Gray, "Off the Map: Defense Planning after the Soviet Threat," *Strategic Review* (Spring 1994), pp. 28–29.

54. David Callahan, "Saving Defense Dollars," *Foreign Policy*, no. 96 (Fall 1994), p. 102.

55. General Gabriel et al., "Report," p. 10.

CHAPTER 11: WHEN TO USE FORCE?

1. U.S. Congress, Senate, Committee on Appropriations, "Departments of Commerce, Justice, and State, the Judiciary, and Related Agencies Appropriations for Fiscal Year 1994," Hearings before the Subcommittee on Commerce, Justice, State and Judiciary, April 27, 1993, Washington, D.C., p. 352; see also Elaine Sciolino, "Christopher Explains Conditions for Use of U.S. Force in Bosnia," *New York Times*, April 28, 1993.

2. Caspar Weinberger, "The Uses of Military Power," Remarks prepared for delivery to the National Press Club, November 28, 1984, News Release, Office of Assistant Secretary of Defense (Public Affairs), Washington, D.C., no. 609–84.

3. Christopher's four conditions were a clear goal, a strong likelihood of success, an exit strategy, and public support. Weinberger had six: an interest vital to ourselves or our allies; public support; a clear objective; an intention of winning; exhaustion of other remedies; and a clear connection between means and ends.

4. The Catholic doctrine of "just war" originated with Augustine and has evolved over centuries of church teaching. This important body of inquiry into the legal and moral bases of war is today embraced by scholars both within and without the Catholic tradition. The doctrine is divided into two parts: *Jus ad Bellum,* meaning the rules governing the decision to go to war, and *Jus in Bello,* meaning those governing the conduct of combatants. The former has direct bearing on the questions raised by Weinberger and Christopher and discussed in this chapter. It sets seven criteria for recourse to war: just cause; competent authority (to declare war); comparative justice (a compelling case for one's own side); right intention (to redress a wrong, not to use it as a pretext for aggrandizement); last resort; probability of success; and proportionality (between the good to be achieved and the costs of war.)

5. Remarks by President George Bush at the American Legislative Exchange Council, Washington, D.C., March 1, 1991.

6. Thomas L. Friedman, "Global Mandate," *New York Times,* March 5, 1995.

7. *Congressional Record*—Senate, January 11, 1991, S 191.

8. U.S. Congress, Senate, Committee on Armed Services, *Hearings, Crisis in the Persian Gulf Region—U.S. Policy Options and Implications,* 101st Congress, 2d session, S. Hrg. 101-1071, p. 116.

9. *Congressional Record*—Senate, S 269, January 11, 1991.

10. Jacob Weisberg, "Gulfballs," *New Republic,* March 25, 1991, p. 17.

11. Interview with Cyrus Vance, CNN "Newsday," January 10, 1991.

12. George Bush, "Address to the Nation Announcing the Deployment of United States Armed Forces to Saudi Arabia," August 8, 1990, *Weekly Compilation of Presidential Documents,* p. 1108.

13. George Bush, "Address before the 45th Session of the United Nations General Assembly in New York City," October 1, 1990, *Weekly Compilation of Presidential Documents,* p. 1496. For other iterations of this point, see other entries in the *Weekly Compilation* for the following dates and pages: August 29, 1990, p. 1174; September 25, 1990, p. 1275; September 26, 1990, p. 1461; October 23, 1990, p. 1640; November 8, 1990, p. 1790; and November 17, 1990, p. 1853.

14. George Bush, "Address before a Joint Session of the Congress on the Persian Gulf Crisis and the Federal Budget Deficit," *Weekly Compilation of Presidential Documents,* vol. 26, no. 37, September 11, 1990, p. 1359.

15. *Congressional Record*—Senate, S 370, January 12, 1991.

16. Roger Cohen, "Peace in the Balkans Now Relies on Man Who Fanned Its Wars," *New York Times,* October 31, 1995.

17. Stephen Engelberg and Eric Schmitt, "Western Officials Say Serbia Helps Bosnian Comrades," *New York Times,* June 11, 1995.

18. John Pomfret, "Serbia Seen Still Aiding War Effort," *Washington Post,* July 4, 1995.

19. Michael R. Gordon, "U.S. Says Belgrade Joined in Attacks," *New York Times,* April 18, 1993.

20. John Pomfret, "Serbs Push into Zepa 'Safe Area,'" *Washington Post,* July 17, 1995.

21. Engelberg and Schmitt, "Western Officials Say Serbia Helps Bosnian Comrades"; Pomfret, "Serbia Seen Still Aiding War."

22. Engelberg and Schmitt, "Western Officials Say Serbia Helps Bosnian Comrades."

23. At a press conference, General Shalikashvili said, "We need to . . . go on the assumption that the Bosnian Serbs have a very effective integrated air defense system [which is] closely linked to various radars throughout the region," London, England, June 28, 1995, Office of the Chairman of the Joint Chiefs of Staff, Public Affairs, Washington, D.C., p. 1.

24. Dan Oberdorfer and John Lancaster, "U.N. Chief Weighs Use of U.S.

Troops in Somalia; Security Council to Consider Options for Protecting Relief Supply Lines," *Washington Post,* November 27, 1992.

25. Paul Lewis, "U.N. Will Increase Troops in Somalia," *New York Times,* March 27, 1993.

26. The figure *at least 750,000* is given by Alex de Waal and Rakiya Omaar, "The Genocide in Rwanda and the International Response," *Current History,* April 1995, p. 156; the words *upward of a million* are from Holly J. Burkhalter, "The Question of Genocide," *World Policy Journal,* vol. 11, no. 4 (Winter 1994–1995), p. 44.

27. Donatella Lorch, "A Year Later, Rwandans Stay and Chaos Looms," *New York Times,* July 15, 1995.

28. Burkhalter, "The Question of Genocide," p. 47.

29. Douglas Jehl, "Officials Told to Avoid Calling Killings 'Genocide,'" *New York Times,* June 10, 1994.

30. Ibid.

31. Security Council Resolution 940, adopted July 31, 1994.

32. Chester A. Crocker, "The Lessons of Somalia," *Foreign Affairs,* vol. 74, no. 3 (May–June 1995), p. 3.

33. President Bill Clinton, Address to the General Assembly of the United Nations, September 27, 1993.

34. Remarks by Anthony Lake at Johns Hopkins University, Baltimore, April 7, 1994.

35. See Kalevi J. Holsti, *Peace and War: Armed Conflicts and International Order 1648–1989* (Cambridge: Cambridge University Press, 1991), p. 308, table 12.2.

36. See Boris Yeltsin, "Peace Keeping Burden in the Former Soviet Union Lies upon the Russian Federation," *Vital Speeches,* October 15, 1994, pp. 5–8; and Russell Watson, "A Yeltsin Doctrine?" *Newsweek,* October 10, 1994, p. 42.

37. *A National Security Strategy of Engagement and Enlargement,* White House, July 1994, p. 7.

38. I have not compiled my own list but borrowed from extant compilations, of which there are many. I have consulted the following: J. D. Singer, *Resort to Arms* (Beverly Hills: Sage, 1977); J. D. Singer and M. Small, "Conflict in the International Systems, 1816–1977: Historical Trends and Policy Futures," in C. Kegley and P. McGowan, eds., *Challenges to America* (Beverly Hills: Sage, 1979); Herbert K. Tillema, *International Armed Conflict since 1945* (Boulder, Colo.: Westview Press, 1991); Michael Clodfelter, *Warfare and Armed Conflicts: A Statistical Reference to Casualty and Other Figures, 1618–1991* (Jefferson, N.C.: McFarland and Co., 1992); Kenneth Macksey and William Woodhouse, *The Penguin Encyclopedia of Modern Warfare* (New York: Viking Press, 1991); International Institute of Strategic Studies, *Strategic Survey* (London: Brassey's, 1992, 1993, 1994); and

Stockholm International Peace Research Institute, *SIPRI Yearbook* (Oxford: Oxford University Press, 1993–1994). Since, however, these sources do not all agree, I am counting those "interstate" wars that are listed by at least three of them. The resulting list of twenty-five appears as an appendix to this chapter.

39. I doubt that the U.S. invasion of Grenada should be classified as an aggression, because of the breakdown of legal order there, the threat to American nationals, and the obvious absence of any American designs on or against Grenada. But others have categorized it this way.

40. Ian Brownlie, *International Law and the Use of Force by States* (London: Oxford University Press, 1963), p. 57.

41. See chap. 6.

42. Rosalyn Higgins, "The New United Nations and Former Yugoslavia, *International Affairs,* vol. 69, no. 3 (1993), p. 471.

43. Holsti, *Peace and War,* p. 251.

44. Anthony Eden, *The Memoirs of Anthony Eden Earl of Avon,* vol. 2, *The Reckoning* (Boston: Houghton Mifflin, 1965), p. 517.

CHAPTER 12: FOSTERING DEMOCRACY

1. Paul Gottfried, "At Sea with the Global Democrats," *Wall Street Journal,* January 19, 1989; and Patrick Buchanan, "America First—and Second, and Third," *The National Interest,* no. 19 (Spring 1990), p. 81.

2. See Howard M. Sachar, *A History of Israel: From the Rise of Zionism to Our Time* (New York: Alfred A. Knopf, 1982), pp. 315–18.

3. Jack F. Levy, "Domestic Politics and War," *Journal of Interdisciplinary History,* vol. 18 (Spring 1988), pp. 653–73.

4. Bruce Russett, *Grasping the Democratic Peace: Principles for a Post–Cold War World* (Princeton: Princeton University Press, 1993), p. 11.

5. Ibid., p. 30.

6. See appendix to chapter 11.

7. When I say that Israel's war was reactive, I am not referring to the shelling that immediately preceded it but to the fact that the PLO, an organization sworn to Israel's destruction, had taken over southern Lebanon, on Israel's border, and emplaced its military machine there. Turkey invaded Cyprus in response to a coup, engineered by the military junta ruling Greece, designed to unite Cyprus with Greece.

8. According to the *New York Times* (March 24, 1991), the countries that had sent forces or medical teams to the Persian Gulf region by the time the ground war started were Afghanistan, Argentina, Australia, Bangladesh, Belgium, Britain, Canada, Czechoslovakia, Denmark, Egypt, France, Greece, Gulf countries (Bahrain, Oman, Qatar, United Arab Emirates), Hungary, Italy, Kuwait, Morocco, Netherlands, New Zealand, Niger, Norway, Paki-

stan, Philippines, Poland, Romania, Saudi Arabia, Spain, Senegal, Sierra Leone, Singapore, South Korea, Sweden, and Syria. Of these, those listed as "free" by Freedom House (in its 1992 survey, which covers 1991) were Argentina, Australia, Bangladesh, Belgium, Britain, Canada, Czechoslovakia, Denmark, France, Greece, Hungary, Italy, Netherlands, New Zealand, Norway, Poland, Spain, South Korea, and Sweden.

9. The "Bangkok Declaration" was adopted at the meeting of ministers and representatives of Asian states, in Bangkok, March 29–April 2, 1993. Its point 8 states: "while human rights are universal in nature, they must be considered in the context of a dynamic and evolving process of international norm-setting, bearing in mind the significance of national and regional particularities and various historical, cultural and religious backgrounds."

10. Joseph C. Grew, Memorandum of conversation, May 28, 1945, in U.S. Department of State, *Foreign Relations of the United States,* vol. 6, p. 545. Cited in Theodore Cohen, *Remaking Japan* (New York: Macmillan, 1987), p. 17.

11. Arnold J. Toynbee, "Things Not Foreseen at Paris," *Foreign Affairs,* vol. 12, no. 3 (April 1934), p. 478.

12. Samuel P. Huntington, *The Third Wave: Democratization in the Late Twentieth Century* (Norman: University of Oklahoma Press, 1991), p. 76.

13. Ibid., p. 310.

14. Seymour Martin Lipset, "The Centrality of Political Culture," *Journal of Democracy,* vol. 1, no. 4 (Spring 1990), p. 80.

15. Remarks at a luncheon at the American Enterprise Institute, Washington, D.C., January 27, 1993.

16. Carroll J. Doherty and John R. Crawford, "Where the Money Goes: Foreign Operations FY94," *Congressional Quarterly,* December 11, 1993, p. 75.

17. World Commission on Environment and Development, *Our Common Future* (New York: Oxford University Press, 1987), p. 14.

18. Herbert Stein and Murray Foss, *An Illustrated Guide to the American Economy* (Washington, D.C.: AEI Press, 1992), p. 10.

19. Remarks by Lech Walesa before RFE/RFL Fund, Washington, D.C., November 1989.

20. Remarks by Vaclav Havel to the Czechoslovak service of Voice of America, Washington, D.C., February 20, 1990.

21. Commission on Broadcasting to the People's Republic of China, September, 1992, p. 2.

22. In addition to carrying out its own program, the NED serves as an umbrella for four companion institutes created by the same legislation that created the NED: one affiliated with each of the major political parties and one each affiliated with the AFL-CIO and the U.S. Chamber of Commerce.

The theory is that these institutes will give special support to their analogues within target countries. The NED's budget of $34 million in FY 1995 included allocations for each of these institutes. In addition, the institutes raise some other funds or carry out programs for U.S. AID. The total of the budgets of the NED and companions in 1994 was about $60 million.

23. Ariel Cohen, "The Purposes of Russian Aid: Supporting Democratic Capitalism," *Backgrounder,* Heritage Foundation, Washington, D.C., July 17, 1995, p. 8.

24. Andrew J. Nathan, *China's Crisis: Dilemmas of Reform and Prospects for Democracy* (New York: Columbia University Press, 1990), p. 122.

25. Ibid., p. 207.

26. President Bill Clinton, News conference, Washington, D.C., May 26, 1994, in *U.S. Department of State Dispatch,* vol. 5, no. 22, May 30, 1994.

27. Anthony Lake, "Confronting Backlash States," *Foreign Affairs,* vol. 73, no. 2 (March–April 1994), pp. 48–51.

28. Julia Preston, "U.N. Offers Plan to Ease Oil Embargo on Iraq for Humanitarian Reasons," *Washington Post,* April 14, 1994.

29. Interview by Peter Tarnoff, Worldnet TV, USIA, December 21, 1994.

30. U.S. Congress, House of Representatives, Subcommittee on Europe and the Middle East of the Committee on Foreign Affairs, *Hearing on Developments in the Middle East,* March 1, 1994.

31. State Department Report on the People's Mujahadeen of Iran, October 28, 1994.

32. Thomas M. Campbell and George C. Herring, *The Diaries of Edward R. Stettinius, Jr., 1943–1946* (New York: New Viewpoints, 1975), pp. 339–40.

33. Bernard Lewis, "The Roots of Muslim Rage," *Atlantic Monthly,* vol. 266, no. 3 (September 1990), p. 48.

CHAPTER 13: FREE TRADE

1. For a cogent critique of this idea, see Daniel Pipes, "It's Not the Economy, Stupid," *Washington Post,* July 2, 1995.

2. Anne O. Krueger, *American Trade Policy: A Tragedy in the Making* (Washington, D.C.: AEI Press, 1995), p. 7.

3. Quoted in John Mashek, "Preview '80: Texas' Connally: Bucking Odds, Coming Up Fast," *U.S. News and World Report,* July 2, 1979, p. 30.

4. *New York Times,* October 13, 1982. Cited in Jagdish Bhagwati, *Protectionism* (Cambridge, Mass.: MIT Press, 1989), p. 64.

5. Theodore White, "The Danger from Japan," *New York Times Magazine,* July 28, 1985, p. 23. Cited in ibid.

6. William Pfaff, "Redefining World Power," *Foreign Affairs,* vol. 70, no. 1 (America and the World 1990–1991), pp. 37–38.

7. For example, Clyde V. Prestowitz, Jr., *Trading Places* (New York:

Basic Books, 1988); or James M. Fallows, *More like Us: Making America Great Again* (Boston: Houghton Mifflin, 1989).

8. Norman J. Ornstein and Mark Schmitt, "Post–Cold War Politics," *Foreign Policy*, no. 79 (Summer 1990), p. 177.

9. John E. Rielly, "Public Opinion: The Pulse of the 90s," *Foreign Policy*, no. 82 (Spring 1991), p. 80.

10. Prestowitz, *Trading Places*, p. 2.

11. Krueger, *American Trade Policy*, p. 41.

12. See Laura D'Andrea Tyson, *Who's Bashing Whom? Trade Conflict in High Technology Industries* (Washington, D.C.: Institute for International Economics, 1992).

13. See, for example, Alan Tonelson, "Beating Back Predatory Trade," *Foreign Affairs*, vol. 73, no. 4 (July–August 1994), pp. 123–35.

14. See, for example, Paul R. Krugman, "The Narrow and Broad Arguments for Free Trade," *American Economic Review*, vol. 83, no. 2 (May 1993), pp. 362–66.

15. Paul Krugman, "Competitiveness: A Dangerous Obsession," *Foreign Affairs*, vol. 73, no. 2 (March–April 1994), p. 30.

16. Jagdish Bhagwati and Vivek H. Dehejia, "Freer Trade and Wages of the Unskilled—Is Marx Striking Again?" in Jagdish Bhagwati and Marvin Kosters, eds., *Trade and Wages* (Washington, D.C.: AEI Press, 1994), p. 38.

17. See, for example, United Nations, *Towards a New Trade Policy for Development*, Report by the Secretary-General of the United Nations Conference on Trade and Development, E/COF. 46/3, 1964.

18. Robert W. Crandall, "The Effects of U.S. Trade Protection for Autos and Steel," *Brookings Papers on Economic Activity*, vol. 1(1987), p. 276.

19. U.S. International Trade Commission, *The Economic Effects of Significant U.S. Imports Restraints*, USITC Publication 2699 (November 1993), pp. 11–21, cited in Joe Cobb, "A Guide to the New GATT Agreement," *Backgrounder* 985, Heritage Foundation, Washington, D.C., May 5, 1994, p. 18.

20. Krueger, *American Trade Policy*, p. 3.

21. Isaiah Frank, "Towards Freer Trade among Nations: A US Perspective," in John Nieuwenhuysen, ed., *Towards Free Trade between Nations* (Oxford: Oxford University Press, 1989), p. 60.

22. Krueger, *American Trade Policy*, p. 3.

23. James Bovard, *The Fair Trade Fraud* (New York: St. Martin's Press, 1991), pp. 75–76.

24. Clyde V. Prestowitz, Jr., "Beyond Laissez Faire," *Foreign Policy*, no. 87 (Summer 1992), p. 74.

25. Ibid., p. 78.

26. C. Fred Bergsten, "The Primacy of Economics," *Foreign Policy*, no. 87 (Summer 1992), pp. 14, 12.

27. Prestowitz, "Beyond Laissez Faire," p. 77.

28. Henry R. Nau, *Trade and Security: U.S. Policies at Cross-Purposes* (Washington, D.C.: AEI Press, 1995), p. 99.

29. On this point, see Francis Fukuyama, "Virtue and Prosperity," *The National Interest,* no. 40 (Summer 1995), pp. 22–23.

30. I am grateful to Franklin Lavin, who first made this point to me.

31. Paul Krugman, "The Myth of Asia's Miracle," *Foreign Affairs,* vol. 73, no. 6 (November–December 1994), p. 78.

32. Council on Competitiveness, *Competitiveness Index 1994,* Washington, D.C., July 1994, pp. 12–21.

33. "Can America Compete?" *Economist,* January 18, 1992.

34. Frances Williams, "US Displaces Japan as Most Competitive Nation," *Financial Times,* September 7, 1994. The United States continued to hold this lead a year later. See Guy de Jonquieres, "U.S. Ranked as 'Most Competitive' Nation," *Financial Times,* September 6, 1995.

35. Roger C. Altman, "Why Pressure Tokyo?" *Foreign Affairs,* vol. 73, no. 3 (May–June 1994), pp. 4–5.

36. Bhagwati, *Protectionism,* p. 70.

37. Daniel Williams and Clay Chandler, "U.S. Aide Sees Relations with Asia in Peril," *Washington Post,* May 5, 1994.

38. Altman, "Why Pressure Tokyo?" p. 3.

39. Surveys by the Gallup Organization (U.S.) and the Yomiuri Shimbun (Japan), latest that of September 24–October 13, 1992 (U.S.) and September 25–26, 1992 (Japan). Surveys by Louis Harris and Associates and the Asahi Shimbun, latest that of May 23 and 26, 1994 (U.S.) and May 28–29 (Japan).

40. Jim Hoagland, "A Soft Deal with Japan," *Washington Post,* July 5, 1995.

41. Jagdish Bhagwati, "The Diminished Giant Syndrome," *Foreign Affairs,* vol. 72, no.2 (Spring 1993), p. 25.

42. Hobart Rowen, "Cozying Up to the Chinese Dictators," *Washington Post,* September 1, 1994.

43. Congressman Richard A. Gephardt, "Speech on the North American Free Trade Agreement," Delivered to the National Press Club, Washington, D.C., September 21, 1993, p. 3.

44. Ibid., p. 9.

45. The basic principles of GATT are "nondiscrimination," meaning that any import barriers a nation creates must be applied equally to all nations; "national treatment," meaning that once they have legally entered the country, foreign goods must not be treated differently from domestic ones; protecting domestic industries only by using tariffs, not quotas; refraining from specified unfair practices; and participating in successive rounds of talks about reducing barriers further.

46. Franklin L. Lavin, "Clinton and Trade," *The National Interest,* no.

32 (Summer 1993), p. 37.

47. Alfred E. Eckes, "Trading American Interests," *Foreign Affairs,* vol. 71, no. 4 (Fall 1992), p. 135.

48. See, for example, Prestowitz, "Beyond Laissez Faire," or Bergsten, "The Primacy of Economics."

CHAPTER 14: CONCLUSION

1. Quoted in Norman J. Ornstein and Mark Schmitt, "Post–Cold War Politics," *Foreign Policy,* no. 79 (Summer 1990), p. 179.

2. See chap. 9, p. 117.

INDEX

Abdic, Fikret, 116
Abyssinia (Ethiopia), 59–60, 81, 167, 168
Achille Lauro, 64
Adams, Gordon, 47
Afghanistan, 146
Africa, 177, 203
Agency for International Development, U.S. (USAID), 182, 186
Agenda for Peace, An (Boutros-Ghali), 72, 75
Aggression. *See* Cooperative and collective security
AID. *See* Agency for International Development
Aideed, Mohammed Farah, 159
Ailleret, Charles, 63
Akashi, Yasushi, 107, 110, 117, 125, 127, 207
Albanians and Albania, 87, 129
Albrecht-Carrie, Rene, 59, 60
Albright, Madeleine, 73, 74, 75, 76, 117, 158
Altman, Roger, 201, 202
Anti-Ballistic Missile Treaty of 1972, 150
Aristide, Jean Bertrand, 160

Armitage, Richard, 82
Arms and technology sales, 65, 69, 78
Aspin, Les, 146, 148
Austria, 57, 131

Badinter Commission, 95, 97–98, 119
Badinter, Robert, 95
Bahr, Egon, 66–67
Baker, James, 11, 89–90, 99–100, 120, 181–82
Balance of power, 30–31, 145, 151
Belarus, 187
Belgium, 57, 60, 61
Benoit, Emile, 47
Bergsten, Fred, 198–99
Bertram, Christoph, 128
Bhagwati, Jagdish, 197, 201, 202–3
Biden, Joseph, 136
Bi-Partisan Commission on Entitlement and Tax Reform, 41
Blomberg, Werner von, 60
Bolshevism, 25–26, 58
Borah, William, 23
Bosnia and Herzegovina: arms embargo, 101, 102, 108, 117–19,

121, 126, 131; Dayton (Ohio) settlement, 111, 112, 129; deaths in, 119; dispute over Kosova, 85–87; ethnic issues in, 98, 101, 109, 110, 112, 114; European activities in, 32, 88, 119–24; Gorazde, 107, 110–11, 117, 122, 126, 128, 157; Joint Action Program, 103; leadership and lessons of, 112–30, 207; NATO activities, 105–8, 110, 111, 115, 117, 120, 122, 128–29, 130; proposed divisions of, 103, 105, 108, 109–10, 112; recognition and independence of, 97–98; safe/no fly/exclusion zones, 103, 104, 105, 109, 110–11, 114–15, 117, 126–27, 157; sanctions, 109, 110, 114, 120; Sarajevo, 100, 105–6, 109, 110, 111, 116, 117, 122, 127; Srebrenica, 102, 110, 115, 117, 157; as a state, 158; UN activities, 76, 80, 97, 99, 100, 103, 106, 108, 109, 110, 114–15, 121, 124–25, 126–27, 128, 169; U.S. activities, 88, 89–90, 102, 118, 119–20, 122, 123, 128, 130, 131; war crimes tribunals, 112, 126; Zepa, 115, 117, 157. *See also* Serbs and Serbia; United Nations; Vance-Owen Plan

Boutros-Ghali, Boutros: Bosnia, 99, 124, 128, 131; defense planning, 138; peacekeeping, 76; role and mission of, 1, 72, 75, 80, 82; Somalia, 74, 158–59

Bretton Woods Accord, 24, 33

Britain. *See* Great Britain

Brookings Institution, 16

Brown, Ron, 203

Brownlie, Ian, 168

Brzezinski, Zbigniew, 15, 155

Buchanan, Patrick, 10, 136, 206

Budget, federal: budget deficit, 38, 49–50; defense spending, 38–39, 43, 44, 45–47, 140–42; discretionary spending, 40–42; entitlements, 39–40, 41–43, 141; foreign policy, 12, 13, 15, 36–37, 39, 40–41, 44–45, 206; interest on national debt, 40, 41

Bush, George: Bosnia, 100, 101, 156; defense spending of, 11; "new world order," 155–56; Persian Gulf War, 32, 68–69, 154, 155–56; policies of, 10–11; Somalia, 74, 158

Bush (George) administration: Bosnia, 99–101, 117, 131; defense planning guidance, 136–37, 146; Yugoslav disintegration, 89, 90

Carnegie Endowment for International Peace, 16, 24, 31

Carrington, Lord Peter, 94, 96

Carter, Jimmy, 67, 155, 160

CBO. *See* Congressional Budget Office

Cedras, Raoul, 160

Chamberlain, Austen, 81

Chamberlain, Neville, 61, 103, 129

Chile, 176

China, 59. *See also* People's Republic of China

Christianity, 178

Christopher, Warren: Bosnia, 102, 103, 105, 108–9, 117; criteria for the use of force, 152, 153, 154; isolationism and, 18; Thatcher, Margaret and, 122

Churchill, Winston, 25–26, 59, 61, 169

Clark, Wesley, 126

Claude, Innis, 81, 82

Clinton, Bill: Bosnia, 101, 103, 105, 106, 118, 122, 209; defense policy, 139–46, 147, 149, 150; defense budgeting and spending, 11, 139–42; deficit reduction, 38, 41; GATT, 203; isolationism and, 11, 18; NAFTA, 203; People's Republic of China and, 187; Republican Party and, 18, 206; Rwanda, 159; United Nations and, 73–75, 80, 162

Clinton (Bill) administration: Bosnia, 101–5, 131; foreign policies of, 3, 139, 183, 188, 206; Haiti, 159; health care reform, 42; Presidential Decision Directive, 75; Somalia, 157–58, 158–59, 162; trade issues, 195; United Nations and, 74–75

Cohen, Roger, 127

Cold war: "doves" and "hawks," 20–21; effects of, 53; end of, 166–67; post–cold war period, 3, 5, 14, 25, 44, 53–56, 68–70, 155; Reagan Doctrine, 65; Soviet Union and, 174; United States and, 16, 23, 24, 174, 181; Western Europe during, 62–68

Commerce. *See* Economic issues; individual countries

Commission on Human Rights (UN), 78

Commission on Improving the Effectiveness of the United Nations (U.S.), 72

Communism, 26, 53, 65, 87, 187

Concert of Europe, 54, 56

Conference on Security and Cooperation in Europe (CSCE), 91, 92, 97

Congress, U.S., 11–12, 74

Congressional Budget Office (CBO), 39, 140, 143

Congressional Quarterly, 11, 182

Congressional Research Service, 142

Connally, John, 192

Conservatism, 17–18, 47–49. *See also* Republican Party

Cooperative and collective security, 16–17, 29–30, 63, 138–40, 168–70

Council on Foreign Relations, 13

Cranston, Alan, 136

Croats and Croatia, 80, 87–88, 89, 96, 98, 111, 116. *See also* Bosnia

Crocker, Chester, 161

Czechoslovakia, 60, 61, 103

Daily Telegraph (London), 126

Dallaire, Romeo, 159

Danforth, John C., 41, 42

Defense spending. *See* Economic issues

De Gaulle, Charles, 62–63

Dchejia, Vivek, 197

Delors, Jacques, 91, 92

Democracy: areas of strategic interest, 185–90; in Catholic countries, 178; in China, 187–88; European, 174–75; in Haiti, 162; nature of, 173–80, 186; role of, 4; spread of, 33, 164–65, 177–80, 184–85, 190, 208; United States and, 175, 180–81, 208; war and peace in, 173–75; waves of, 179–80

Deng Xiao Ping, 56

Deterrence, 146–47, 149

Diesing, Paul, 34

Domestic problems and policies, 15–16, 19, 47–50, 209. *See also* United States

Eagleburger, Lawrence, 89, 101

Eckes, Alfred E., 205

Economic issues: costs of defense strategies, 137–38, 141, 145–46; costs of restoring order, 3; free and strategic trade, 191–205;

growth over historical time, 183; isolationism and, 15–16; military spending, 45–47, 54; opportunity costs, 47; "peace dividend," 141; political power and, 54; post–World War II period, 32–33; protectionism, 192, 193, 194–95, 196–98; sanctions, 78, 97, 109, 110, 113, 153, 187; security issues and, 145–46; standard of living, 37, 50; trading blocs, 203; use of force, 163–64. *See also* Commerce; individual countries
Economist, 90, 92, 94, 96, 97, 100, 114–16, 117, 120, 124, 128
Eden, Anthony, 169
Egypt, 131, 174
Elections, 10–11, 18, 101, 176
England. *See* Great Britain
Environmental issues, 203
Escapism, 12–13
Ethnic cleansing. *See* Bosnia; Rwanda
European Community (EC): Bosnia, 99, 101, 105, 108–9, 116–17, 123–24; disintegration of Yugoslavia, 89, 90–95, 96–97; German role in, 96
Europe, Eastern, 69
Europe, Western: during the cold war, 62–68; economic factors, 33; missile deployments, 66–68; NATO and, 63–64; standard of living, 37; as a superpower or leader, 53–54, 56–70, 82; trade with Eastern Europe, 69; U.S. forces in, 142; during World War I, 56–58; during World War II, 58–61. *See also* Bosnia and Herzegovina

Fascism, 58
Federal Reserve Board, 199
Finland, 81, 173

Force. *See* Foreign aid and policies, U.S.
Foreign Affairs, 14
Foreign aid, 12, 13, 15, 36–37, 39, 44–46, 54, 182–84, 185
Foreign policies, U.S., 3–4; Bosnia, 100; containment, 24, 62, 64, 65, 210; costs of, 43–47, 205; democracy and, 173–90; domestic policies and, 15–16, 19, 209–10; "doves" versus "hawks," 20–21; "fortress America," 30; humanitarian actions, 22–23, 161–62; *imperial overstretch,* 46; justification for force, 160–63; military actions, 22; role of elite opinions, 13–15; spending on, 12, 13, 15, 36–37, 39, 44–46, 54; use of force, 152–70; Washingtonians and Wilsonians, 20–35. *See also* Isolationism; United States
Foreign Policy, 14, 15
Foss, Murray, 46, 183
France: arms sales, 69; attitude toward the United States, 2; Bosnia, 101, 108, 116, 117, 118, 120–21, 124; during the cold war, 65; "force de frappe," 63; leadership of, 2; NATO and, 62–63, 65; recognition of Croatia and Slovenia, 96; refugees, 131; United Nations and, 77; during World War I, 57; during World War II, 60
Frank, Barney, 5
Freedom House surveys, 164, 177
Friedman, Thomas, 154
Fukuyama, Francis, 4–5

Gallucci, Robert, 149
Galvin, John, 90
GATT. *See* General Agreement on Tariffs and Trade
General Accounting Office, 140, 143

General Agreement on Tariffs and Trade (GATT), 124, 191, 194, 195, 203–4
Genocide. *See* Bosnia and Herzegovina; Rwanda
Genscher, Hans-Dietrich, 68
Gephart, Dick, 203
Germany: arms sales, 69; Bosnia, 119–20; during the cold war, 23–24, 66; neo-Nazi violence, 131; during World War I, 57; during World War II, 29, 31, 60, 61; economic factors, 33; recognition of Croatia and Slovenia, 95–96; United States and, 138
Ghandi, Indira, 176
Gligorov, Kiro, 88
Goals, national, 2. *See also* individual countries
Gold, David, 47
Gompert, David, 88, 90, 91, 101, 121
Gorazde. *See* Bosnia and Herzegovina
Gorbachev, Mikhail, 67, 174
Government, role of, 5, 183, 198–200, 209
Gray, Colin, 150–51
Great Britain: Bosnia, 101, 115–16, 118, 121–22, 124; democracy and, 180; European integration, 96; leadership of, 2, 31; NATO and, 65; during World War I, 28–29, 57–58; during World War II, 60, 61, 173; recognition of Croatia and Slovenia, 96
Greece, 97, 124, 129
Grenada, 65, 160, 166, 167, 174

Haiti, 160, 162, 164
Halperin, Morton, 17
Hamilton, Lee, 28
Harkin, Tom, 142
Harries, Owen, 14, 16, 17, 207

Hashimoto, Ryutaro, 202
Havel, Vaclav, 130, 184
Health care, 42, 198
Helms, Jesse, 206
Hendrickson, David C., 23
Heritage Foundation, 185
Higgins, Rosalyn, 169
Hitler, Adolph, 1, 29, 58, 60, 61. *See also* Germany
Hoagland, Jim, 73, 202
Hoar, Joseph, 140–41
Holbrooke, Richard, 111
Honecker, Erich, 66
Hormats, Robert, 49
Human rights, 27, 48, 78, 187
Human Rights Conference, UN (Vienna, 1993), 176
Hungary, 131, 166
Huntington, Samuel, 178, 179–80
Hurd, Douglas, 91, 121–22
Hussein, Saddam, 31, 153, 155, 188. *See also* Iraq; Persian Gulf War
Hyland, William, 13–14, 15, 17

Idealism, 33–35
India, 174
Inouye, Daniel, 144
International law: Bosnia and, 130; of states, 158; UN Charter, 160; war and, 167; Wilsonians and, 22; Yugoslavia and, 94–95
Iran, 27, 31, 188, 190
Iraq, 29, 31, 69, 77, 181–82, 188. *See also* Muslims; Persian Gulf War
Islamic issues. *See* Muslims
Isolationism, 3, 9–19, 22. *See also* individual countries
Israel, 29, 32, 64, 80, 160, 166, 173, 174
Italy, 58, 59–60, 61, 64, 76–77, 81, 131, 167, 168
Izetbegovic, Alija, 88, 96, 97, 101, 102, 117, 118, 125

Jansa, Janez, 89–90
Janvier, Bernard, 110
Japan: automobile industry, 197, 202; democracy in, 178, 199; during the cold war, 23–24; economic factors, 12–13, 33, 55–56, 192–94, 196, 199–203; gross national product, 13; Japan bashing, 193, 195, 196, 201, 202; standard of living, 37; as a superpower or leader, 54, 55–56; United States and, 138, 200–3, 204; during World War II, 29, 59, 81, 167-68
Jaruszelski, Woijcech, 65
Jefferson, Thomas, 22
Johnson, Lyndon, 63
Jovic, Boris, 157
Juster, Kenneth, 90

Kantor, Mickey, 195, 201, 202
Karadzic, Radovan, 102, 103, 116, 126
Kellogg-Briand Pact of 1928, 34
Kennan, George, 24, 34
Kennedy, Edward, 156
Kennedy, Paul, 46, 54
Kenney, George, 90
Kerrey, Bob, 10, 41, 42
Kirkpatrick, Jeane, 71, 149
Kirstof, Nicholas, 26
Kissinger, Henry, 64, 78
Kohl, Helmut, 65, 96, 119
Kondracke, Morton, 71, 72
Korb, Lawrence, 145
Korea, North, 29, 149–50
Korean War, 28, 63, 81, 153
Kozyrev, Andrei, 103
Krauthammer, Charles, 17
Krieger, Wolfgang, 95
Krueger, Anne, 191, 197
Krugman, Paul, 196, 200
Kuchma, Leonid, 187
Kuwait. See Persian Gulf War

Lake, Anthony, 107, 125, 144, 162, 188
Lavin, Frank, 204
Leach, James, 72
Leadership: in Bosnia, 127–29; economic factors and, 55; failures of, 2; military strength and, 135; need for, 2, 131; political, 137; shared, 53–70; use of force and, 153, 169–70. See also individual countries
League of Nations: charter, 61; as peacekeeper, 59–60, 81; U.S. refusal to join, 13–14, 23; war and, 168
Lebanon, 80, 173, 174
Lewis, Bernard, 189
Libby, I. Lewis, 137
Liberalism, 16, 17–18, 47–49, 138
Libya, 64–65, 160
Lind, Michael, 16, 17
Lipset, Seymour Martin, 180
Lodge, Henry Cabot, 18, 23
Lord, Winston, 202
Los Angeles Times, 127
Luck, Edward, 29–30

Maastricht summit, 96
Macedonia, 88, 97, 124
Major, John, 96
Manchuria, 59, 81, 167, 168
Mandela, Nelson, 32
Marshall Plan, 23
Maynes, Charles William, 14
Medicare and Medicaid, 39–40, 42
Mesic, Stipe, 88, 89, 92
Mexico, 32, 138, 164, 196–97
Michelis, Gianni De, 91
Middle East, 64. See also individual countries
Mihajlov, Mihajlo, 122–23
Milosevic, Slobodan, 87–88, 92, 109–10, 112–13, 157
Minority issues, 94–95

"Mission creep," 23, 80
Mitterrand, François, 120
Mladic, Ratko, 110, 126, 157
Modernization, 142–43
Mogadishu. *See* Somalia
Mondale, Walter, 192
Montenegro, 97
Moral issues: aggression, 168; budget deficit, 50; democracy, 175–76; foreign policies, 22–26, 34–35, 209–10; use of force, 161–64
Morgenthau, Hans, 34
Mrksic, Mile, 157
Muslims, 27, 130–31, 188–90. *See also* Bosnia
Mussolini, Benito, 58, 59–60

NAFTA. *See* North American Free Trade Agreement
Nasser, Gamal Abdel, 79–80
Nathan, Andrew, 187
Nationalism, 114
National Commission on America and the New World. *See* Carnegie Endowment for International Peace
National Endowment for Democracy (NED), 25, 185, 186, 190
National Interest, The, 14
National Journal, 74–75
National Security Revitalization Act of 1995, 38
NATO. *See* North Atlantic Treaty Organization
Nau, Henry, 199
Nazism, 58–59
NED. *See* National Endowment for Democracy
Newhouse, John, 96, 119, 120–21
New York Times, The: Bosnia, 100, 102, 107, 110, 120, 121, 126, 128, 157; defense planning guidance, 136; domestic issues, 15;

role of the United States, 16, 28; Rwanda, 159
Nicaragua, 65
Nigeria, 76–77
Nixon, Richard, 11, 54
North American Free Trade Agreement (NAFTA), 11, 32, 203
North Atlantic Treaty Organization (NATO): Europe and, 63–65; Korean War, 63; membership in, 32, 62; Persian Gulf War, 68–69; two-track missile strategy, 67–68; United States and, 62, 63–65; Yugoslavia and, 90; "zero option" for missiles, 67. *See also* Bosnia and Herzegovina
Nuclear Nonproliferation Treaty, 148–49
Nuclear weapons: Anti-Ballistic Missile Treaty of 1972, 150; anti-nuclear movement, 68; French, 63; intermediate-range nuclear missiles, 67; neutron bomb, 66–67; proliferation of, 29–30, 148–49; self-defense and, 161; SS-20 missiles, 67, 68; strategic forces, 142
Nunn, Sam, 77, 143, 154–55

OAS. *See* Organization of American States
Oil. *See* Petroleum
O'Neill, William, 29
Operation Desert Storm. *See* Persian Gulf War
Organization of American States (OAS), 165
Owen, Lord David, 91, 101, 102, 105, 116, 122
Ozal, Turgut, 181–82

Pakistan, 174
Panama, 166, 174
Parsons, Anthony, 78

Payne, James, 46
Peace, 28–31
"Peace dividend," 44, 141
Pelletreau, Robert, 188
People's Republic of China: economic factors, 55–56; as a future threat, 26–27, 147–48; as a superpower or leader, 53–54, 55–56; trade with, 22; United States and, 187–88, 190. See also China
Perez de Cuellar, Javier, 72
Perle, Richard, 67
Perot, Ross, 11, 196–97
Perry, William J., 16, 106, 107, 109
Persian Gulf War, 154–55; causes of, 153; conservative views of, 17; economic sanctions and, 153, 155; effects of, 90, 146; Gulf War syndrome, 154; Hussein, Saddam and, 31–32; isolationism and, 14–15; NATO and, 68–69; oil and, 28; opposition to, 154–55; United Nations and, 71, 81
Peterson, Peter, 41
Petroleum: Iranian, 188; Iraqi, 69; Middle East issues, 64, 138; Persian Gulf War and, 28, 155–56; World War II and, 60
Petrovsky, Vladimir, 72–73
Pfaff, William, 53, 55, 193
Pickering, Thomas, 91
Plato, 2
Poland, 60, 61, 65, 176, 184
Poos, Jacques, 91
Portugal, 64
Powell, Colin, 28, 151
Prestowitz, Clyde, 193, 198–99, 200
Public opinion: on balancing the budget, 38, 39; economic powers, 193; elite opinion, 13–15; on foreign policies, 3; toward isolationism, 11–12; use of force and, 153; U.S.-Japanese relations, 202

Public opinion polls: ABC News/ Washington Post, 12; Asahi Shimbun, 202; Chicago Council on Foreign Relations, 12, 193; Gallup, 12–13, 193, 202; Harris, Louis, 202; Yomiuri Shimbun, 202; Times Mirror, 12

Racial issues, 48
Radio Free Europe/Asia, 184–85, 188
Reagan Doctrine, 65
Reagan, Ronald, 24–25, 150
Reagan (Ronald) administration, 4, 189
Realism, 22, 24, 30, 33–34
Refugees, 131, 159
Republican Party, 18, 38, 43, 206
Republika Sepska, 112, 129. See also Bosnia
Research and development, 145
Rhodesia, 78
Ribbentrop, Joachim von, 60
Ricks, Thomas, 77
Rifkind, Malcolm, 121–22
Rise and Fall of the Great Powers, The (Kennedy), 45–46
Rogue states, 149–50
Rose, Michael, 115, 117, 122, 125–27
Russell, Bertrand, 64
Russett, Bruce, 45, 174
Russia (modern): aid for, 11; Bosnia, 118, 122–23, 130; Chechnya, 130, 185, 187; foreign policy, 166–67; Haitian invasion, 164; as a leader, 56; as a future threat, 26; Serbs and, 121–22; United States and, 185–87, 190. See also Soviet Union
Russia (pre-Soviet), 57, 58
Rwanda, 22–23, 75, 77, 80, 159–60, 162

Sachs, Jeffrey, 26

Sahu, Anandi, 46
Samuelson, Robert J., 29
Sanctions. *See* Economic issues
Santiago Declaration, 165
Sarajevo. *See* Bosnia and Herzegovina
Schifter, Richard, 89
Schlesinger, James, 15, 155
Schlieffen Plan, 57
Schmidt, Helmut, 66, 67, 68
Scowcroft, Brent, 140
SDI (Star Wars). *See* Strategic Defense Initiative
Selassie, Haile, 59
Serbs and Serbia: Bosnia and, 98, 102–4, 115–16, 124–27, 129, 156–58; Croatian, 87–88, 98; during World War I, 57; embargo on, 78; Slovenia, 92, 96; United Nations and, 126–27; Yugoslavian military, 118, 157; Yugoslavian settlement, 95. *See also* Bosnia and Herzegovina; Yugoslavia
Shalikashvili, John, 117, 125, 157
Shinn, David, 74
Skelton, Ike, 140
Slocombe, Walter, 149
Slovenia, 89–90, 91–92. *See also* Bosnia and Herzegovina
Snyder, Glenn H., 34
Social security, 39–40, 41, 42–43
Solidarity (Poland), 65
Somalia, 22, 32, 73–74, 76–77, 80, 158–59, 161, 162
Sorenson, Theodore, 15
South Africa, 32, 78
Soviet Union (USSR): during the cold war, 174; collapse of, 3, 5, 9, 54; post–World War I period, 25–26; threat of, 4, 23; United States and, 9–10, 31; during World War II, 31, 60, 81. *See also* Russia
Spain, 65, 124

Spending, government. *See* Budget, federal
Stalin, Joseph, 1, 29, 34, 61, 189. *See also* Soviet Union
Stambolic, Ivan, 87
Star Wars. *See* Strategic Defense Initiative
Stein, Herbert, 46, 183
Stephanopoulos, George, 136
Stokesbury, James, 63
Strategic Defense Initiative (SDI; Star Wars), 150
Superpowers, 53–54

Talbott, Strobe, 68, 118–19
Tarnoff, Peter, 3, 188
Thatcher, Margaret, 65, 69, 122
Third Reich. *See* World War II
Third Wave, The (Huntington), 179
Third world, 177, 191–92, 197
Thornburg, Richard, 10
Toynbee, Arnold, 178
Trade. *See* Economic issues
Trade Act of 1974, 194
Truman, Harry S., 63, 189
Tudjman, Franjo, 87, 88
Turajlic, Hakija, 115
Turkey, 128, 131, 174, 190
Tyson, Laura D'Andrea, 195

Ukraine, 187
United Nations: charter of, 78–79, 81, 117, 155, 160, 162, 165, 168–69, 170; economic sanctions, 78; Haiti, 159; isolationism and, 17; Korean War, 63; Military Staff Committee, 78–79; multilateral military action, 77–79; peacekeeping, 38–39, 72, 75–77, 79–81, 98, 115, 162–63; Persian Gulf War, 71; post–cold war period, 71–73, 80; Rapid Deployment Force, 72, 73; role of, 16, 72–73, 81, 82,

169–70; Rwanda, 75, 159; Somalia, 73–74, 76–77, 163; United States and, 16, 33, 38–39, 64, 74, 81, 82; Yugoslavia, 91. *See also* Bosnia and Herzegovina

United States: allies of, 147; attitudes toward, 2; commercial factors, 3; decline of, 53–54; defense planning, 136–51; democracy and, 178–79, 180–81; economic factors, 10, 12–13, 32–33, 36–50, 55–56, 191, 197, 198, 200, 204–6; goals of, 21, 24, 30, 208–10; imperialism of, 1; isolationism and neutrality of, 1–2, 9–19, 22, 25, 28, 70, 153, 206; leadership of, 2–3, 5, 33–35, 49, 70, 82, 204–5, 207–10; military capabilities, 137–45; mistakes of, 70, 208, 210; nondefense projects, 142–43; power of, 3–5, 16–19, 30–33, 62, 82, 135–36, 148–49, 168; role of, 1–2, 12, 16, 32, 33, 90, 131, 138, 146–47, 161–64; security of, 24–25. *See also* Bosnia and Herzegovina; Domestic problems and policies; Economic issues; Elections; Foreign policies, U.S.; individual countries and wars

USAID. *See* Agency for International Development, U.S.

U.S. News and World Report, 126

USSR. *See* Soviet Union

Vance, Cyrus, 99, 101, 155

Vance-Owen Plan, 101, 102–3, 123, 128

Versailles Peace Treaty of 1919, 21, 23, 27, 60

Vietnam syndrome, 152, 154

Vietnam War, 4, 29, 64, 146, 154

Voice of America, 184–85

Walesa, Lech, 184

Walker, Stephen, 101, 105

Wallace, Henry, 4

Warner, John, 77

Warnke, Paul, 66

Wars, 28–30, 34, 165–66, 170, 173–74, 208–9. *See also* individual wars

Washington, George, 21, 210

Washingtonians, 20–35, 53

Washington Post: Bosnia, 106, 108, 117, 125, 127, 128; Clinton, Bill, 11, 73; Somalia, 158; United Nations, 73, 76, 77

Wattenberg, Ben J., 33

Weinberger, Caspar, 65, 152, 153, 154

West European Union (WEU), 120, 124

Weyrich, Paul, 18

White, Theodore, 192–93

Williams, Carol, 127

Wilson, Woodrow, 22, 24, 25–26, 182, 211

Wilsonians, 20–35, 210

Wofford, Harris, 10

Wohlstetter, Albert, 127

Wolfers, Arnold, 21, 164

Wolfowitz, Paul D., 137

World Commission on Environment and Development, 183

World Competitiveness Report, 200

World organizations, 81–82. *See also* League of Nations; United Nations

World Trade Organization (WTO), 195, 201, 203, 204

World War I: Europe and, 56–59; pan-Slavism and, 123; postwar period, 2, 4, 23, 25, 27, 181; U.S. response to, 28, 181, 206–7. *See also* Versailles Peace Treaty of 1919; individual countries

World War II: causes of, 10, 23, 25,

28, 29, 59, 153; effects of, 49, 167, 191; Europe and, 59–61; postwar period, 4, 23, 24, 25, 32, 45, 174–75, 177, 181; U.S. response to, 4, 28, 29, 181, 210. *See also* individual countries

World War III, 30

WTO. *See* World Trade Organization

Yeltsin, Boris, 121

Yom Kippur War of 1973, 64

Yugoslavia: arms embargo, 78, 94, 123; disintegration of, 88, 89, 90–95, 120; European Community in, 89–97; military, 92, 94, 98, 117, 157; nationalism in, 87; United Nations, 94; United States and, 89–90, 91, 97–98, 121; unrest in Slovenia and Croatia, 87–88; during World War II, 60. *See also* Bosnia and Herzegovina; Croats and Croatia; Serbs and Serbia

Zepa. *See* Bosnia and Herzegovina

Zhirinovsky, Vladimir, 122

ABOUT THE AUTHOR

JOSHUA MURAVCHIK is a resident scholar at the American Enterprise Institute. His articles appear frequently in *Commentary*, the *New Republic*, the *Weekly Standard*, the *New York Times*, and the *Wall Street Journal*, and he has contributed to *Foreign Affairs*, the *New York Times Magazine*, and numerous other magazines and newspapers.

A. M. Rosenthal, writing in the *New York Times*, called his 1991 book, *Exporting Democracy*, "a brilliant analysis of the power of democracy and the folly of realism." Mr. Muravchik's 1988 *News Coverage of the Sandinista Revolution* was called "a magnificent volume on how the media attempt to manipulate public opinion in the United States" (*Journalism Quarterly*). His 1986 book, *The Uncertain Crusade*, was praised in the *New Republic* as "certainly one of the most important neoconservative foreign policy statements that have appeared to date."

Mr. Muravchik received his Ph.D. in international relations from Georgetown University. In 1986 the *Wall Street Journal* wrote that "Joshua Muravchik may be the most cogent and careful of the neoconservative writers on foreign policy."

A Note on the Book

This book was edited by Dana Lane
of the publications staff
of the American Enterprise Institute.
The index was prepared by Julia Stam Petrakis,
and the figures were drawn by Hördur Karlsson.
The text was set in Sabon.
Lisa Roman of the AEI Press set the type,
and Edwards Brothers Incorporated,
of Lillington, North Carolina,
printed and bound the book,
using permanent acid-free paper.

The AEI Press is the publisher for the American Enterprise Institute for Public Policy Research, 1150 Seventeenth Street, N.W., Washington, D.C. 20036; *Christopher C. DeMuth,* publisher; *Dana Lane,* director; *Ann Petty,* editor; *Leigh Tripoli,* editor; *Cheryl Weissman,* editor; *Lisa Roman,* editorial assistant (rights and permissions).

The Imperative
of American Leadership